IMAGES
of America

ORANGE COUNTY INTERNATIONAL RACEWAY

On the Cover: At Orange County International Raceway, the 1974 Professional Dragsters Association race's final round saw Bob Pickett driving Pete Everett's "Pete's Lil Demon" (foreground) versus Dave Condit driving the Plueger and Gyger Mustang (background). When the Christmas tree flashed green, it was Pickett all the way to the finish line as Condit went up in smoke. Pickett and Everett picked up three big funny car wins at Orange County International Raceway in 1974. (Photograph by the author.)

IMAGES
of America

ORANGE COUNTY INTERNATIONAL RACEWAY

Steve Reyes

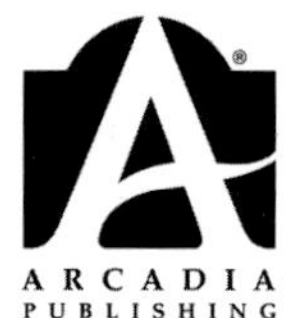

ISBN 978-1-4671-6229-6

Published by Arcadia Publishing
Charleston, South Carolina

Printed in the United States of America

Library of Congress Control Number: 2024945301

For all general information, please contact Arcadia Publishing:
Telephone 843-853-2070
Fax 843-853-0044
E-mail sales@arcadiapublishing.com

Visit us on the Internet at www.arcadiapublishing.com

To the Kelly Bros., Obadiah and Malachi, my wacky little grandsons. I love you guys!

Contents

ACKNOWLEDGMENTS

I would like to thank Don Gillespie, Carl Olson, Bob Frey, Mickey McIver, Lou Hart, and Richard Shute/Auto Imagery. You all made this book possible.

All photographs were taken by the author Steve Reyes unless otherwise noted in the photograph caption.

Introduction

State of the art was the only way to describe Orange County International Raceway (OCIR). It was Southern California's "Taj Mahal" of racing venues. For 16 years, 2 months, 24 days, and 848 Saturdays (weekends) from 1967 to 1983, it was the premier raceway in the United States. OCIR was the first raceway that was purposely built with spectator comfort in mind; the first to offer reserved seating. The layout was the result of lease holders Mike Jones, Bill White, and Larry Vaughan traveling the United States visiting raceways to see what would be best for their racing venue.

The Mike Jones effect was far reaching. He developed the manufacturers' funny car championships, with cars lined up along the racetrack with searchlights and massive fireworks that delighted the packed spectator stands and the racers; it was like P.T. Barnum had staged a drag race. Even the logos, flags, color schemes, stadium lighting, and landscaping were the best and brightest available at the time. OCIR's octagonal tower was a one-of-a-kind design that provided offices, officials' deck, and even a lounge for VIPs.

Also available was equipment for the media to use to report on the racing, which included rooftop access for photographers and television cameras. Besides the manufacturers' funny car event in November, other blockbuster events were staged throughout the year: the Funny Car 500 on Memorial Day weekend and the Nitromethane Championships around the Fourth of July, which featured 16 car fields of top fuel dragsters, funny cars, and fuel altered. One of the largest top fuel dragster events in the country was held at OCIR: Doug Kruse's Professional Dragsters Association, also known as the PDA race. It was an all-dragster show that featured 64 top fuel dragsters at its first OCIR race in March 1968.

Being an international raceway, OCIR had a road course and, in the early years of the track, Sports Car Club of America (SCCA) points meets for open wheel vehicles, including Formula and Super Vee events. Fédération Internationale de l'Automobile (FIA) motorcycle and sidecar racing also used the road course. In OCIR's later years, a Moto X and off-road course was built next to the track, and a Speedway bike track was added. Even in its early years, OCIR played host to air shows with the biggest names in air racing attending the shows.

But as the population continued to expand, the land use, which was taxed as ranch lands, became too valuable as real estate. OCIR's founders, Mike Jones, Bill White, and Larry Vaughan, believed their long-term lease (50+ years) and their proximity to Marine Corps Air Station El Toro would keep the track safe and off-limits to developers. However, East Irvine became an incorporated city in 1971, and plans for the Irvine Spectrum were unveiled, a massive mixed-use complex (food, shopping, and housing) at the apex of the 5 and 405 Freeways. This was right where OCIR was located. It became too lucrative to pass up, and the original OCIR lease holders sold all interest back to the Irvine Company in 1973.

For the next 10 years the track was in turmoil. In those 10 years, the track changed from National Hot Rod Association (NHRA) sanction to American Hot Rod Association (AHRA) sanction and then back to NHRA sanction. Five different track managers tried to make OCIR great again.

The global energy crisis in the 1970s crippled spectators' ability to purchase gas to drive to OCIR events. In 1980, OCIR returned to being an NHRA sanction track; from 1981 to 1983, it hosted the NHRA World Finals. A few weeks after the 1983 NHRA finals, the track would shutter its doors for good. This was the nail in the coffin for drag racing in Southern California.

One

THE OCIR FAST GUYS

98 PERCENT NITRO IN THE TANK

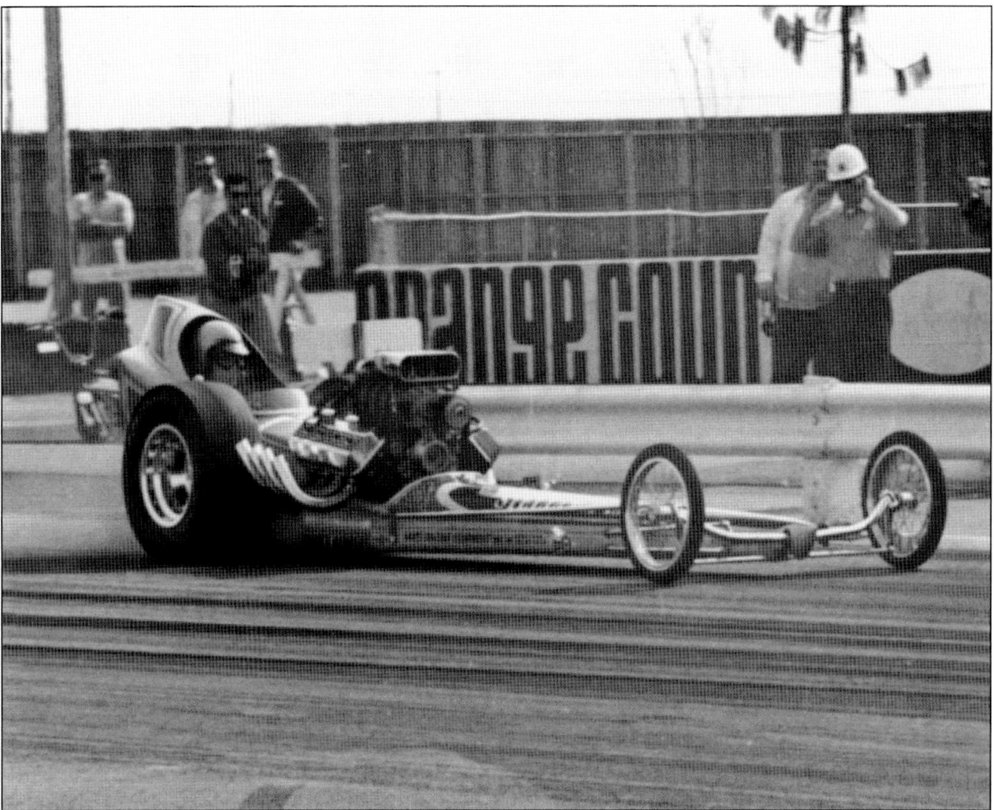

The opening race on August 5, 1967, saw Bobby Tapia in the Stellings and Tapia top fuel dragster beat Tom McEwen driving the Holland and Guedel top fuel dragster. Tapia recorded 223.32 miles per hour to set the miles per hour track record. In the final round, Tapia realized that all was not right with his car. It blew the clutch, damaged the car, and bruised Tapia's feet. Tapia would soon leave drag racing for his other passion in life, computers and computer programming.

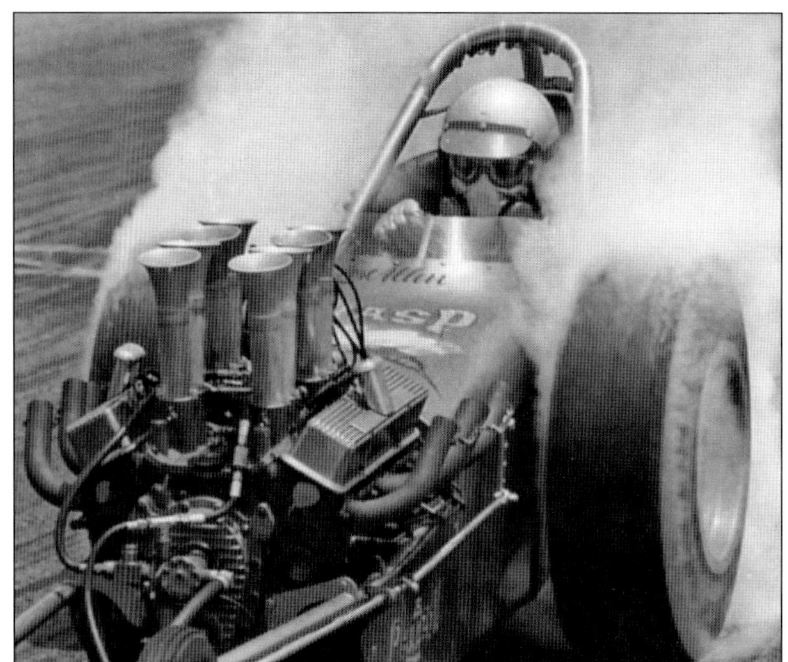

In July 1968, Les Allen drove the Allen family's "Wasp" junior (JR) fuel dragster to an OCIR JR fuel elapsed time (ET) record at 7.82. He also recorded a 7.79 ET to back up his 7.82 ET. In addition, Allen ran 199.10 miles per hour and 196.94 miles per hour to become drag racing's quickest and fastest JR fuel dragster in the country at that time.

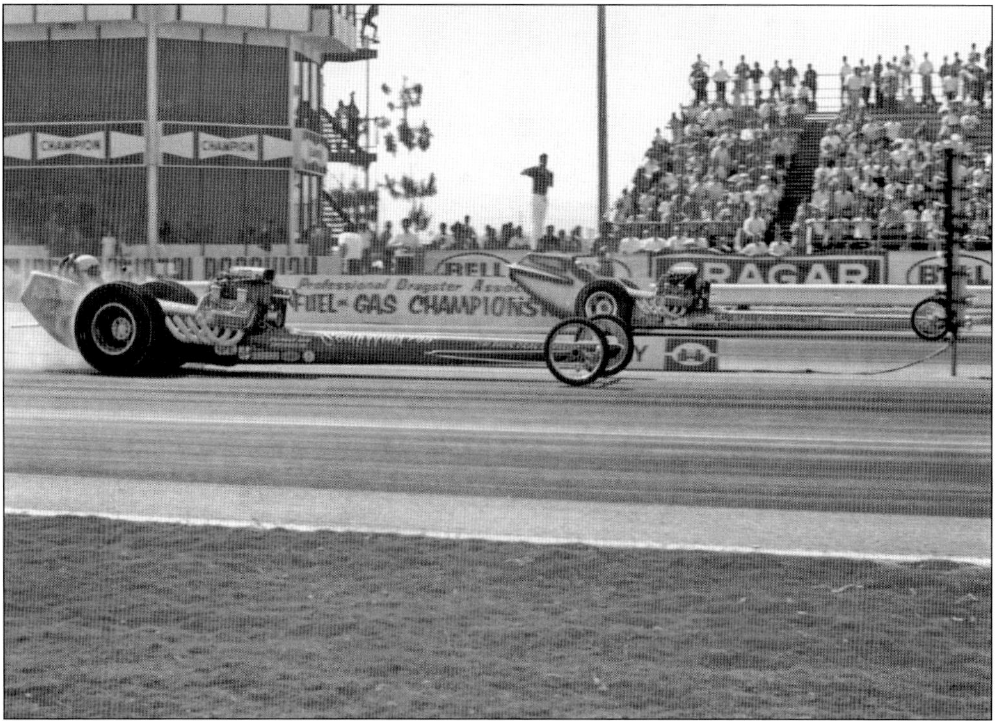

An east versus west battle took place in the first round of the 1968 OCIR PDA race. Don "Mad Dog" Cook in his Southwind top fuel dragster (nearside) took on Ron Rivero driving the K&G Associates top fuel dragster from Pennsylvania. Rivero won the round and advanced to the second round of the competition. The 1968 PDA field of top fuel dragsters was the last 64-car top fuel show held in the country; after this year, it was cut back to a 32-car field.

The extremely popular Southern California (SoCal) team of Tim Beebe and John "Zookeeper" Mulligan set a top fuel dragster record twice in 1967 and the miles per hour record once in 1968 at OCIR (6.83 and 6.79 ETs at 227.84 miles per hour). The duo started 1969 on a high note by winning top fuel eliminator at the NHRA Winternationals in Pomona, California. It all ended tragically the same year when John "Zookeeper" Mulligan died from burns sustained in a horrific fire and crash at the NHRA US Nationals in September.

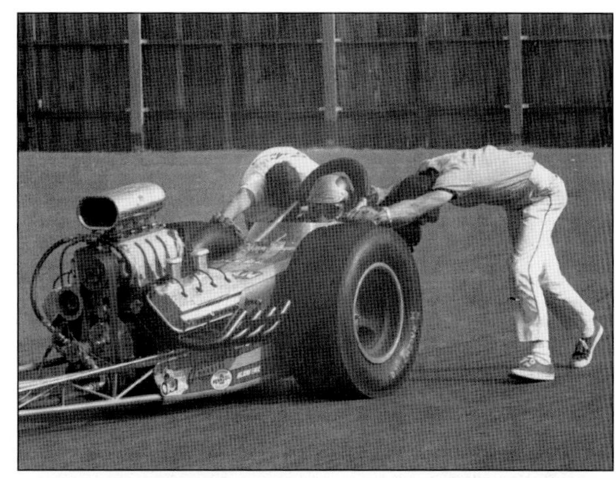

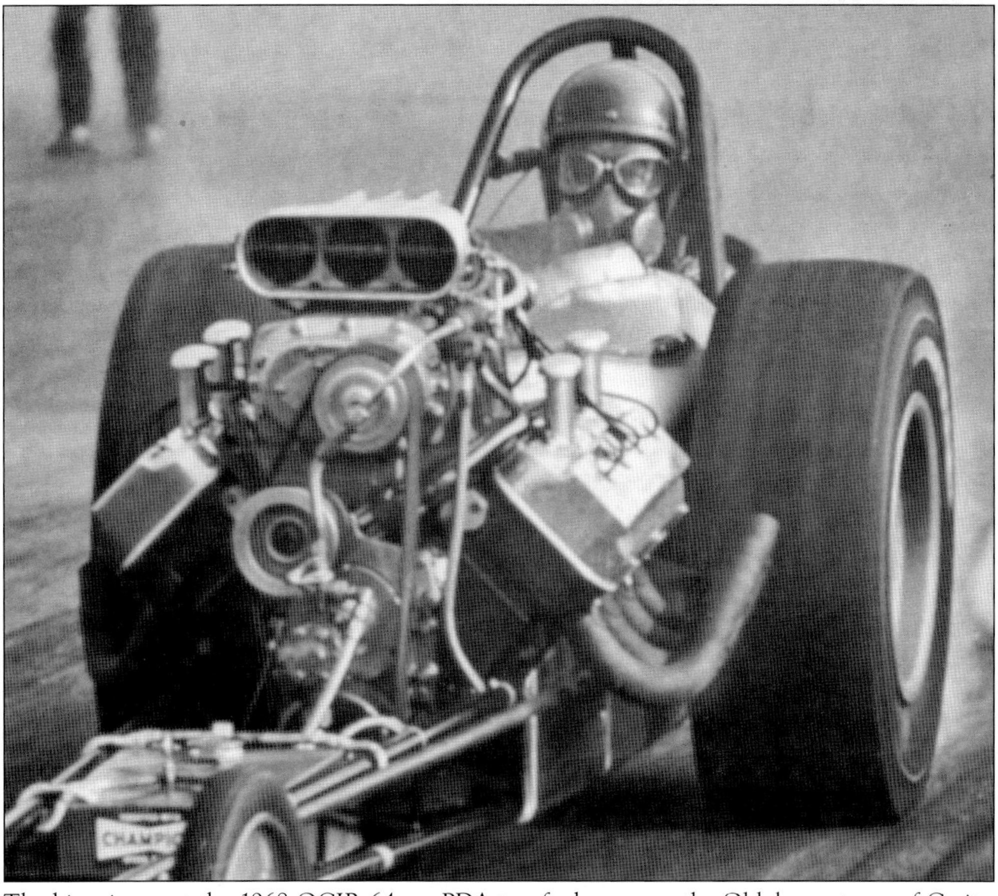

The big winner at the 1968 OCIR 64-car PDA top fuel race was the Oklahoma team of Creitz, Greer, and Donovan with driver Vic Brown. Brown waded through a tough 64-car field to claim the top fuel eliminator title. His last victim was Don Garlits, who broke and red-lighted in the final round. With that PDA win under their belt, Creitz, Greer, and Donovan changed drivers and won the PDA race in Fremont, California. With Vic Brown and Steve Carbone driving, they won two of the three PDA races in 1968. Later, Vic Brown went and drove for Ed Wills and his "Mr. Ed" top fuel dragster based in Fresno, California.

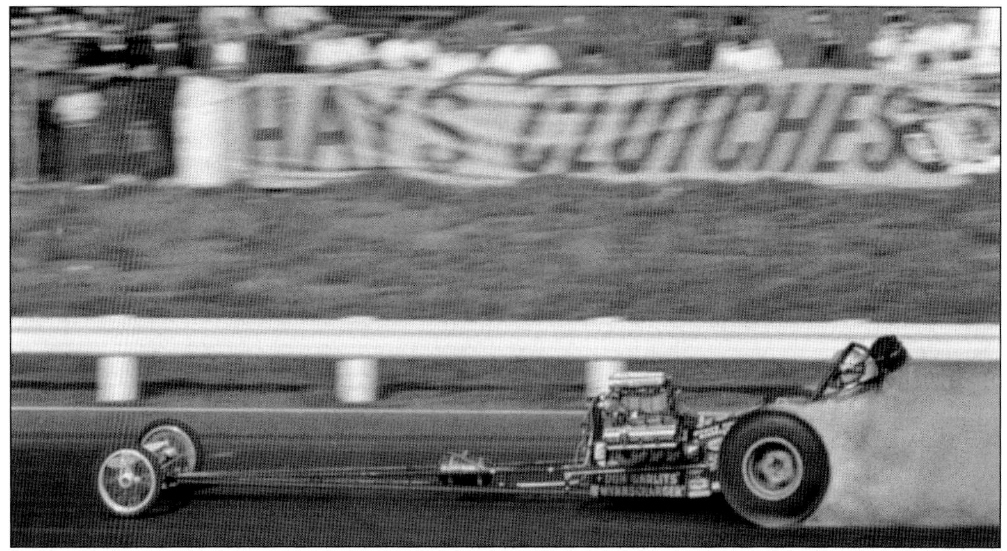

Don Garlits made the long tow from Seffner, Florida, to East Irvine, California, only to fall one round short of a top fuel win at the 1968 OCIR PDA 64-car top fuel show. Garlits was the odds-on favorite heading into the final against Creitz, Greer, and Donovan. However, a broken transmission caused Garlits to red-light, giving the win to driver Vic Brown.

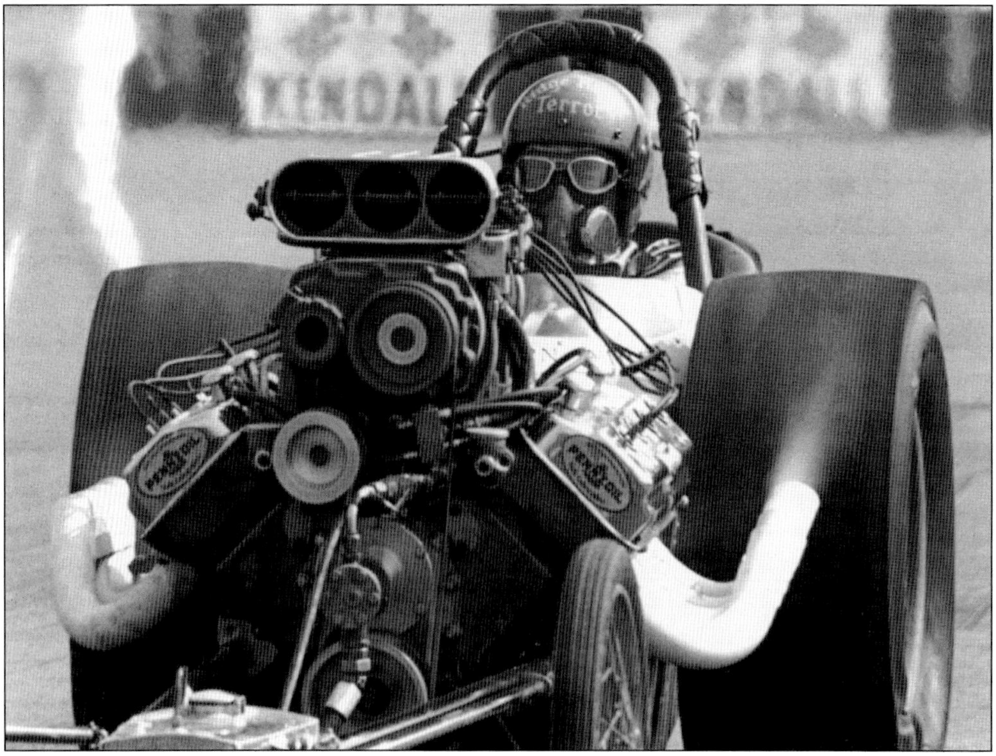

The "Ridge Route Terrors," also known as Warren, Coburn, and Miller, set the OCIR track ET record on opening day as James Warren piloted the top fuel dragster to a 6.89 clocking. The Bakersfield-based trio would set the OCIR ET record three times: 1967, 6.89; 1974, 6.06; and 1975, 5.79. They also won the 1973 OCIR PDA race over Don Garlits.

Making a rare appearance on the West Coast in 1968 was the Ramchargers top fuel dragster, driven by Chuck Kurzawa. The team was escaping the cold winter at its Michigan base for some fun in the California sun at OCIR, Lions, and Irwindale. The following year was the last year that the Ramchargers raced in top fuel; an all-new funny car was debuted in 1970 with Leroy Goldstein at the helm.

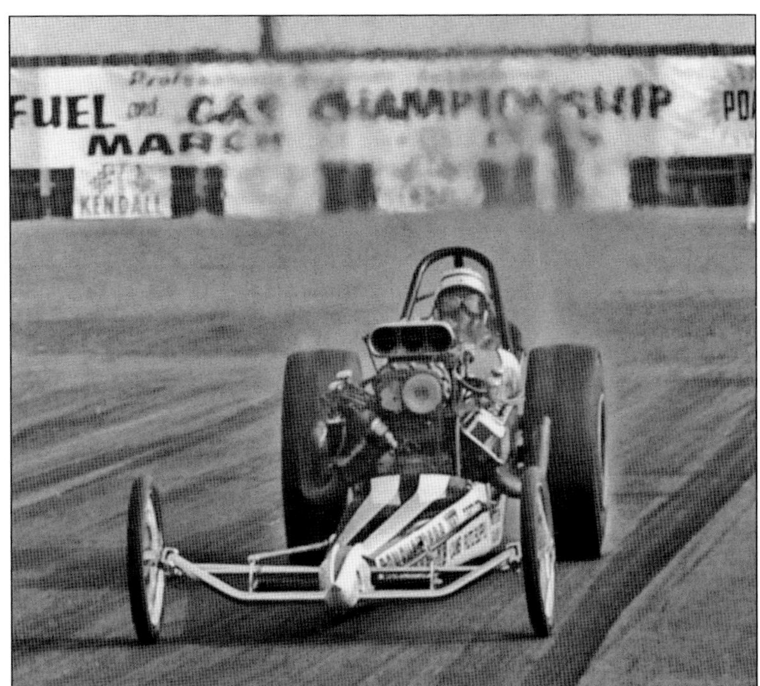

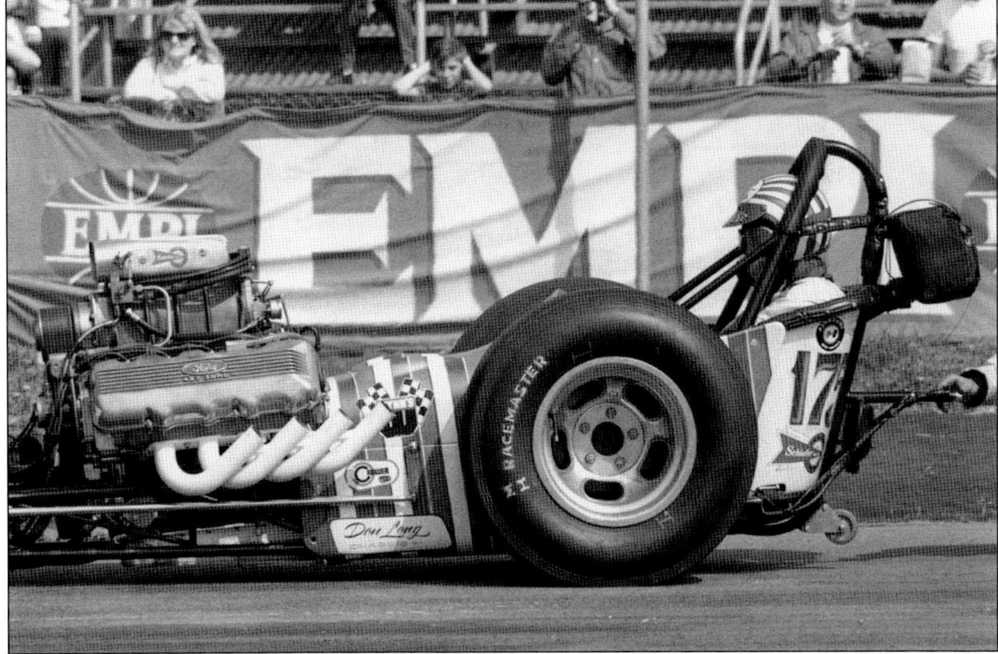

Don "the Snake" Prudhomme won the 1967 NHRA Division 7 race at OCIR, putting away Bob Mayer in the final round. Prudhomme also won the PDA race at Lions in 1967 by defeating Beebe and Mulligan in the final round. He was driving for Lou "Wolfman" Baney and his 429 Ford SOHC (single overhead camshaft)–powered top fuel dragster. Baney's race car would become the "Shelby's Super Snake" top fuel dragster in 1968.

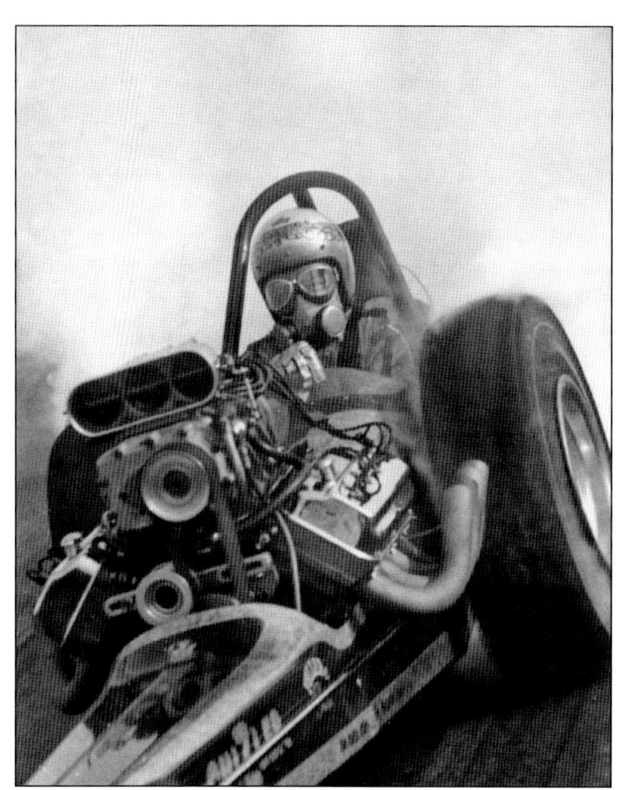

Top fuel legend Chris "the Golden Greek" Karamesines left cold and snowy Chicagoland to race at OCIR in 1968. Karamesines was a welcome sight at top fuel events on the West Coast. With his "Chizler" top fuel dragster, he proceeded to race from SoCal to Washington state. When at OCIR, his pit area was always mobbed with his legions of fans. Many SoCal top fuel racers sought advice from Karamesines because of his many years of experience racing in top fuel, and "the Golden Greek" was happy to share information to new and old top fuel racers.

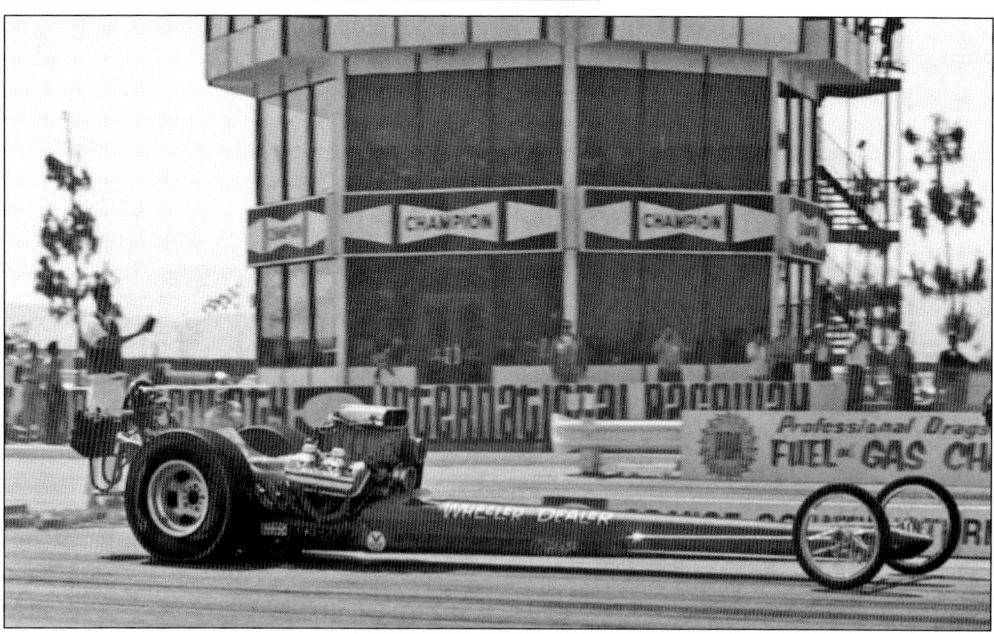

A pleasant surprise at the 1968 OCIR PDA race was the East Coast–based top fuel dragster of Bruce Wheeler. His "Wheeler Dealer" top fuel dragster was driven by Little "Super Jew" Al Friedman. After the PDA race, Wheeler sold his car to Tom Chastang in Virginia, and Friedman went and drove for Harry and Maxine Lehman's "American Way" top fuel dragster. Wheeler moved to Hawaii and opened up a souvenir shop for the tourist trade on the big island.

On April 26, 1969, "Jumpin'" Jeep Hampshire was critically injured in a horrific crash at OCIR. Hampshire was driving the Caspary and Hampshire top fuel dragster when it hit the guardrail almost head-on at high speed. The car disintegrated upon impact with the guardrail, leaving Hampshire in only a roll cage. He had a long recovery, and because of injuries to one of his arms, he retired from driving. His brother Ronnie continued driving in top fuel for Caspary and Robinson, Sid Waterman, and Ted Gotelli.

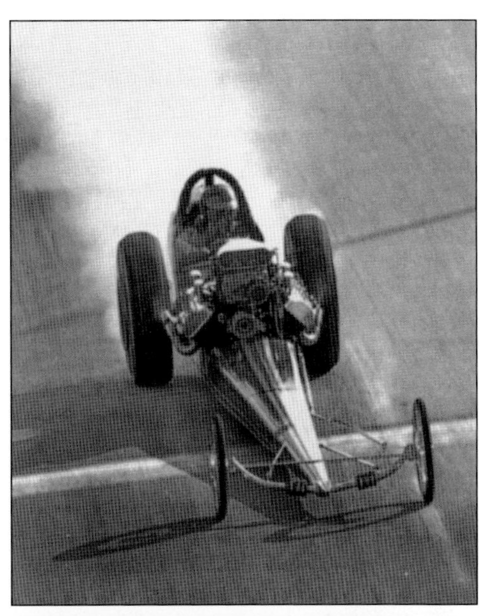

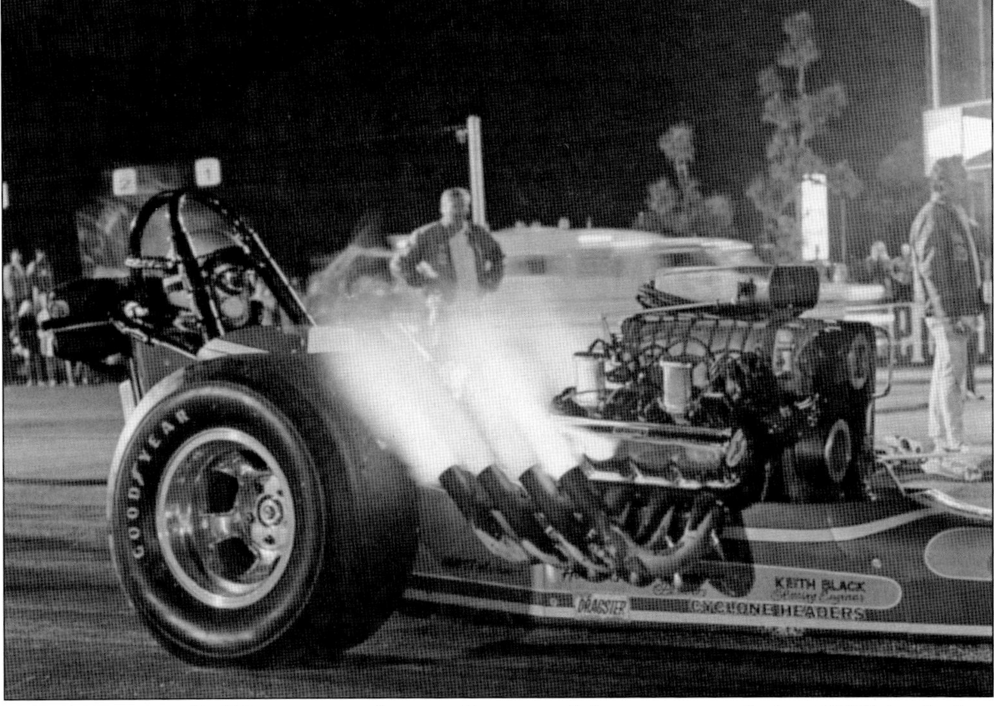

Kelly "the Controller" Brown must have really enjoyed driving in top fuel at OCIR in the late 1960s. He won top fuel eliminator in three different cars. While driving for Dave Mackenzie and his Dean Engineering top fuel dragster, he won the 1968 NHRA Division 7 World Championship Series races at OCIR. In 1969, he drove Lou "Wolfman" Baney's top fuel dragster to a big win at the OCIR fuel tournament. Again in 1969, he won top fuel in Leland Kolb's top fuel dragster (pictured); this time it was the OCIR anniversary race. Driving top fuel dragster was not what Brown did for a living, though. He was a stuntman and stunt coordinator for the motion picture business in Hollywood.

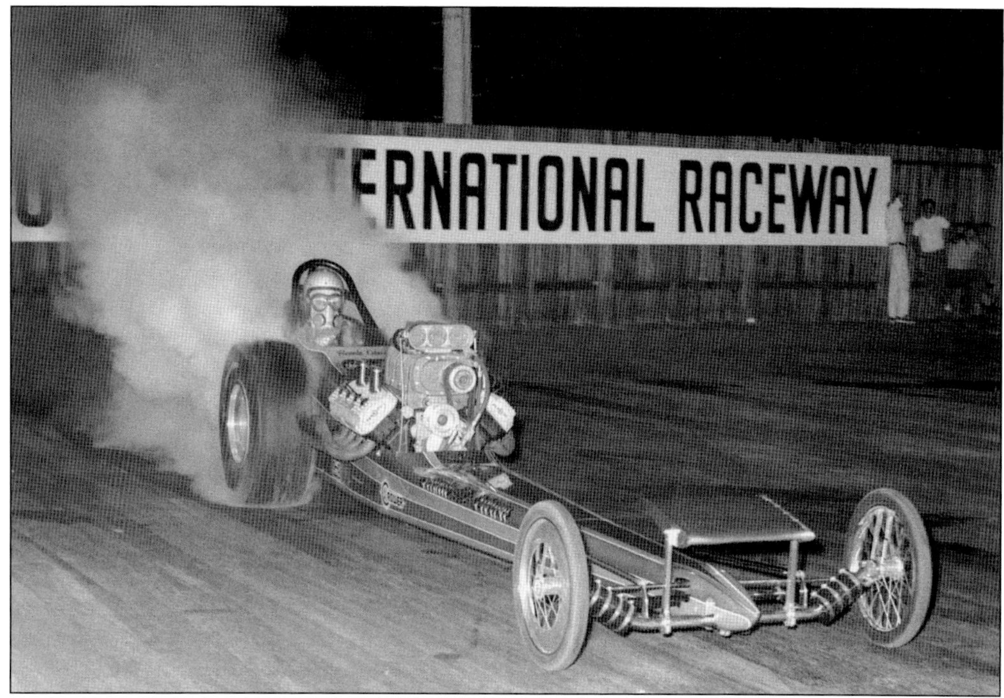

It is the one-year anniversary of OCIR, and the two low ETs are racing for a winner takes all purse of $14,000. The two quickest cars of the year were Oklahoma's Bennie "the Wizard" Osborne and local SoCal hero Tom "Mongoose" McEwen. When the smoke and nitro fumes cleared, it was Osborne (pictured) taking home the cash to Oklahoma.

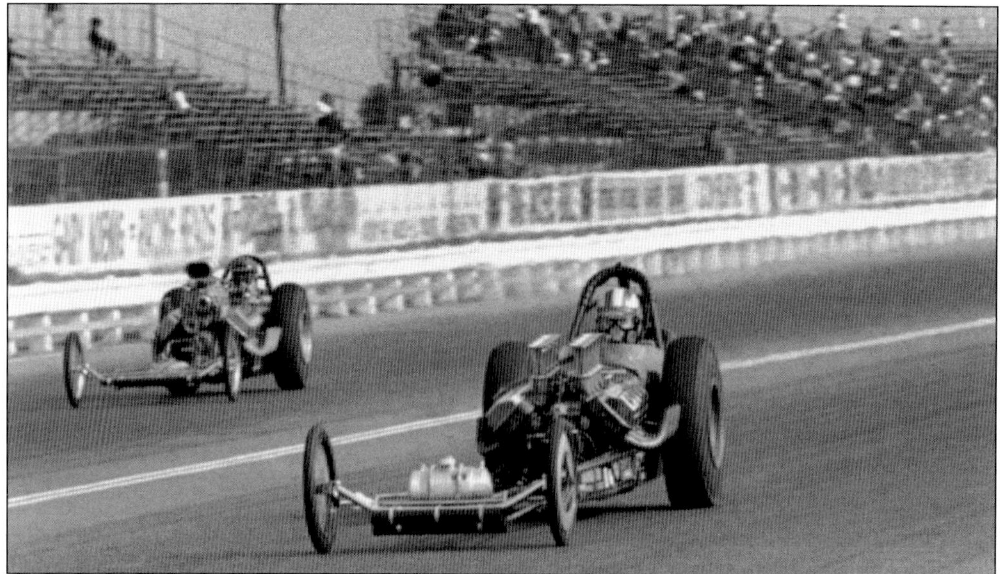

Gene Adams and Don Enriquez were unbeatable at OCIR with their JR fuel dragster from 1969 to 1973. The pair won JR fuel four straight times at the OCIR PDA events. At the 1969 NHRA Division 7 World Championship Series race, they set a new low ET record for JR fuel dragsters at 7.46. In 1971, Don Enriquez drove the Adams and Enriquez JR fuel dragster to a win competition eliminator at the NHRA Winternationals in Pomona, California.

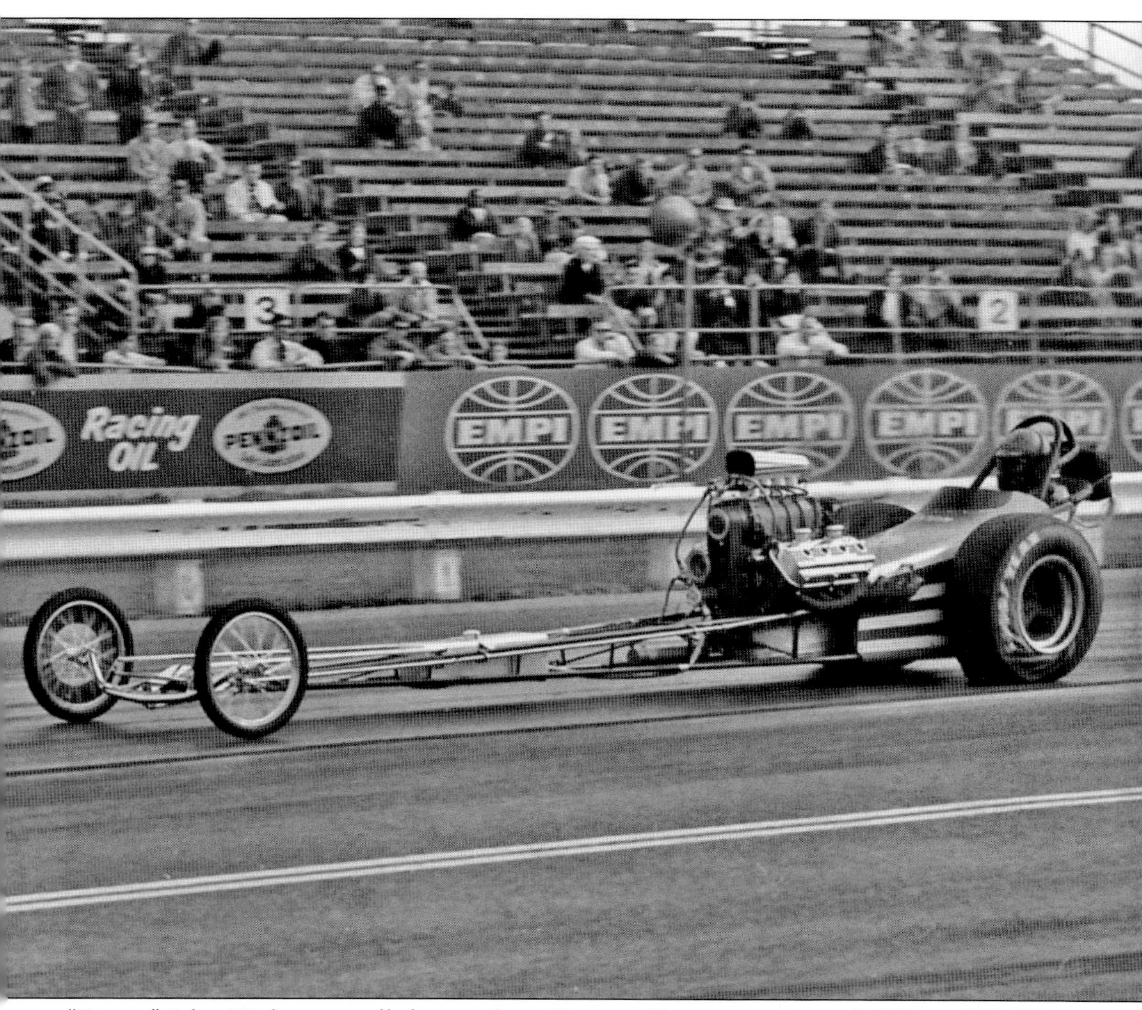

"Kansas" John Wiebe came all the way from Newton, Kansas, to race at OCIR in 1971. The "Weeb" took home top fuel honors at OCIR's All Pro Series Championships. At the event there was a combined total of 60 nitro-burning race cars (top fuel and funny cars). Wiebe won the final round on a hole shot over Larry Dixon. Dixon ran a better 6.76 ET, but Wiebe won with a slower 6.88 ET. He who snoozes, loses.

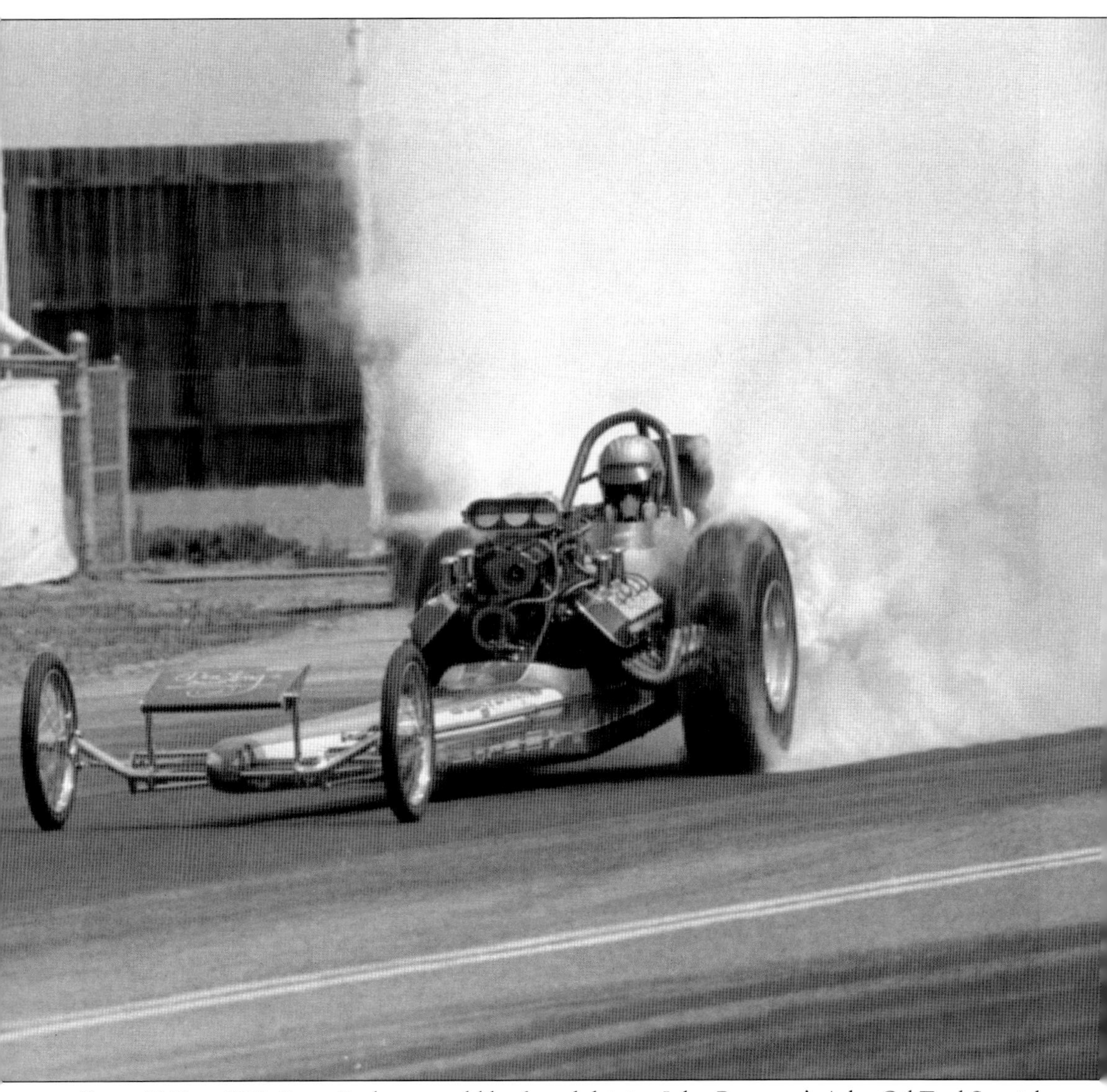

From 1967 to 1971, Steve Carbone could be found driving John Bateman's Atlas Oil Tool Special top fuel dragster, the Creitz and Donovan top fuel dragster (pictured), Mike Kuhl's top fuel dragster, and his own top fuel dragster. Carbone won the Hot Rod Magazine Championships at Riverside, California, in 1968 in Bateman's car, the 1968 PDA race in Fremont in the Creitz and Donovan car, and the 1970 PDA race at OCIR in Mike Kuhl's car. In 1971, Carbone started the year by winning the AHRA Winternationals in Scottsdale, Arizona. Then he beat Don Garlits in the final round to win the NHRA US Nationals. The win at nationals was the last time a front-engine top fuel dragster would win that event.

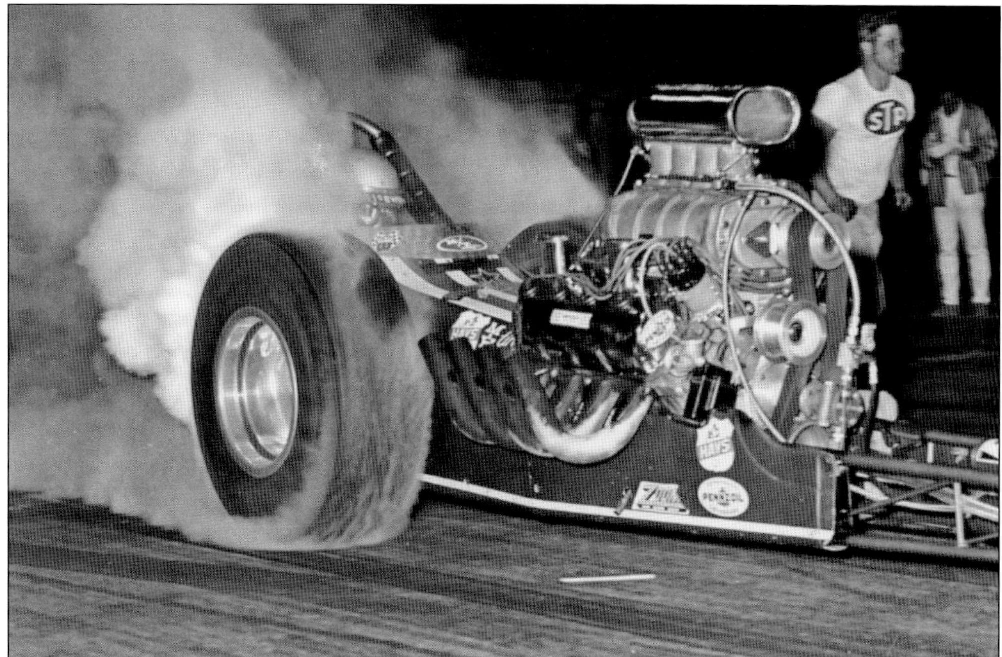

Tom "Mongoose" McEwen could not catch a break racing at OCIR in 1967 or 1968. He was runner-up at the first-ever top fuel dragster event in 1967 while red-lighting in the Guedel and Holland top fuel dragster. Then, in 1968, he lost the big money race ($14,000) to Bennie Osborne. He would rebound in 1972 with his first rear-engine top fuel dragster by winning the Bakersfield Fuel and Gas Championships, his biggest career win in a top fuel dragster.

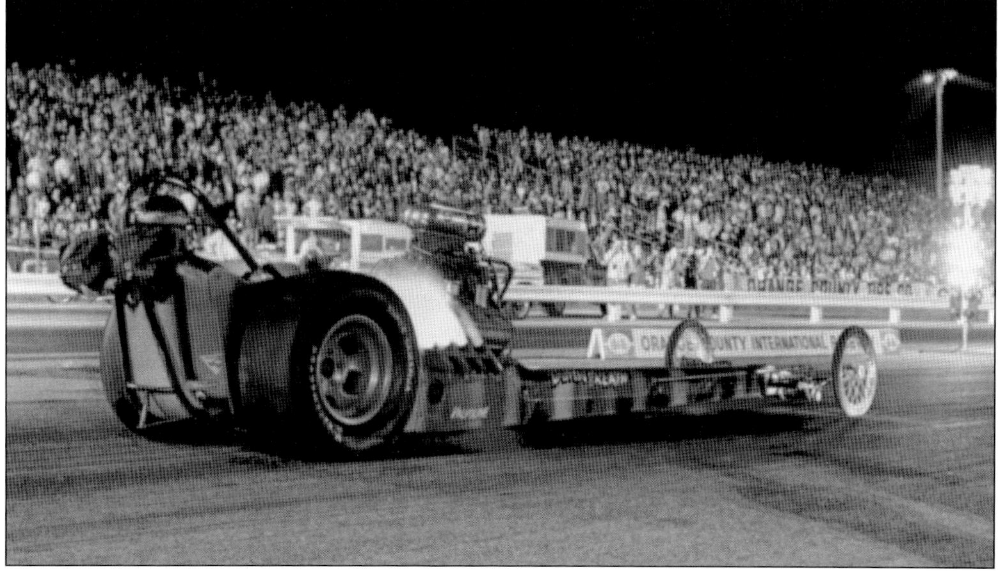

The last day in top fuel racing for Big Jim Dunn and his Dunn and Reath top fuel dragster was August 29, 1970. The La Mirada firefighter would soon take delivery on an all-new Woody Gilmore–chassis, Cuda-bodied funny car. The new car with partner Joe Reath saw action towards the end of 1970. Dunn and Reath learned very quickly the difficulties of SoCal funny car racing, but the team prevailed with some big victories at OCIR, Lions, and Irwindale.

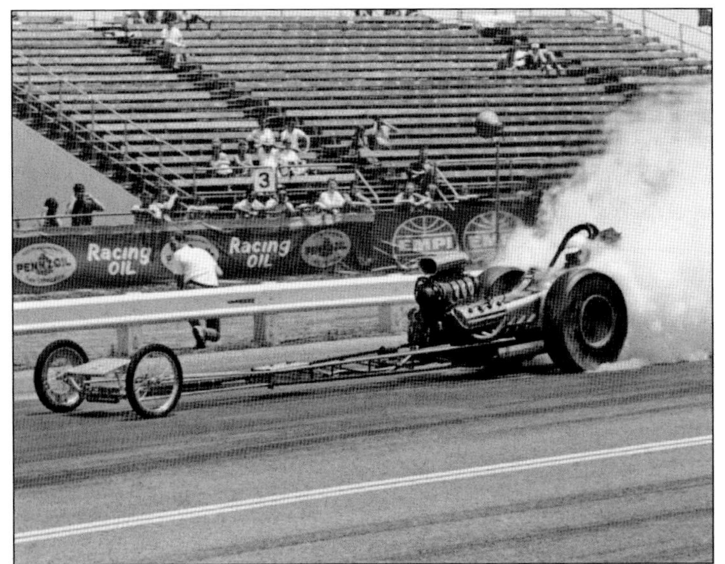

Veteran top fuel driver Don Moody came out of retirement in 1970 to drive the Cerny, Lins, and Manke top fuel dragster. Soon, he was a top fuel terror in SoCal racing; he set three ET top fuel records at OCIR, 6.37 in the front-engine top fueler pictured and twice—6.14 and 6.17—in the Cerny and Lins rear-engine top fuel dragster. He also won back-to-back OCIR NHRA Division 7 World Championship Series races in 1970 and 1971.

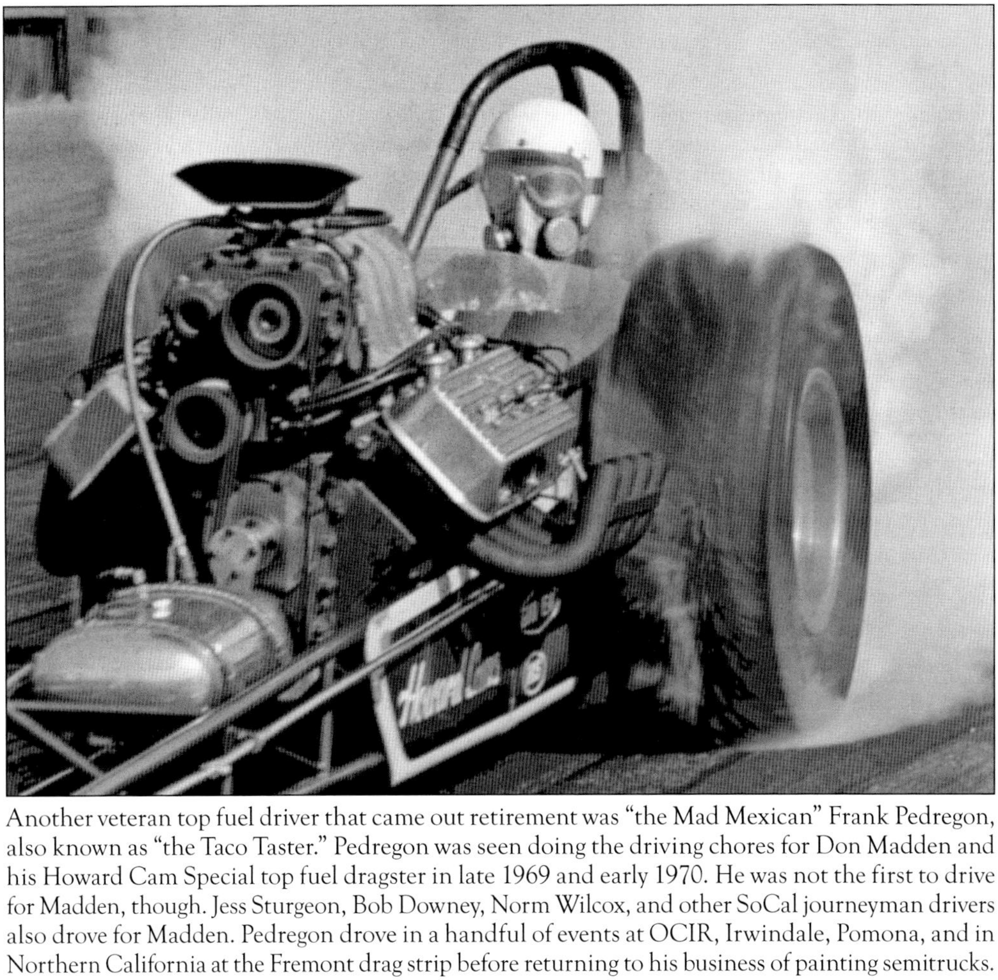

Another veteran top fuel driver that came out retirement was "the Mad Mexican" Frank Pedregon, also known as "the Taco Taster." Pedregon was seen doing the driving chores for Don Madden and his Howard Cam Special top fuel dragster in late 1969 and early 1970. He was not the first to drive for Madden, though. Jess Sturgeon, Bob Downey, Norm Wilcox, and other SoCal journeyman drivers also drove for Madden. Pedregon drove in a handful of events at OCIR, Irwindale, Pomona, and in Northern California at the Fremont drag strip before returning to his business of painting semitrucks.

The Texas Whips, also known as the Carroll Bros., brought their top fuel dragster to OCIR in 1969. Those Texas boys wanted to see what all the fuss was about regarding this new super drag strip in Orange County, California. Driver Buddy Cortines had his hands full with the Carroll's top fuel dragster when their 392 Chrysler Hemi engine decided OCIR had a little too much grip on the track surface.

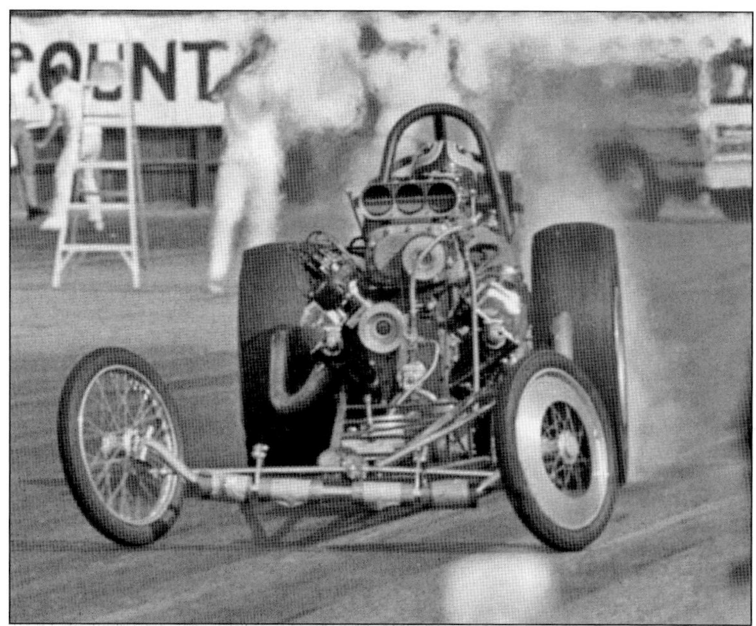

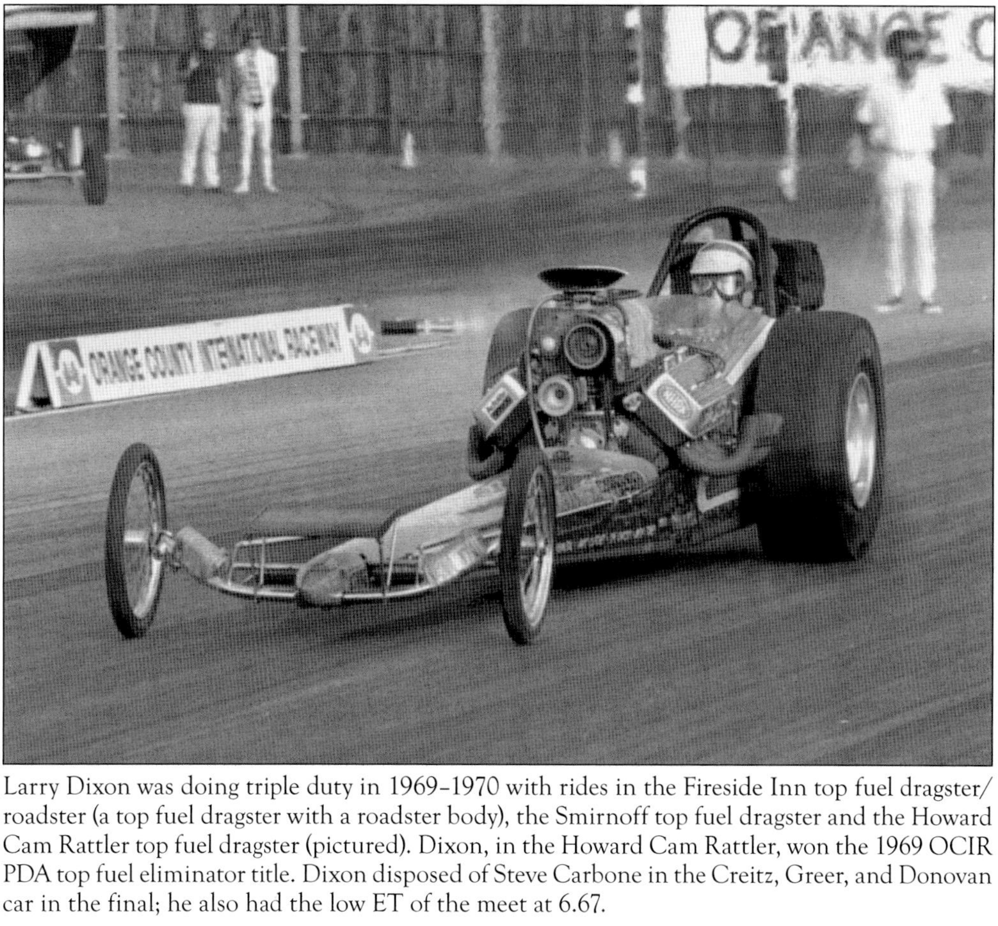

Larry Dixon was doing triple duty in 1969–1970 with rides in the Fireside Inn top fuel dragster/roadster (a top fuel dragster with a roadster body), the Smirnoff top fuel dragster and the Howard Cam Rattler top fuel dragster (pictured). Dixon, in the Howard Cam Rattler, won the 1969 OCIR PDA top fuel eliminator title. Dixon disposed of Steve Carbone in the Creitz, Greer, and Donovan car in the final; he also had the low ET of the meet at 6.67.

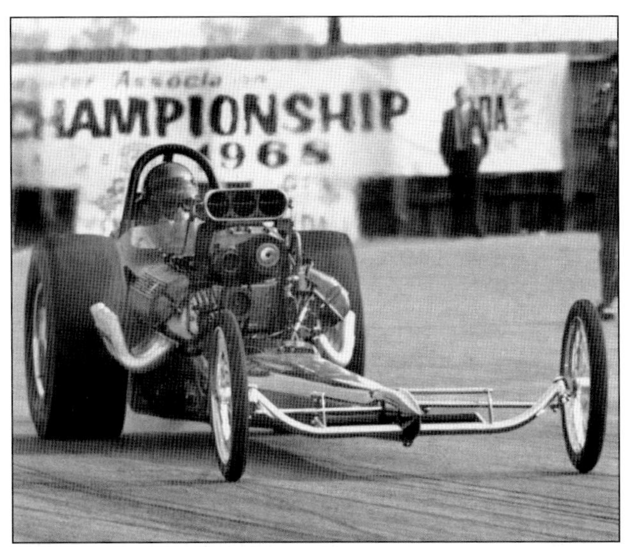

Minnesota-based top fuel racer Tom Hoover brought his 429 Ford SOHC–powered top fuel dragster to OCIR in 1968. Hoover was one of a handful of top fuel racers who used the 429 Ford SOHC engine. Other top fuel racers who used that engine were Connie Kalitta, Lou Baney, Chuck Griffth, Halstead and Dunlap, and Sneaky Pete Robinson. Robinson was the first to win a major NHRA event with the Ford engine. In 1970, Hoover switched from top fuel to funny cars, but his dad still raced the top fuel dragster under Ma and Pa Hoover with Denny Darrah as the driver.

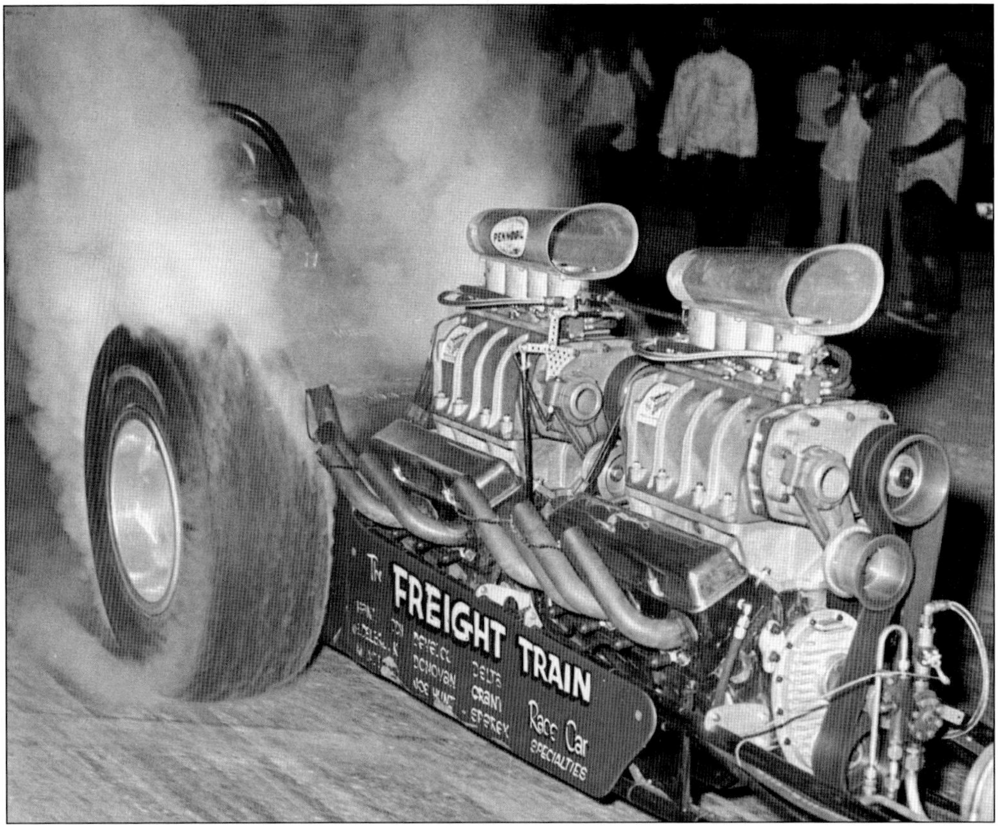

The top gas class was only around OCIR from 1967 to 1971. The first few years the class was dominated by John and Beverly Peters' "Freight Train." The awesome twin engine Chevy dragster was piloted by Bob Muravez or Billy "the Kid" Scott. With Muravez driving, the Freight Train cranked out a new national record at OCIR of 7.56 at 198.66 miles per hour. Then Scott got in the car and ran 207.84 miles per hour in December 1967. Early in 1968, Scott drove the Freight Train to a new OCIR top gas ET record at 7.36. In 1971, the NHRA dissolved the top gas class at its events.

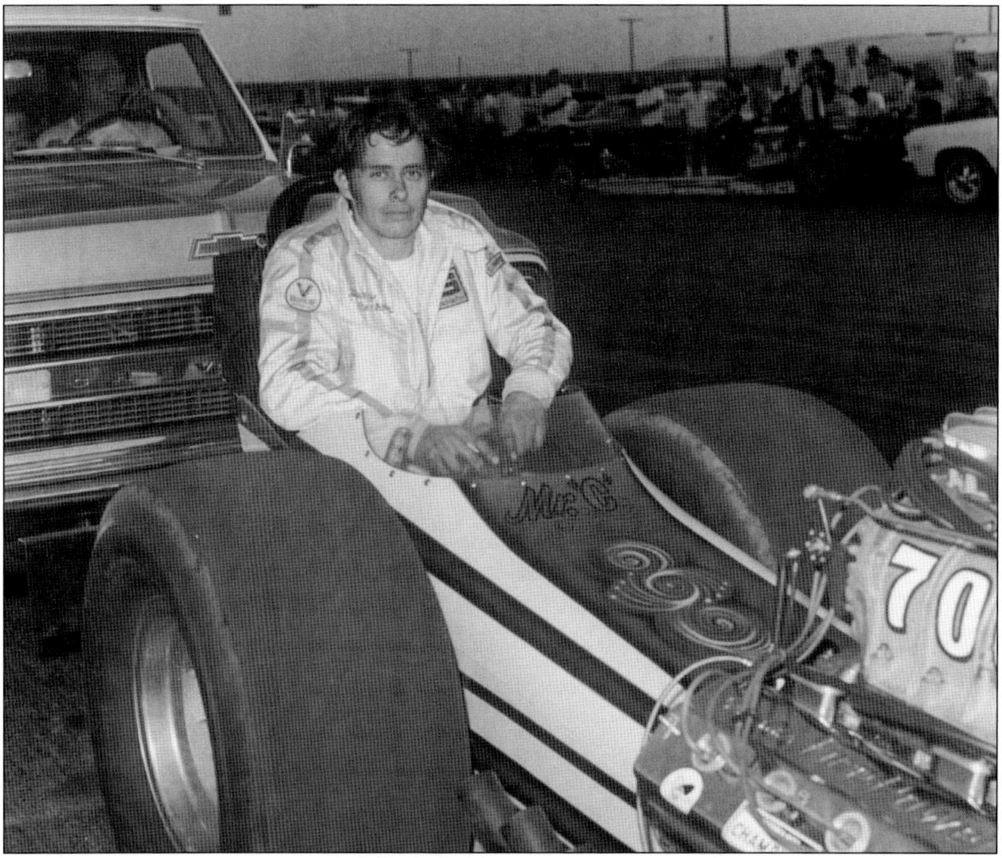

Top gas standout Gary Cochran made the switch to top fuel in late 1970 with his "Mr. C" dragster. On January 28, 1971, Cochran was the big underdog racing Don Garlits's new rear-engine top fuel dragster in the final of top fuel eliminator. Cochran sent Garlits back to his trailer empty-handed as he beat Garlits with a 6.59 to a losing 6.68. They both ran 223.88 miles per hour. That was the first day in competition for Garlits's rear-engine creation. Garlits would regroup and a week or so later win the 1971 NHRA Winternationals in Pomona, California.

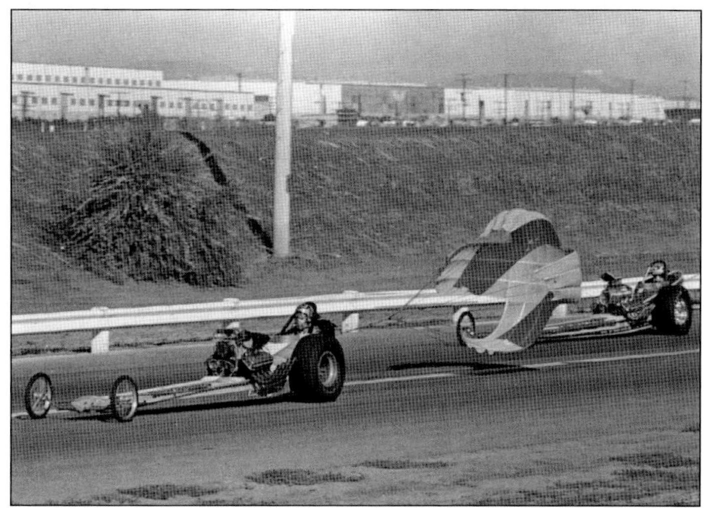

Longtime journeyman top fuel driver Tom Tolar slows down the unknown top fuel dragster of Rodney Kirchhoff in the OCIR shutdown area. In this photograph, it is not the car that is interesting but the background. Those are large industrial buildings springing up all around OCIR. The population is growing in East Irvine in early 1971 and moving closer to the racetrack.

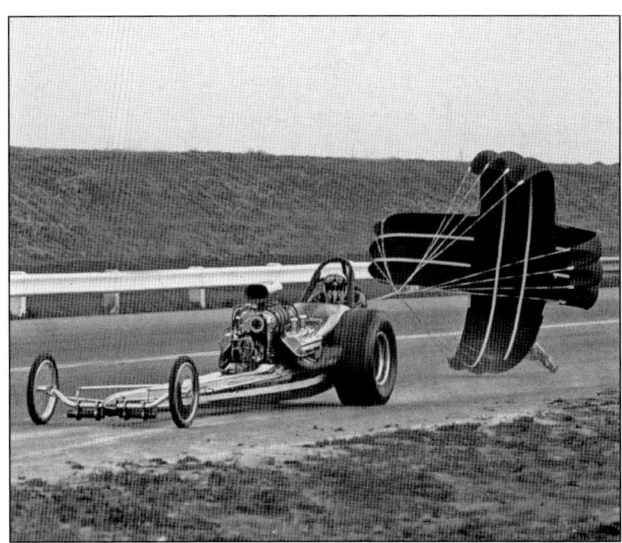

On tour in the winter of 1970 is banker Bruce Dodds and his St. Louis–based "Spirit" top fuel dragster with Bob Murray at the controls at OCIR. The Spirit was a regular at AHRA top fuel shows in the Midwest, but Dodd's front-engine top fueler would soon be replaced by an all-new rear-engine car in early 1971. Murray did the shakedown passes on the new Spirit but relinquished the driver's seat to Arnie Behling. Behling and new crew chief John "Tarzan" Austin put the new Spirit in the winner's circle at the 1971 NHRA Summernationals in Englishtown, New Jersey.

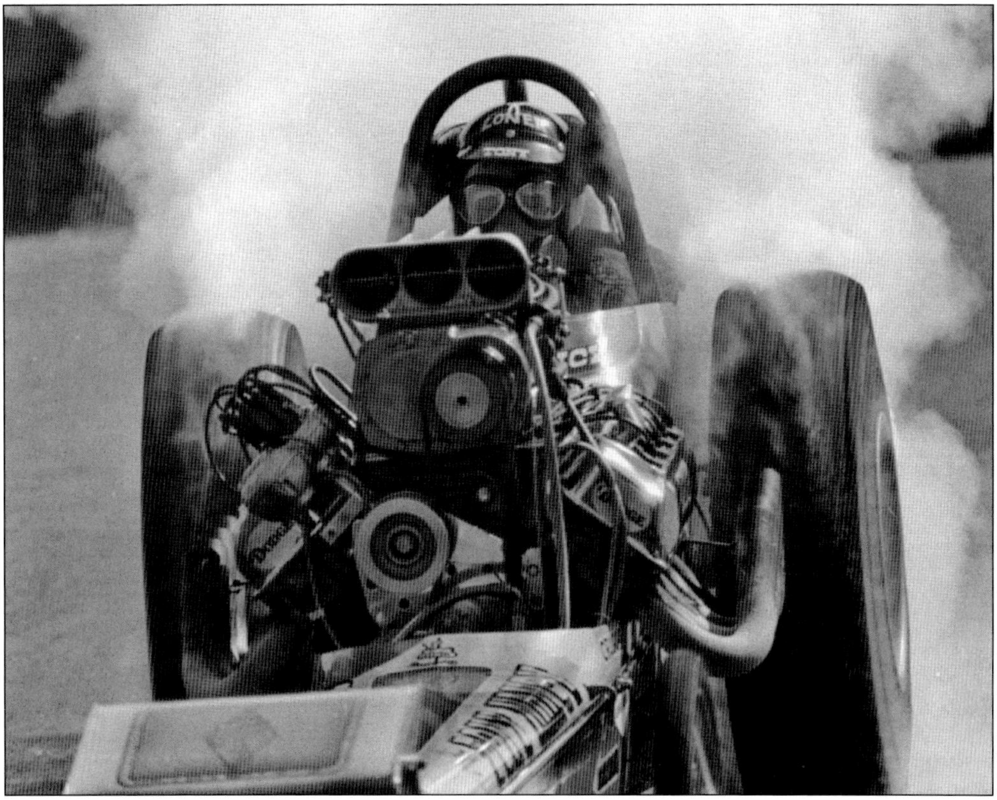

Late in 1969, Tony Nancy listened to his good friend Don Prudhomme about Nancy switching from top gas to top fuel, and he made the leap in 1970. Nancy's all-new "Wynn's Sizzler" top fuel dragster made its debut at OCIR in 1970. On March 27, 1971, Nancy set the OCIR ET record at 6.57. Then on July 23, 1971, he set the OCIR miles per hour record at 234.97. At the 1970 OCIR PDA race, Nancy, runner-up to Steve Carbone, who was driving for Mike Kuhl, also had low ET of the event at 6.69. He did start his top fuel endeavor in 1970 by winning the Bakersfield Fuel and Gas Championships.

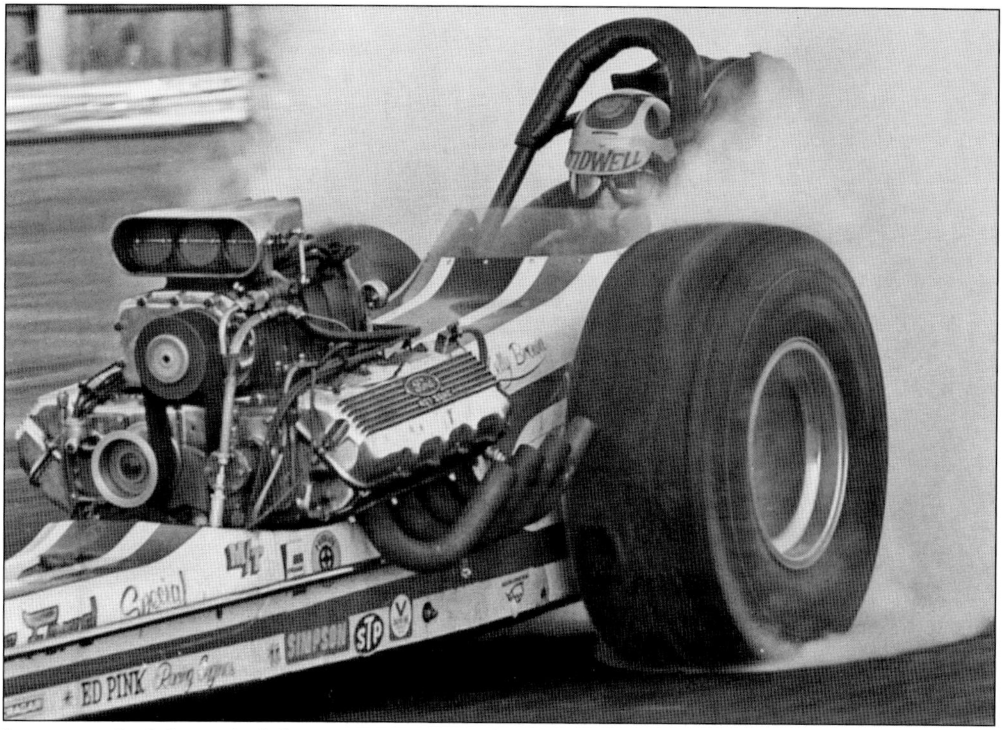

Longtime SoCal top fuel dragster owner Lou "Wolfman" Baney had some incredibly talented drivers in his many top fuel dragsters over the years. Tom "Mongoose" McEwen, Don "the Snake" Prudhomme, Kelly "the Controller" Brown, and "Captain" Billy Tidwell (pictured) all had seat time in Baney's top fuel dragsters. In April 1969, Kelly Brown, in Baney's Ford-powered top fueler, put away Norm Wilcox, Gerry Glenn, and James Warren to win the OCIR fuel tournament. All of Brown's runs were in the 6s: 6.81, 6.86, 6.85, and 6.84 in the final. He also had top speed of the event at 226.70 miles per hour.

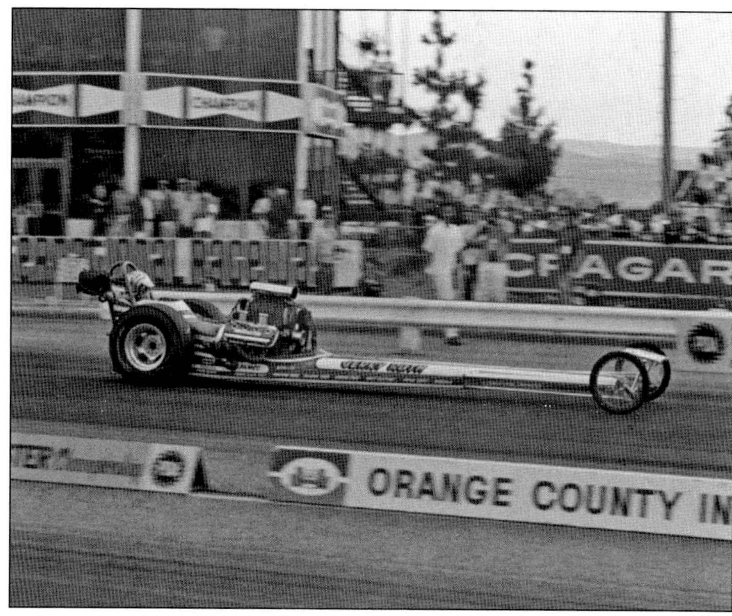

In March 1968, Jerry Ruth ventured down from the Northwest to compete at the OCIR PDA 64-car show. Ruth went away empty-handed, but he returned to SoCal in July for the Lions Drag Strip PDA race. There, Ruth waded through a stout field of the country's best top fuel dragsters and beat Tim Beebe and John Mulligan in the final round to claim that he was indeed king of the country's top fuel dragsters in 1968.

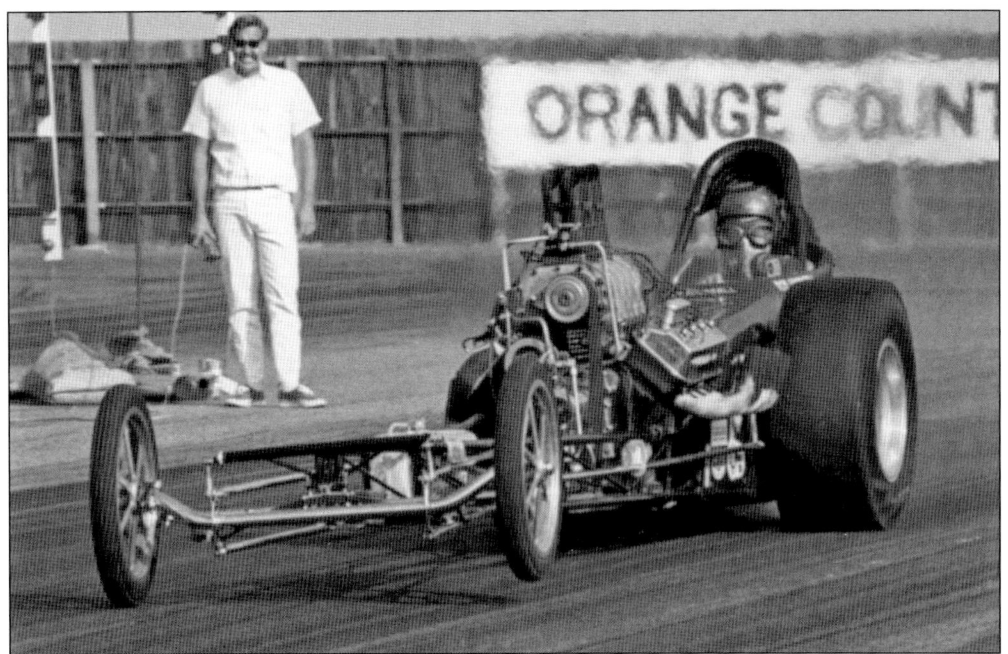

A regular at OCIR top fuel dragster events was Ronnie Goodsell and his "Earthquake" top fuel dragster. Goodsell's car was a one-of-a-kind top fueler that had suspension front and rear; he also used calliope-style injector stacks. Prior to his Earthquake top fueler, Goodsell drove for the Frantic Four and Joe Winter. While driving for the Frantic Four, Goodsell had Don Garlits run into the back of him at an East Coast track; nobody was hurt, just crunched race cars and hurt feelings. Goodsell also tried his hand at driving funny cars, which did not go so well. He had a crash and burn with Don Kirby's Beach City Chevrolet Corvette funny car at OCIR that ended his funny car driving career.

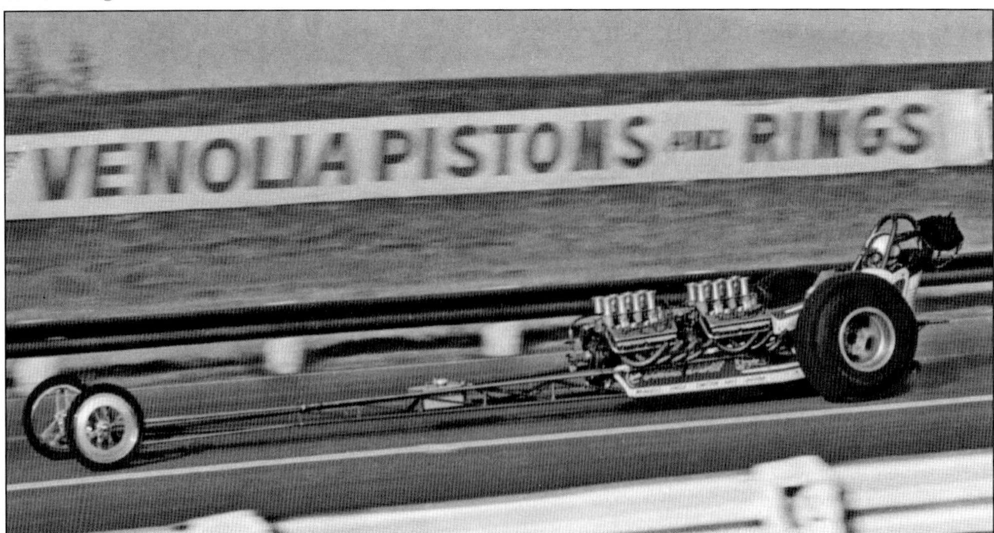

March 1970 at OCIR was the unveiling of the Adams, Rasmussen, and Scoggins "Double Eagle" twin engine top fuel dragster. Driver Don Enriquez laid down an impressive 6.79 ET on the car's first full run. But the twin engine top fuel dragster did not live up to its potential and was quickly parked. Adams and Enriquez returned to the single-engine JR fuel dragster for 1971.

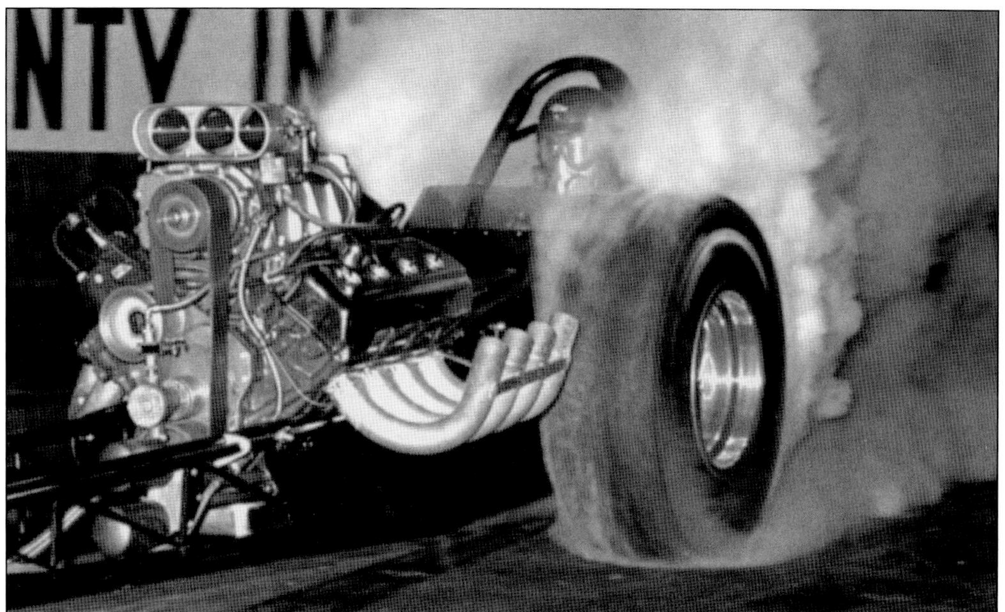

The "Ol' Gray Fox" Jack Ewell had former JR fuel dragster owner/driver Carl Olson at the helm of the Ewell, Bell, and Olson top fuel dragster in 1969–1970. Olson made the best of his top fuel ride by winning the 1969 Irwindale Grand Prix of drag racing, and in 1970, he cranked out 226.13 miles per hour for top speed honors at the OCIR PDA race.

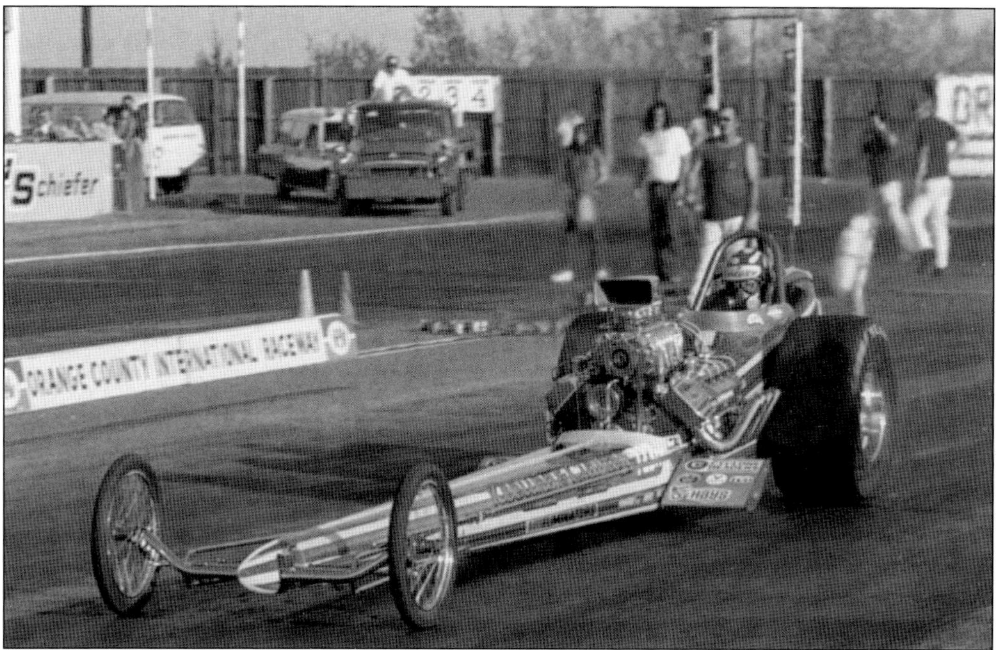

One of the best race cars ever to grace the track at OCIR was the Keeling and Clayton "California Charger" top fuel dragster. With Rick Ramsey as the driver, they had an incredibly good 1970 by winning top fuel eliminator at the first NHRA Supernationals in Ontario, California. In July 1971, the trio set the OCIR track ET record at 6.68. They then lowered their own top fuel ET record at OCIR to 6.42.

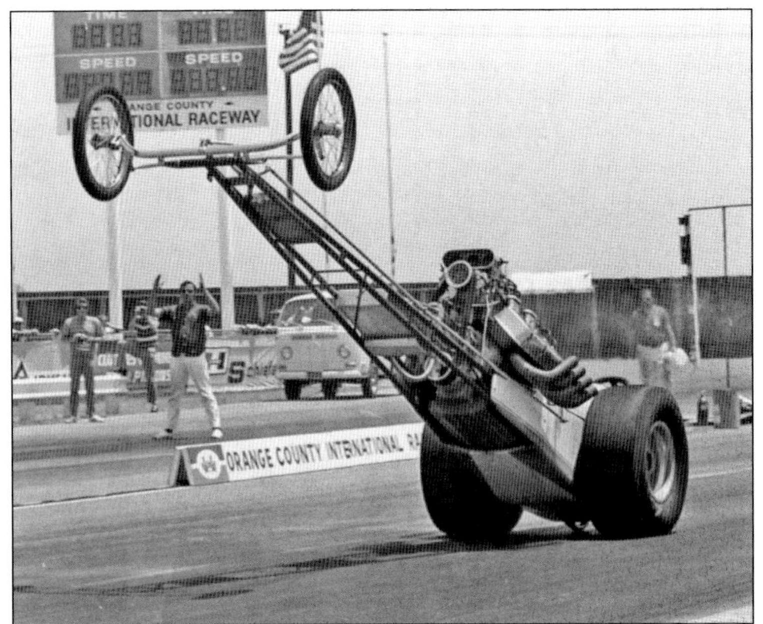

San Diego's Ted Inque found out the hard way about OCIR's track prep with three giant wheelstands that destroyed the front end of his top fuel dragster. Inque loaded up his very broken race car and headed home to San Diego to fix his very broken fueler. OCIR manager Mike Jones took his track prep very seriously, making sure the track was clean and the right amount of traction compound was used.

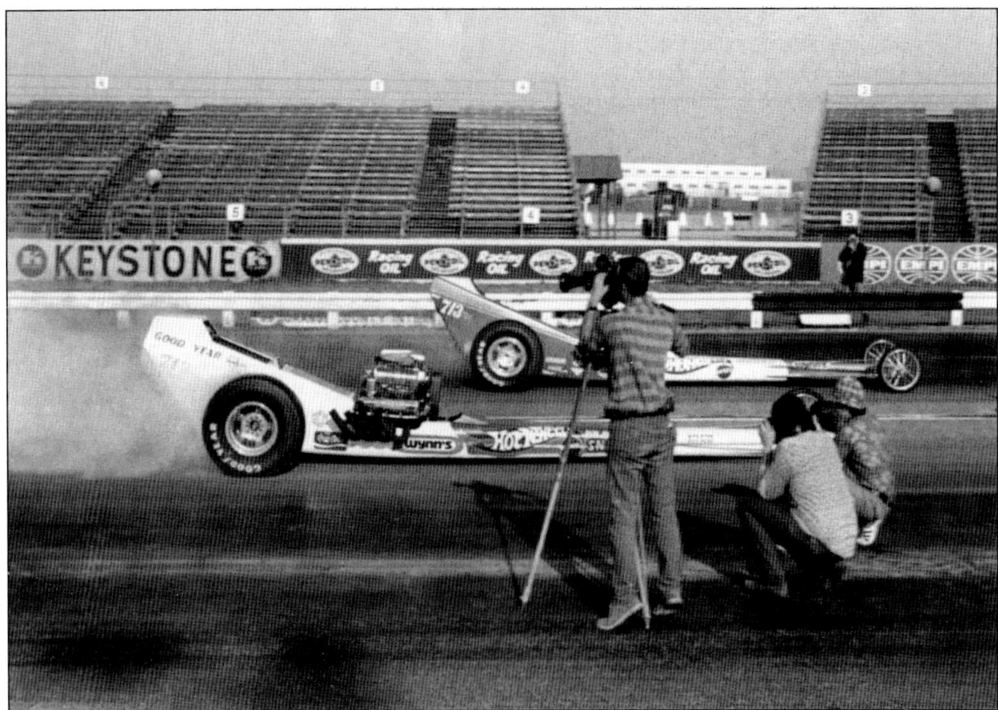

When Mattel, which sells Hot Wheels, entered the world of drag racing, it did so in a big way with the sponsorship of two funny cars and two top fuel dragsters for Don "the Snake" Prudhomme and Tom "Mongoose" McEwen. Here, in 1971, at OCIR, the Mattel film crew is shooting a television commercial for the Snake and Mongoose dragster playset. And yes, the cars are going the wrong way on the track. The video team insisted that the cars burnout toward the back wall of the burnout area because it provided better lighting. Being pros, Prudhomme and McEwen did what had to be done for the film crew and their sponsor.

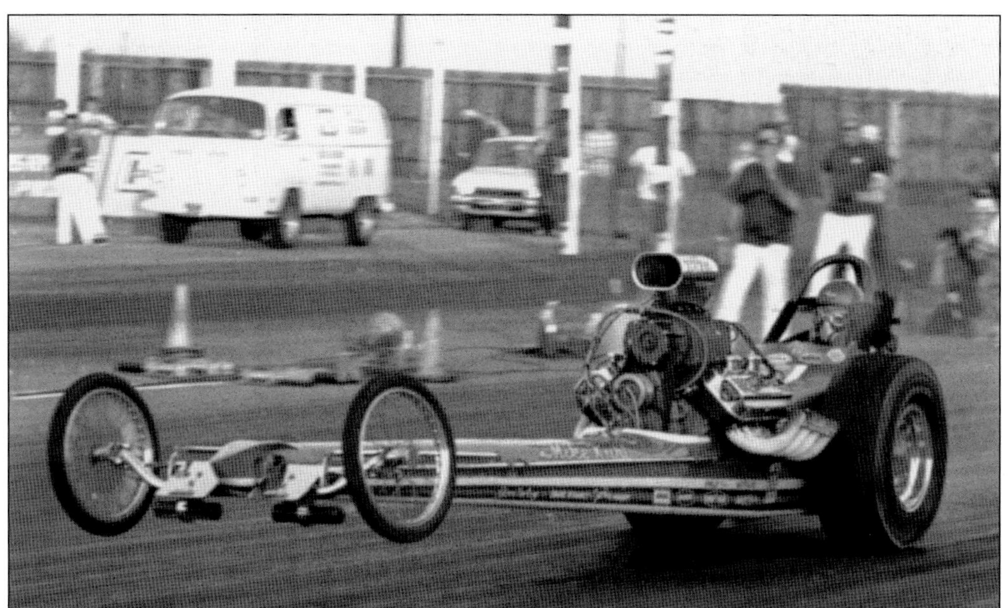

In 1971, Mike Kuhl and Carl Olson teamed up to run the Kuhl and Olson (K&O) top fuel dragster at OCIR. They were racing "Surfer" Hank Westmoreland, who was driving the Allen family "Praying Mantis" top fuel dragster. The Christmas tree flashed green, and Olson jumped to the lead in the K&O fueler, his car riding on its fifth wheel in the rear of the car. Of course, Olson expected the front end to return to earth, but the car had other ideas. He was at the one-eighth mile on the quarter-mile track and still the front wheels are high in the air. The OCIR crowd was on its feet wondering if Olson was going the entire quarter mile with the front end dangling in the air. At just past the one-eighth mile, Olson had to lift off the throttle, which allowed Westmoreland to pass and win the race. That was one of the best crowd-pleasing runs of 1971 at OCIR.

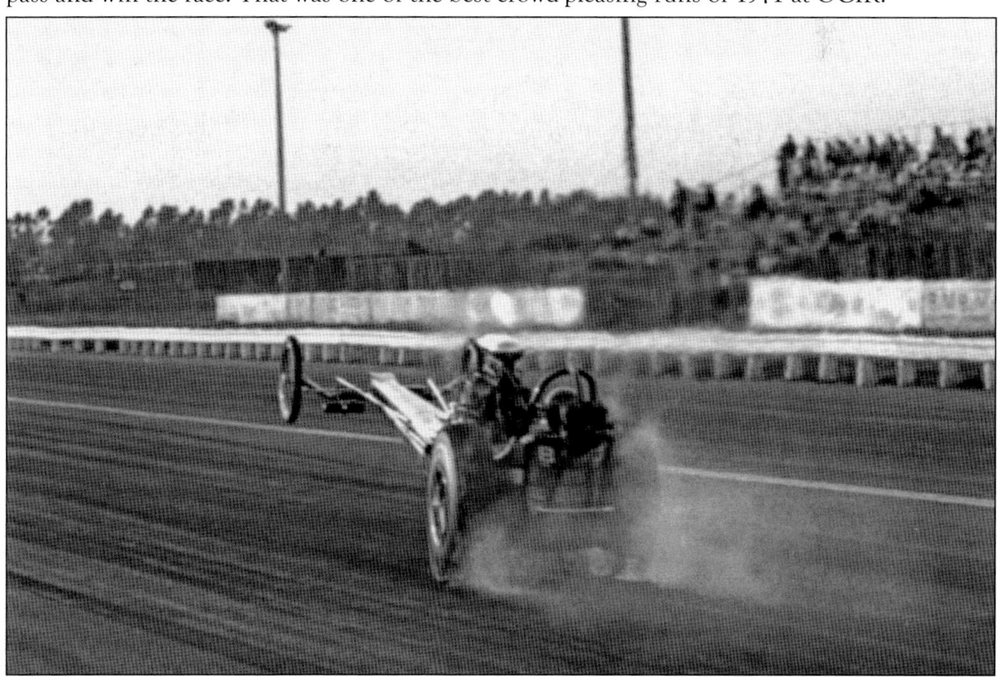

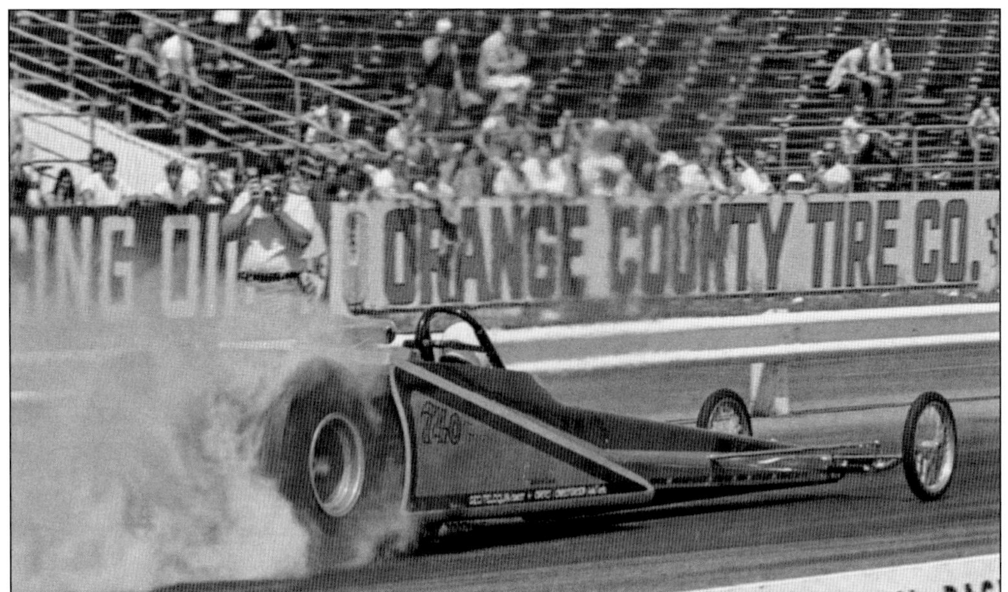

Making its debut in 1971 at OCIR was Leland Kolb's "Polish Lotus," a wedge-bodied, rear-engine top fuel dragster. This wedge-concept body would also be used by Don Prudhomme, Chris Karamesines, Kenney Goodell, Dan Olson, and Pancho Rendon. The body proved to be too heavy for top fuel competition, though, and the bodies would soon be removed or the cars parked. Pancho Rendon's car was destroyed in a spectacular crash at the 1971 NHRA US Nationals in Indianapolis. Rendon's driver, Connie Kalitta, escaped unharmed in the crash.

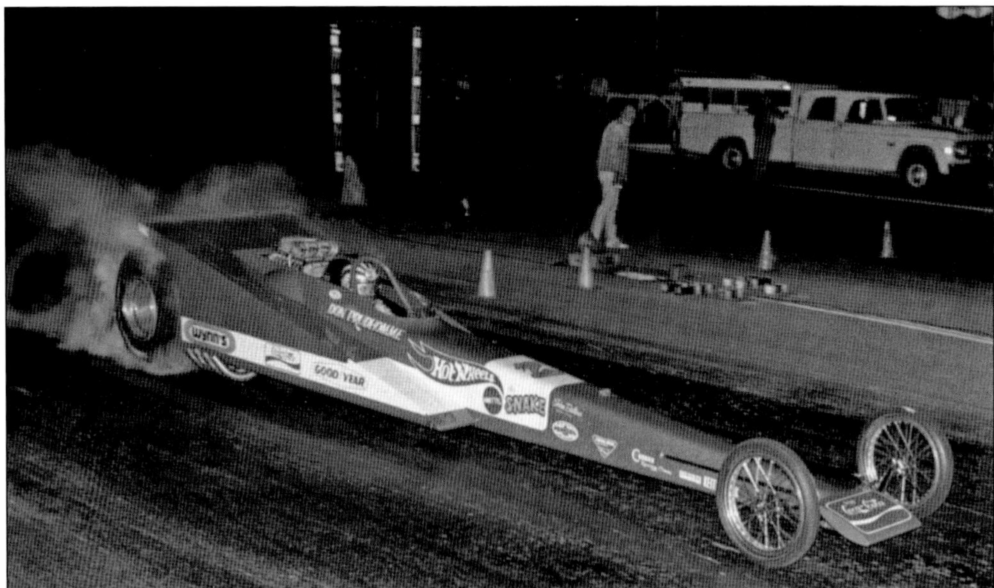

After much fanfare and hype, Don Prudhomme's wedge-style, rear-engine top fuel dragster made its debut at OCIR in May 1971. Prudhomme tried to make the overweight top fuel dragster work but to no avail. By the time the NHRA US Nationals rolled around in September, Prudhomme had removed the wedge body to compete with lighter cars in top fuel. The car, in its full wedge-body glory, appeared on the cover of *Drag Racing USA* magazine and on an OCIR race program before being stripped.

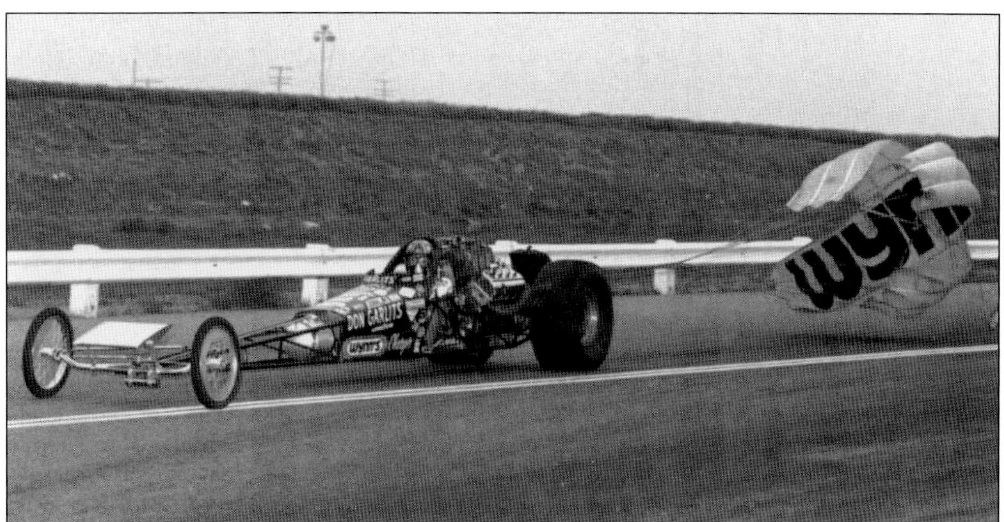

It was a cool, overcast day at OCIR on January 28, 1971, when Florida's Don Garlits unveiled his new rear-engine top fuel dragster. This was the car's first day in competition, and it proved to be a successful outing for Garlits. Garlits was beaten in the final round of the top fuel eliminator by local boy Gary Cochran, 6.59 to a losing 6.62. About a week or so later, Garlits took his new car to the 1971 NHRA Winternationals in Pomona, California, and won top fuel eliminator over a field of front-engine top fuelers.

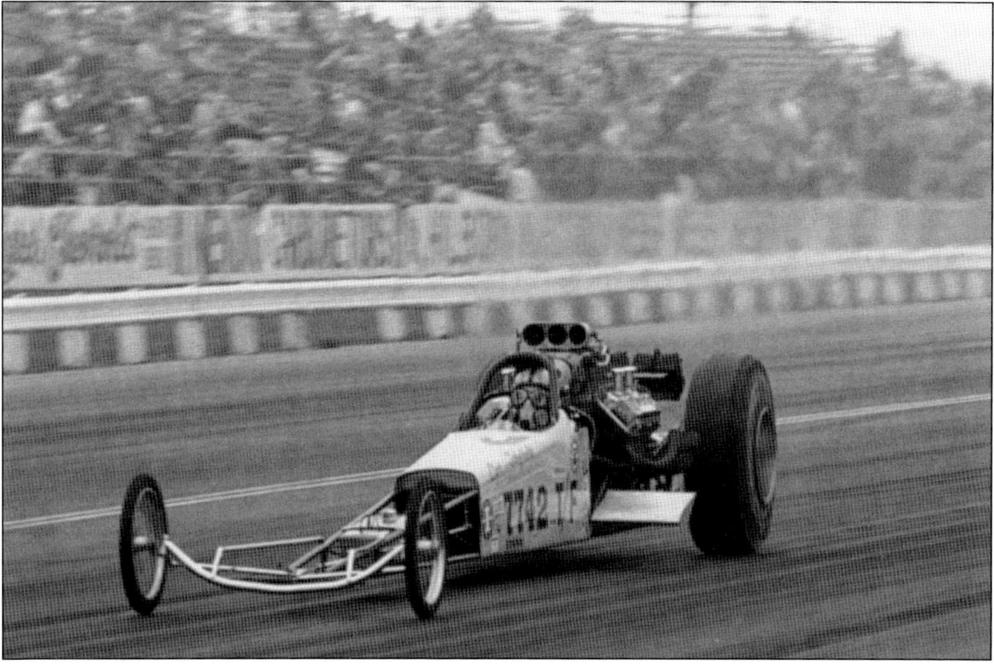

Like many top fuel racers, Ted Cyr and Flip Schofield parked their front-engine top fueler and built a new rear-engine top fuel dragster. On its second run at OCIR in 1971, the car staged, and when the Christmas tree went green, Flip Schofield hit the throttle. But new car gremlins overtook the car and the transmission exploded, spreading pieces everywhere on the starting line and throwing pieces into the second story of the OCIR tower, just missing track manager Mike Jones. It was a very forgettable day at OCIR for Cyr, Schofield, and Jones.

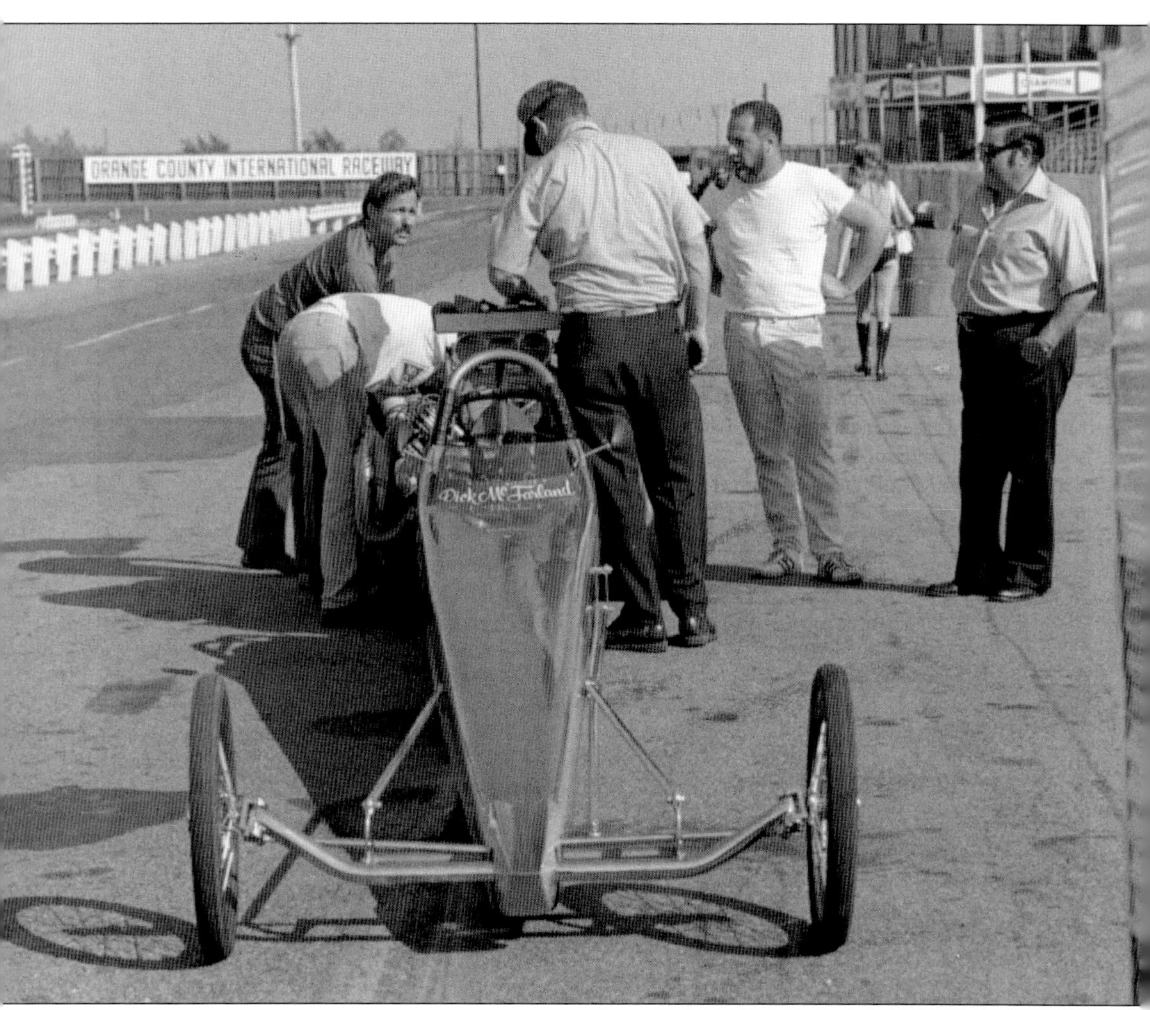

New car testing at OCIR in 1971 was quite common. Here, Florida's Dick McFarland (at left with mustache) is getting ready to take laps with his all-new Woody Gilmore and Keith Black–powered top fuel dragster. McFarland readies his new car for its maiden voyage with, from left to right, an unidentified crew member, Keith Black, Woody Gilmore, and Lou Baney. McFarland made check out runs under those watchful eyes before packing up and heading back to Florida.

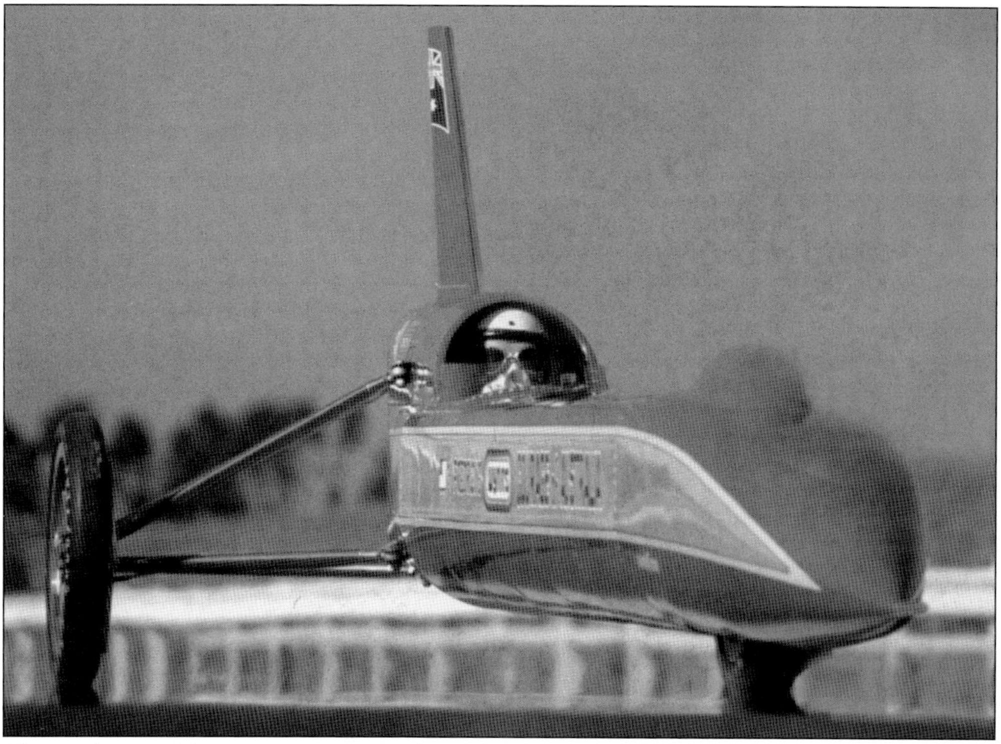

The quickest and fastest car ever to run down the racetrack at OCIR was Bill Fredrick's "Courage of Australia," a hydrogen peroxide/silver screen catalyst rocket car. On November 11, 1971, Vic Wilson piloted the sleek three-wheeled purple rocket to a 5.10 at 311.41 miles per hour. It would take 21 years for a nitro-powered top fuel dragster to clock 300 miles per hour. Kenny Bernstein would run 301.70 miles per hour in his "Budweiser King" top fuel dragster on March 20 at the 1992 NHRA Gatornationals in Gainesville, Florida.

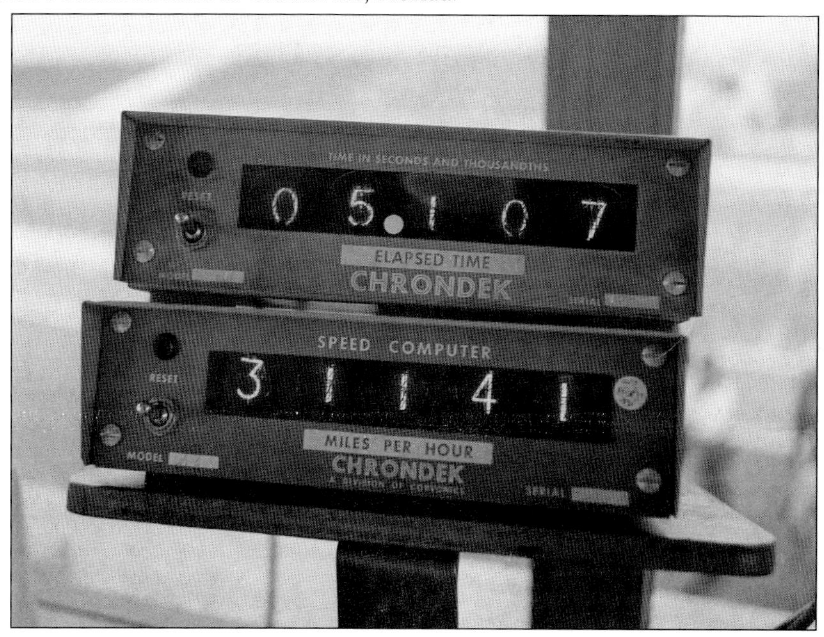

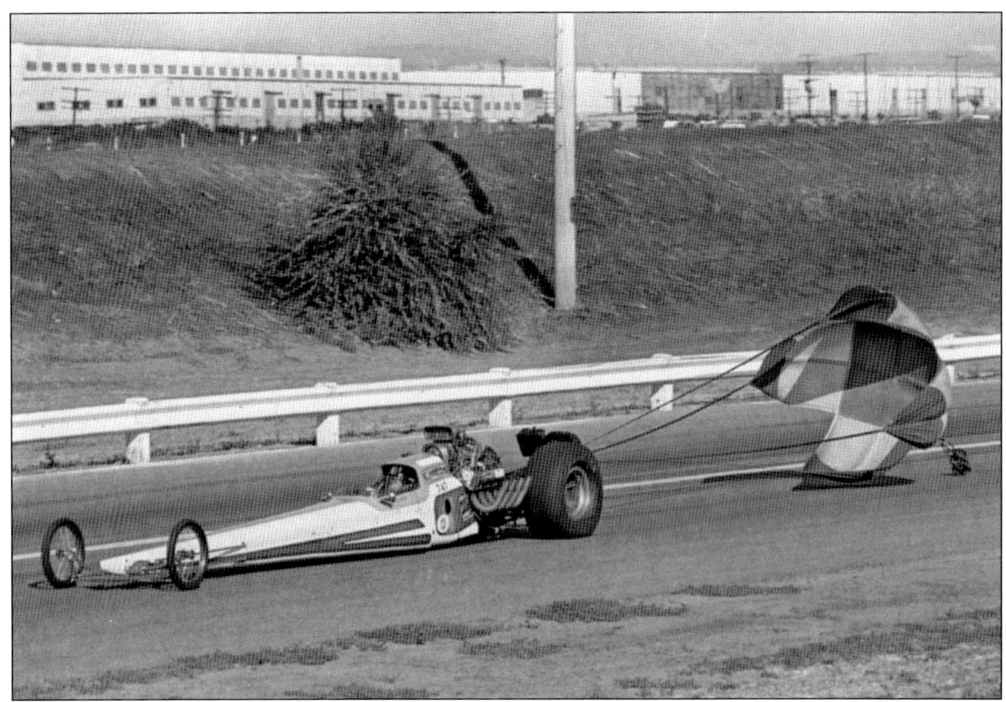

The adventures of Harry Hibler at OCIR in 1971–1972 are legendary. While on a pass in a new top fuel dragster, Hibler had a chute failure. No big deal because OCIR has a sand trap at the end of the track. But what if it had rained, and the sand was packed solid? Hibler hit the sand trap, and instead of slowing the car down, the sand catapulted the car end over end. Hibler crawled out with a fractured left arm. It was no big deal for Hibler, though, as later that same night he drove Don Green's "Rat Trap" fuel altered with that broken arm. Hibler got well, and the dragster was fixed and renamed "the Sandman." Then, in 1972, Hibler blew the clutch out of the car just past the starting line (yes, that is the bell housing in midair). He was not injured, but he did live up to his nickname of "Hand Grenade Harry."

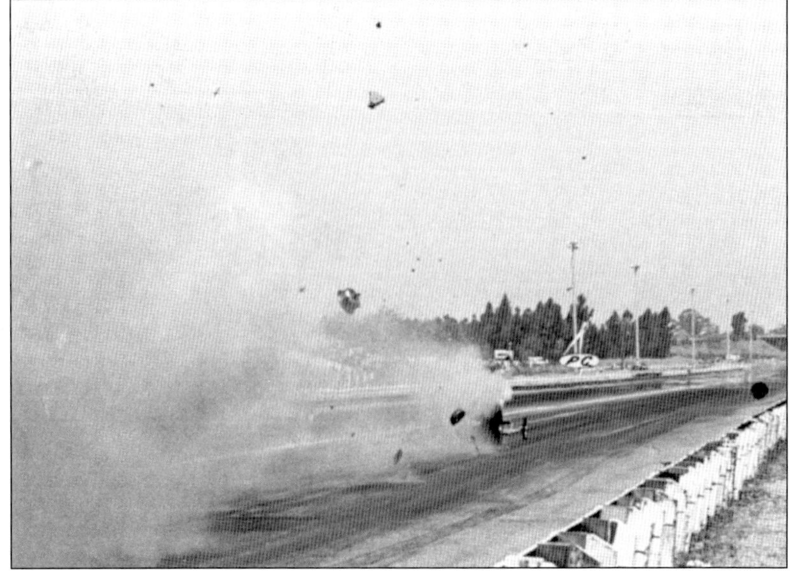

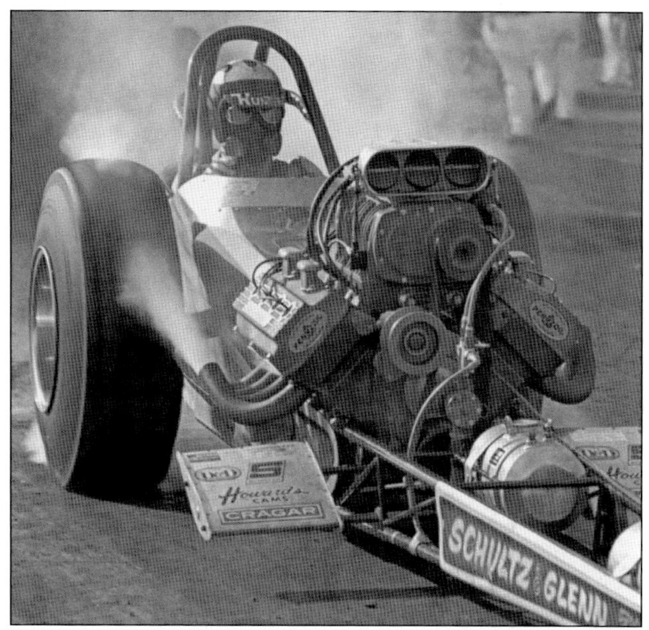

The dynamic duo of Bill Schultz and Gerry Glenn had a surprisingly good year in 1971. With their shiny, new top fuel dragster, the pair won the OCIR PDA race by beating Keeling and Clayton in the final round: 6.50 at 220.58 miles per hour to a losing 6.72 at 185.13 miles per hour. Schultz and Glenn then headed to Amarillo, Texas, for the 1971 NHRA World Finals, where they met Don Garlits in the final round. Garlits redlighted his chances away, and Glenn streaked to a 6.59 victory at 227.27 miles per hour. Not too bad for a new top fuel car. This duo also owned the last front-engine top fueler that would win the NHRA World Finals.

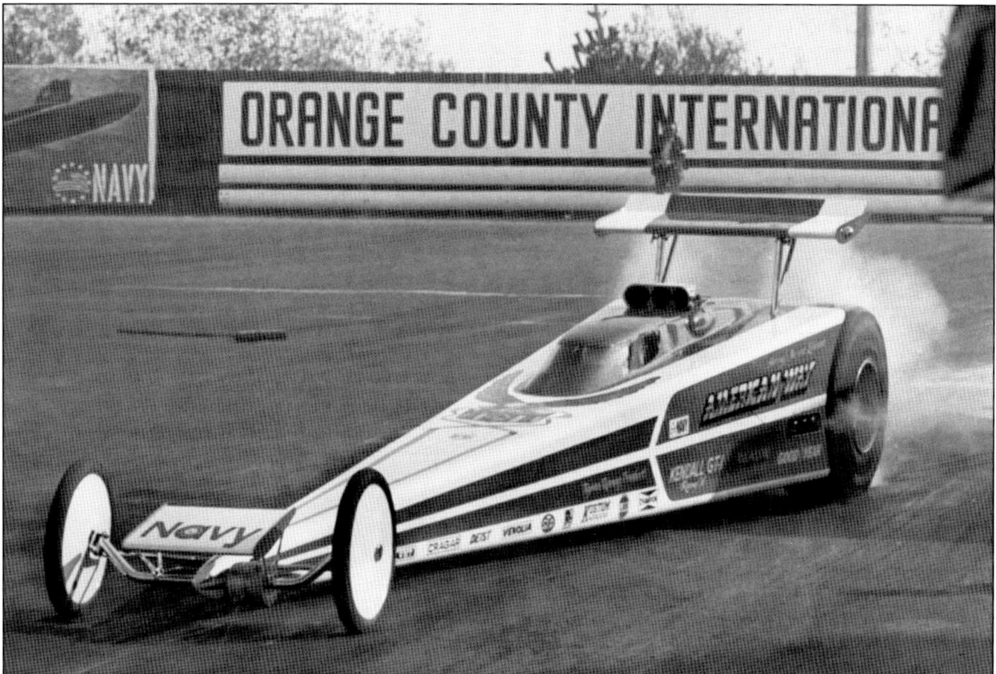

Sadly, running a top fuel dragster can be very trying at times. Harry and Maxine Lehman found this out firsthand with their "American Way" top fuel streamline dragster in 1972. The car was built around their driver Al Friedman. Friedman was a smaller than the average driver, so the cockpit of the car was small and a very tight fit for anyone else but him. Unfortunately, Friedman passed away, leaving the Lehmans with a big problem. Who could fit into their all-new streamliner? West Coast journeyman driver Howard Haight squeezed into the car for its debut at OCIR's Navy-sponsored race. Haight continued to drive the car a few more times until it was crashed in a finish line accident in 1974 at Maple Grove, Pennsylvania. The Lehmans did not rebuild the car.

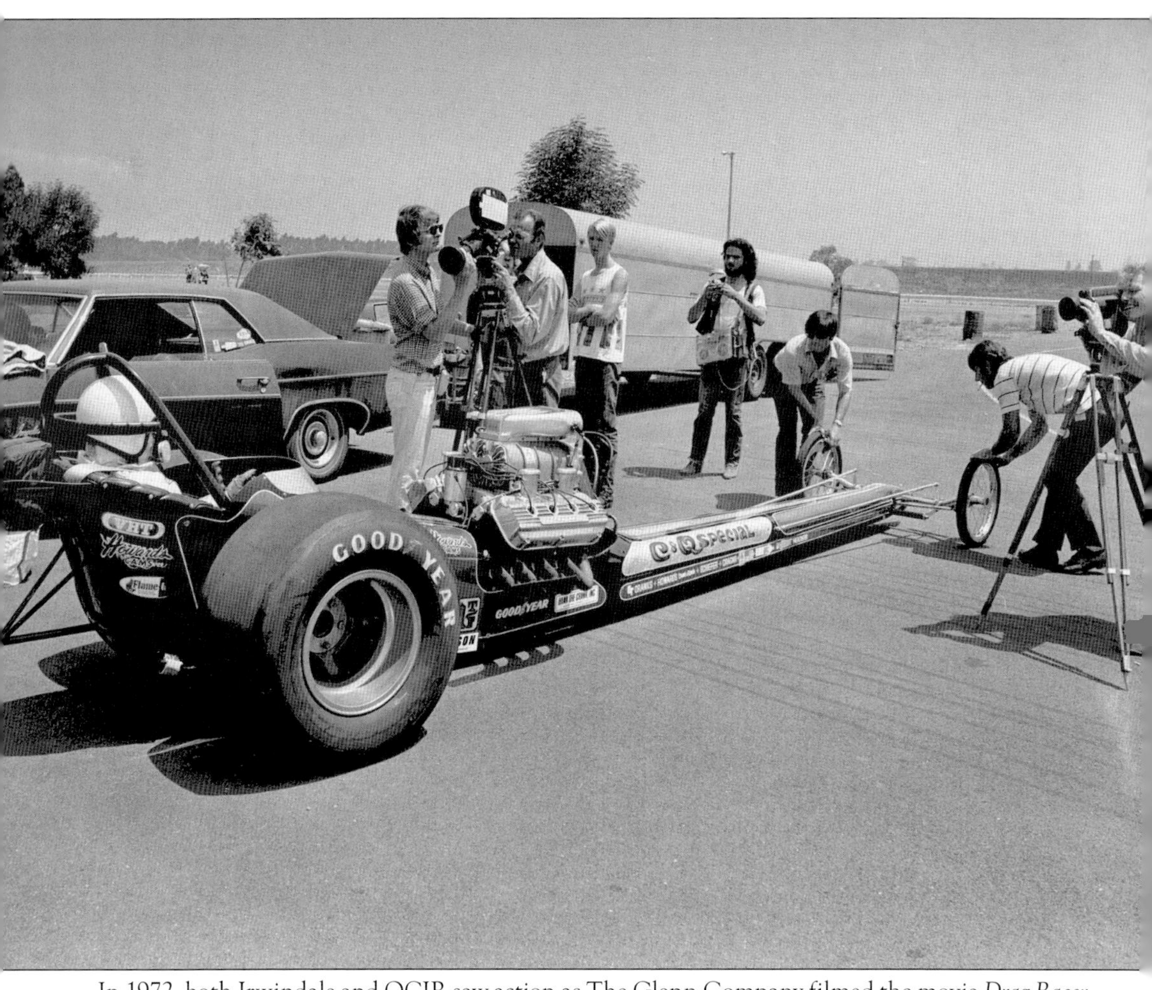

In 1972, both Irwindale and OCIR saw action as The Glenn Company filmed the movie *Drag Racer* at the tracks. The movie starred Mark Slade, Jeremy Slate, and Deborah Walley. It also featured the top fuel dragsters of Annin and Snively, Bill Simpson, and Schultz and Glenn. The funny cars of John Lombardo and Mert Littlefield were also featured, as were the altereds of Sherm Gunn and Dennis Giesler. John and Beverly Peters brought their "Freight Train" out of retirement for a starring role in the movie. The main "star" car in the movie was the 1970 front-engine Schultz and Glenn top fuel dragster, which was rebranded as the "C&O Special."

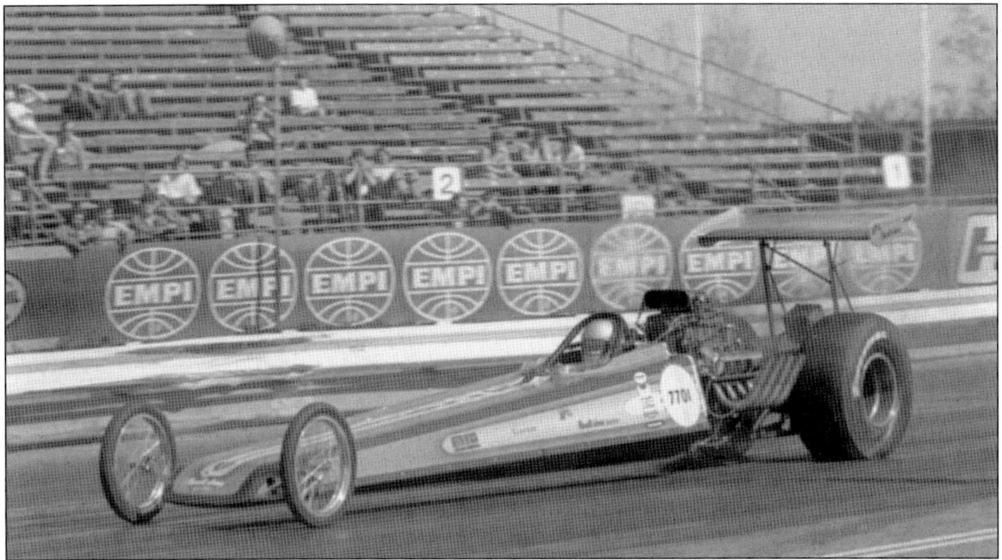

The team of Lisa and Rossi introduced their top fuel streamliner at OCIR in 1972 with the "Flyin' Hawaiian" Danny Ongais in the driver's seat. The OCIR fans referred to it as the "Flying Doorstop" because of its strange shape. The car would soon change owners and became a Vels/ Parnelli Jones top fuel dragster with Billy Tidwell in the driver's seat. Jack "Mosquito" Martin took over the driving duties in 1973.

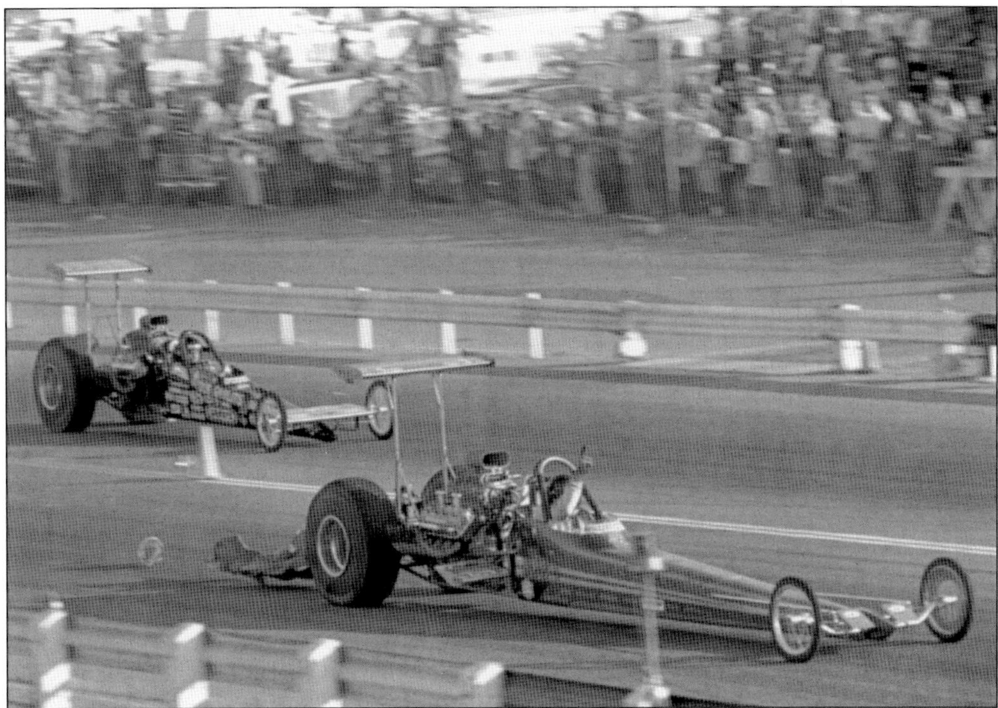
Heading down to OCIR from Washington state was the top fuel team of Petersen and Fitz. With Herm Petersen at the controls of the Northwest-based top fuel dragster, the duo won the 1972 OCIR PDA race. Petersen defeated Don Garlits and his shorty top fuel dragster in the first round and took care of Tom McEwen with a 6.75 at 215.82 miles per hour in the final round.

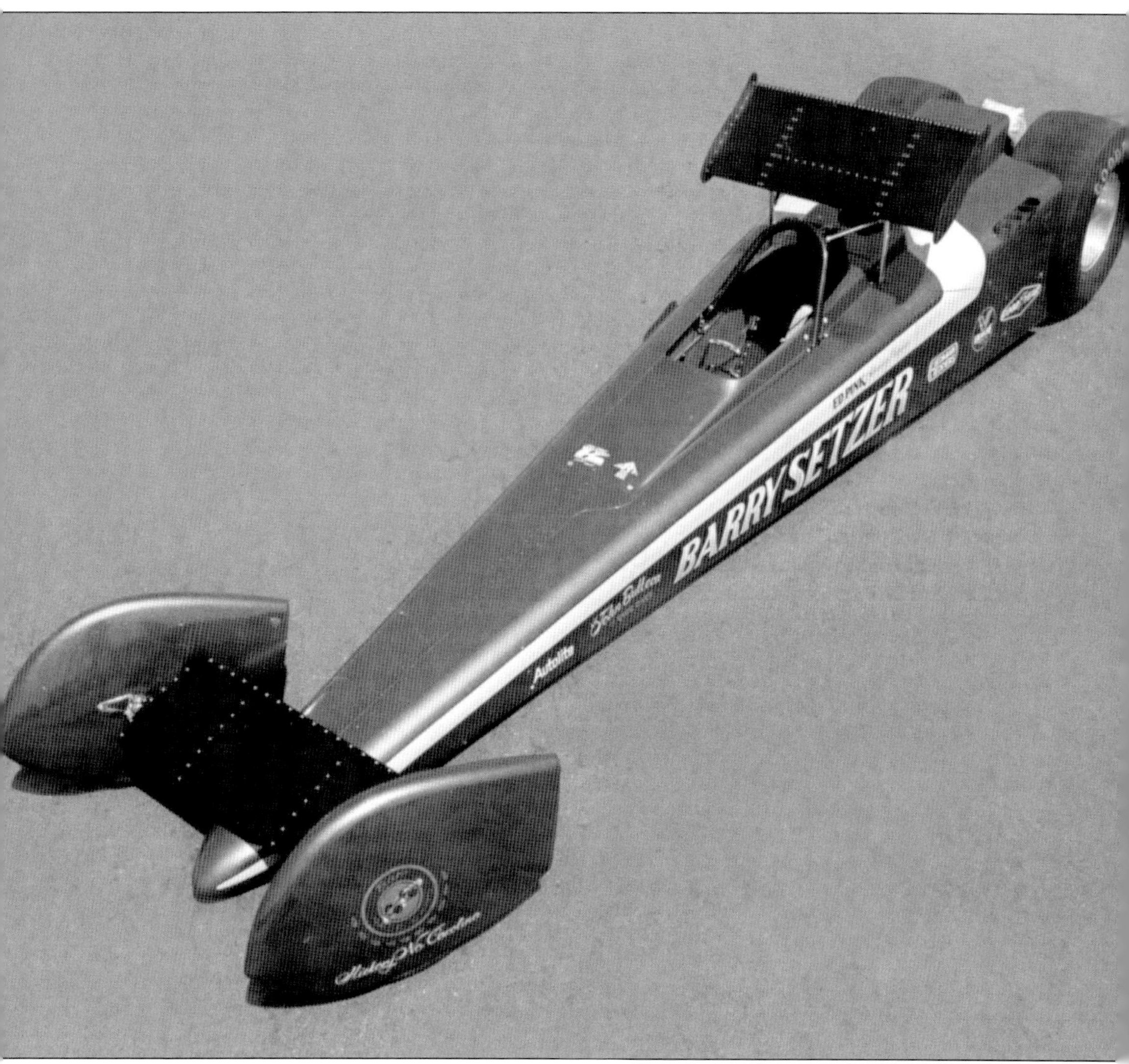

North Carolina's Barry Setzer had master craftsman John Buttera build a one-of-a-kind, wedge-shaped, monocoque-style chassis top fuel dragster. The car had .050-gauge magnesium sheet riveted together. After all the publicity around this one-of-a-kind top fuel dragster, it was time to see if the car would work. In hush-hush secret testing during the week at OCIR, driver Pat Foster was to make the shakedown runs of the candy-red wedge. Unfortunately, things did not go as planned. On the third try to get the car to go down the racetrack, it did a giant wheelstand and came down, damaging the car. The car was parked and considered a failure. It was later repaired and sold to Russell Mendez and Ramon Alvarez. They were going to put a rocket engine in it, but Mendez was killed in their other rocket car in Gainesville, Florida. Alvarez sold it to Don Garlits, who restored it. The car now resides in the Don Garlits Museum of Drag Racing in Ocala, Florida.

The Alabama-based team of Jack Mackay and Clayton Harris brought their "New Dimensions" top fuel dragster to OCIR in 1971–1972. Those Alabama boys showed how they run a top fuel dragster when on February 13, 1972, Clayton Harris set both ends of the OCIR records for top fuel dragsters with a 6.22 at 235.60 miles per hour.

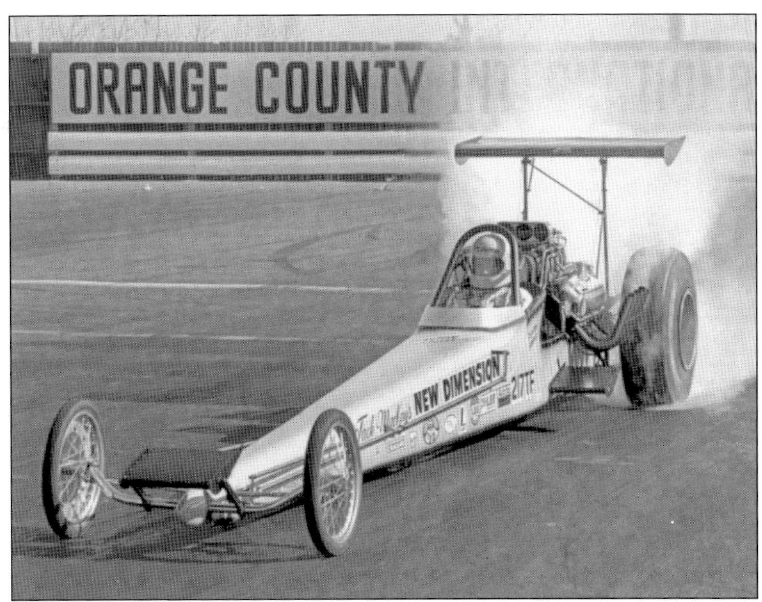

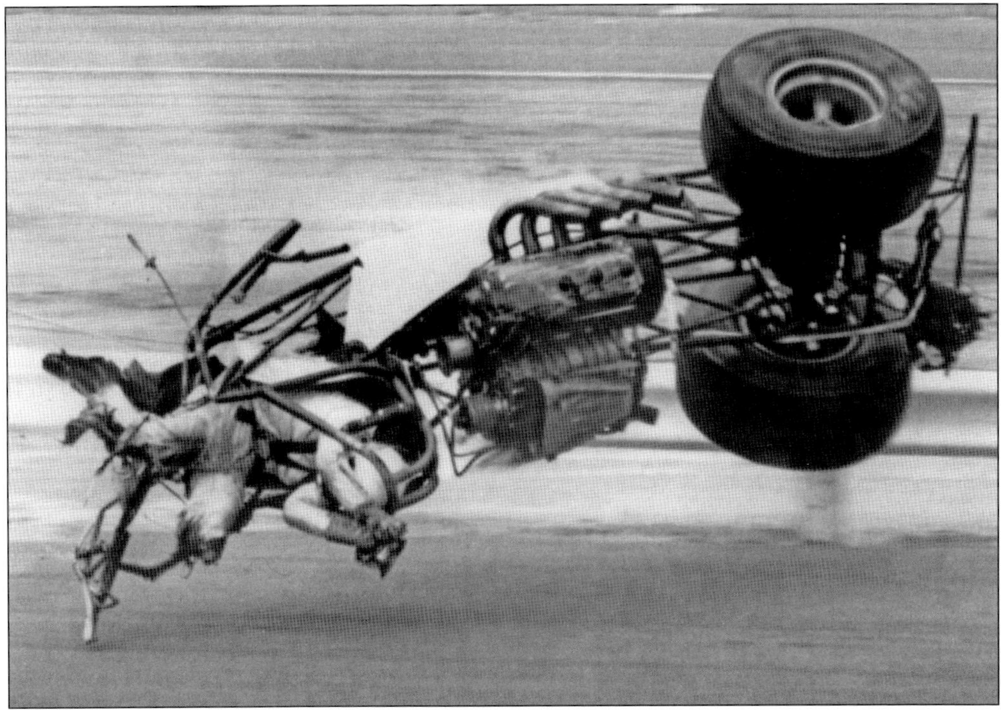

The worst scenario for a rear-engine top fuel dragster happened in early 1972 at OCIR. Kenny Logan hit the OCIR guardrail head on at speed with his top fuel dragster. The ensuing crash cost Logan his legs and right hand. He was dead at the scene, but the OCIR emergency crew had a new respirator and used it to bring Logan back to life. Logan's accident was one of the primary reasons that racetracks around the United States installed concrete barriers and got rid of the Armco guardrails. Thankfully, Kenny Logan is still with us, and he attends nostalgia drag races on the West Coast.

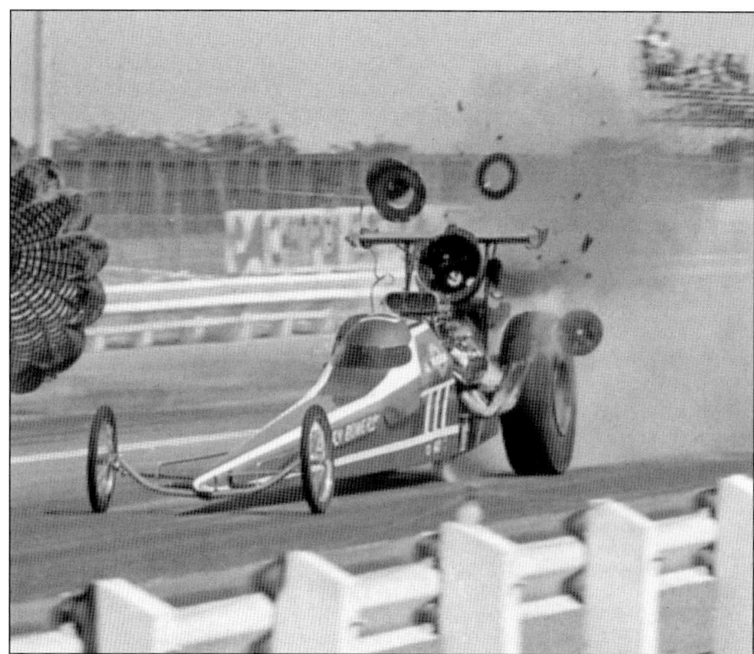

The onset of the rear-engine top fuel dragster proved to be a great breakthrough for driver safety and performance. Here, at OCIR in 1972, Larry Bowers's top fuel dragster had a massive clutch failure, but Bowers was not injured in the explosion. Five years earlier, in Tony Waters's front-engine top fuel dragster, Mike Sorokin was killed when Waters's car had the same type of clutch failure at OCIR on December 30, 1967.

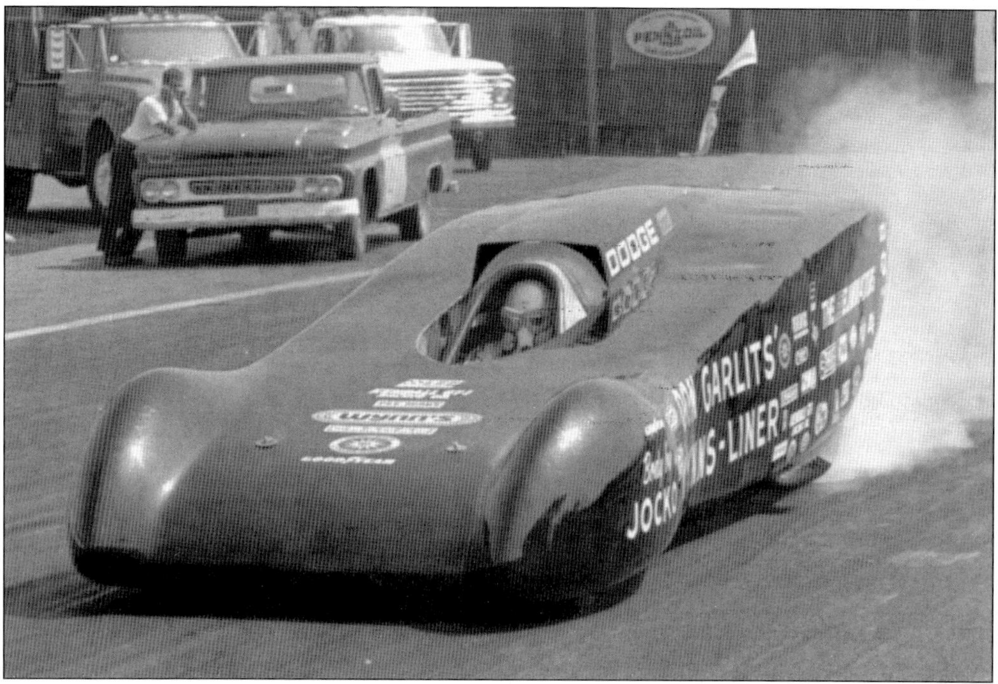

Don Garlits tried going to a streamliner in the mid-1970s. Garlits and crew chief T.C. Lemons brought his Wynns-Liner to OCIR for some test and tune-up runs. Veteran top fuel and funny car driver Butch Maas was at the controls of the black beauty. The car had been run in Florida with Don Cook driving, but it had problems with the front end floating at the finish line. OCIR had a different track surface so maybe that would make a difference in the car's performance. Maas and Garlits made three very ho-hum runs with the car, and it was trailered back to Florida and remained parked until Garlits opened his drag racing museum, where it is now on display.

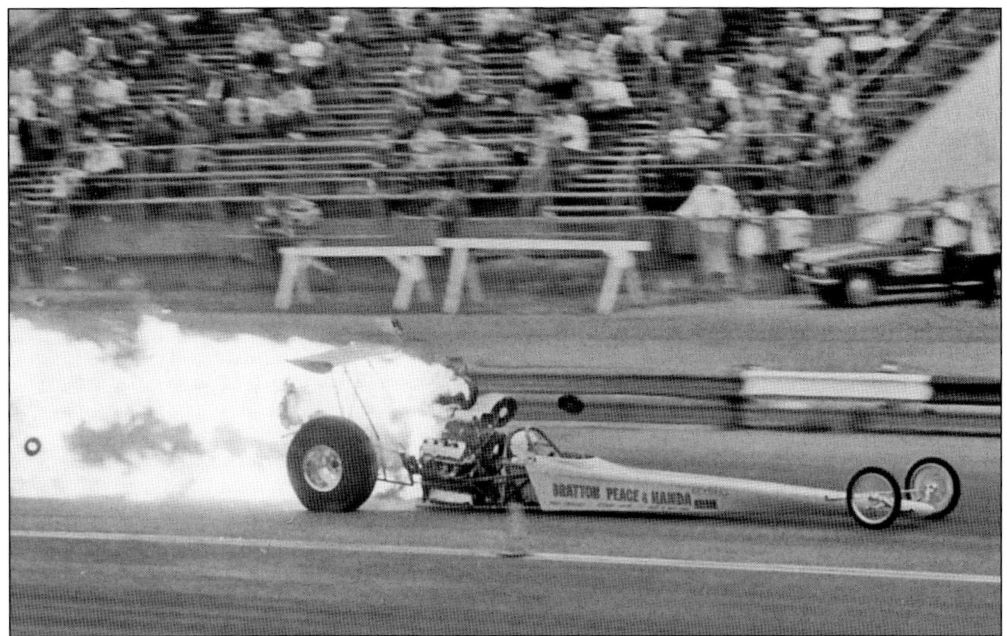

The Northern California team of Bratton, Peace, and Handa proved they could blow up parts just like the top fuel racers in SoCal. Here, at OCIR in 1973, their car, piloted by Jim Peace, had a massive transmission and clutch failure that cut the frame rails behind the driver. Peace was not injured, but the trio's wallet took a beating that day.

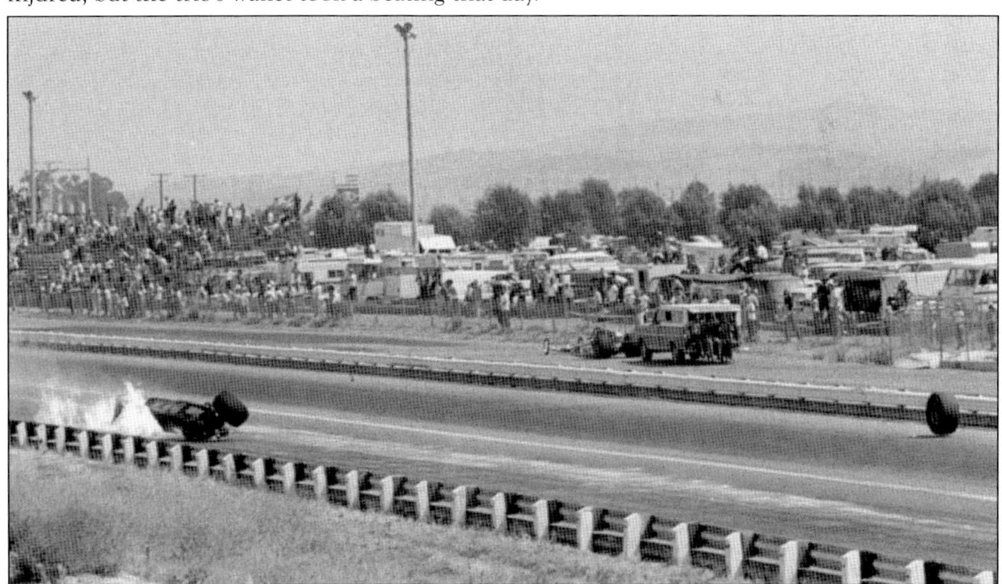

The OCIR PDA race was incredibly great for the team of Petersen and Fitz in 1972. But 1973 was a disaster for the team. First-round action saw the Petersen and Fitz top fuel dragster lose a rear wheel and flip upside down, sliding the entire length of the quarter mile on fire. Driver Herm Petersen sustained serious burns to his face and hands in the blaze. The drag racing community rallied around Petersen to try and get the Washington-based driver back on his feet. Petersen is one tough guy and overcame his injuries. One year after his accident, he was driving a top fuel dragster at OCIR.

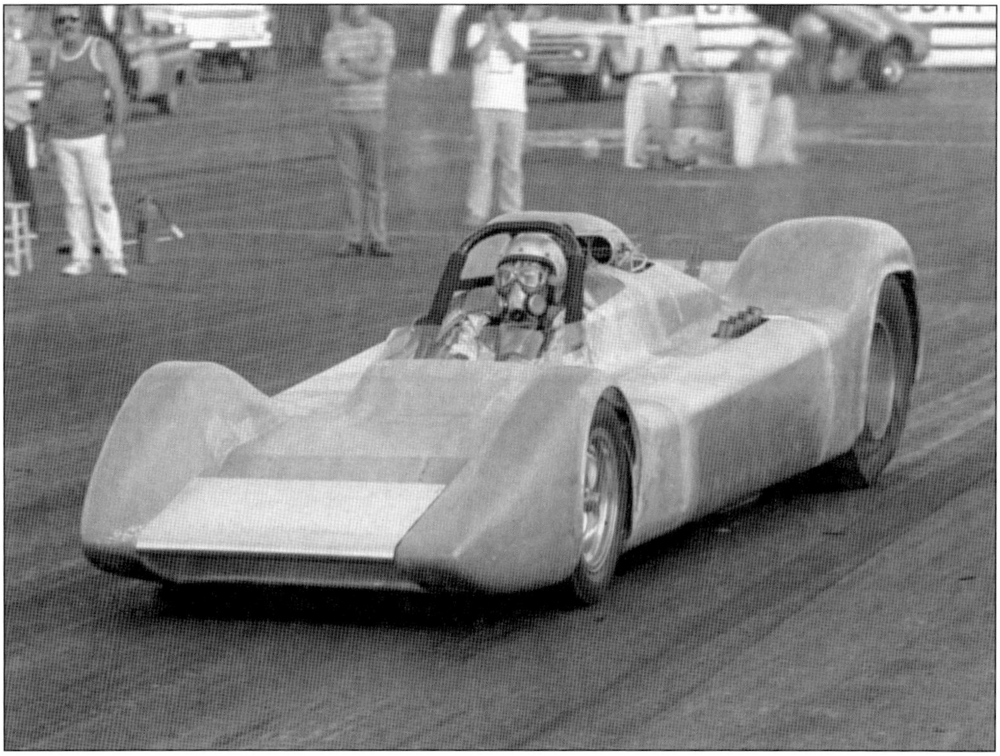

It seemed like for a while everyone was trying to make a streamliner top fuel dragster work at OCIR. Here, in 1973, it is Jim Dunn with a special streamline body built by Doug Kruse atop the Dunn and Reath rear-engine funny car. The car ran a few times with the Kruse body and was used for a magazine shoot, and then it was then discarded. Dunn plopped his Cuda body back on and went back to funny car racing in 1973.

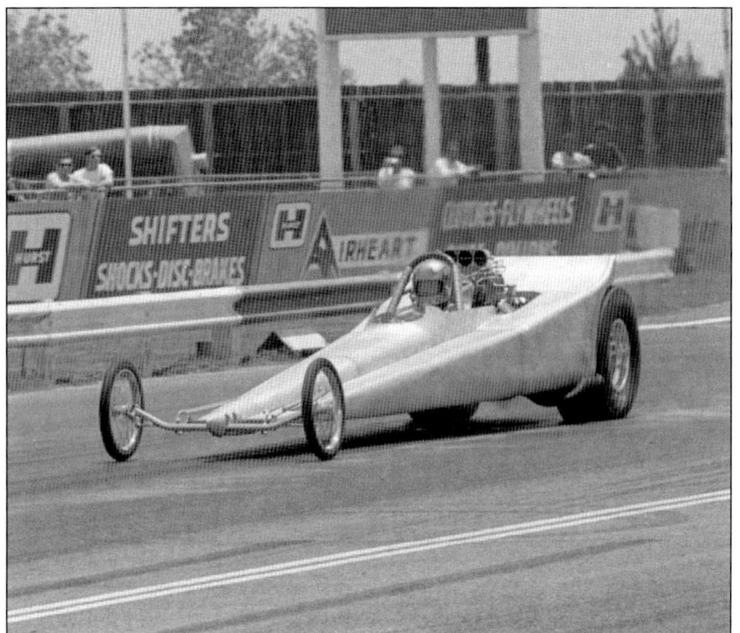

Again in 1973 at OCIR, another streamliner top fuel dragster was making waves. This time it was the Mooneyham and Sons streamliner from Louisiana/California, also known as the California Cajun team. "Fearless" Fred Mooneyham was the driver of the Gene Mooneyham-tuned streamliner. The silver shoehorn-looking top fuel dragster did not perform well and was soon lost in the abyss of forgotten streamline top fuel dragsters.

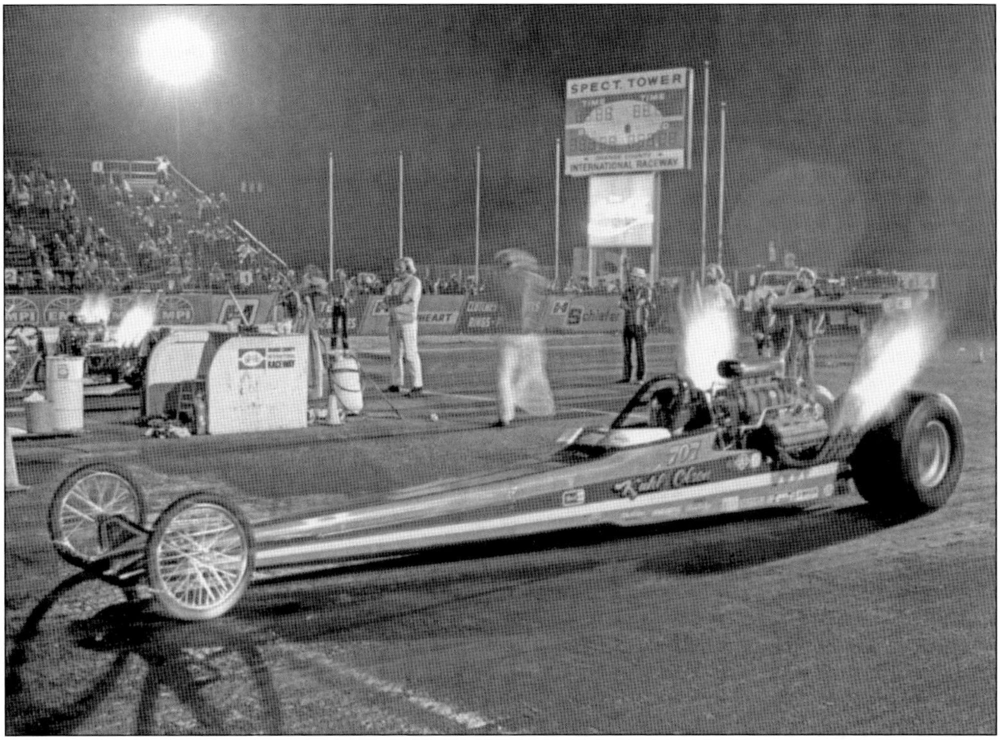

Carl Olson was one of a handful of top fuel drivers who had won at the three weekly running drag strips in SoCal. In 1969, he won top fuel at the Irwindale Grand prix of drag racing while driving for Jack Ewell. In 1972, he won Lions' last drag race in the Kuhl and Olson top fuel dragster. And in 1972 and 1973 at OCIR, he would win the nitro championships and the OCIR All Pro points events (overall points leader); those wins were in the Kuhl and Olson top fuel dragster. Also in 1972, the Kuhl and Olson top fueler won the 1972 NHRA Winternationals in Pomona, California.

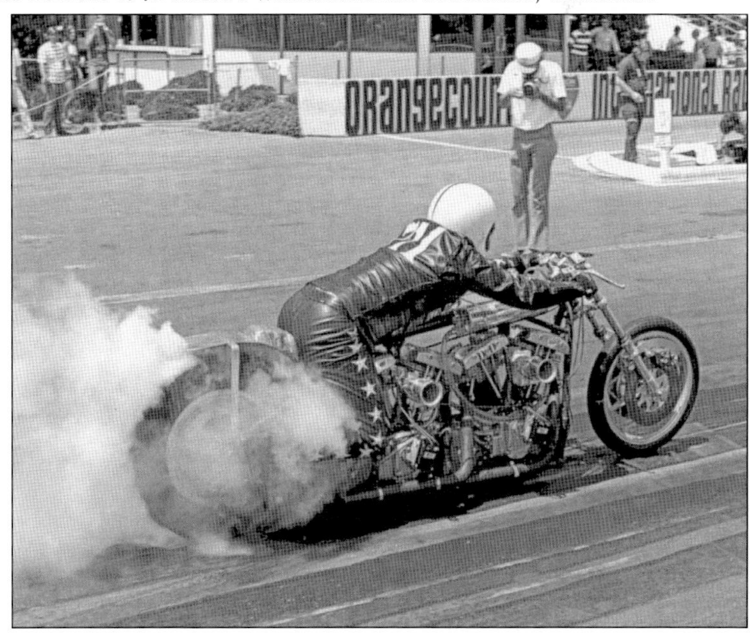

Not all nitro burners at OCIR had four wheels. Here is Joe Smith doing some test and tune on his then new twin engine top fuel Harley-powered drag bike. Although OCIR did not run any top fuel bike events, manager Mike Jones welcomed the fuel motorcycle racers to test and tune at any OCIR event. Smith, at the time, was one of the most well-known of the top fuel Harley owner/riders and an NHRA national event winner.

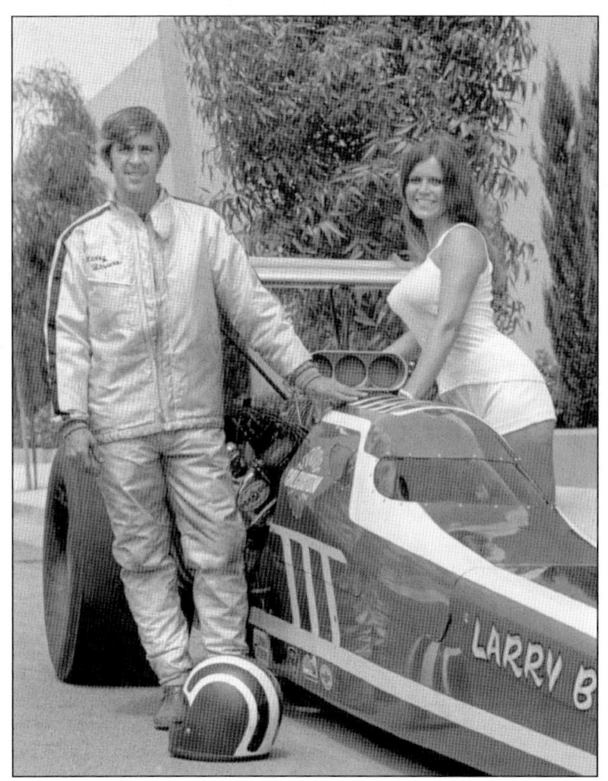

Doug Kruse always promoted his PDA events with drivers and race queens. He felt it put more of a human interest into the events. For his 1974 OCIR PDA event, he had top fuel driver and owner Larry Bowers (left) and race queen Barbara Roufs (right) to promote his OCIR race. Kruse also used other drivers to promote his OCIR PDA race. James Warren, Gary Hazen, Wayne King, Randy Allison, and Gerry Glenn all were included in the promotion of the PDA race.

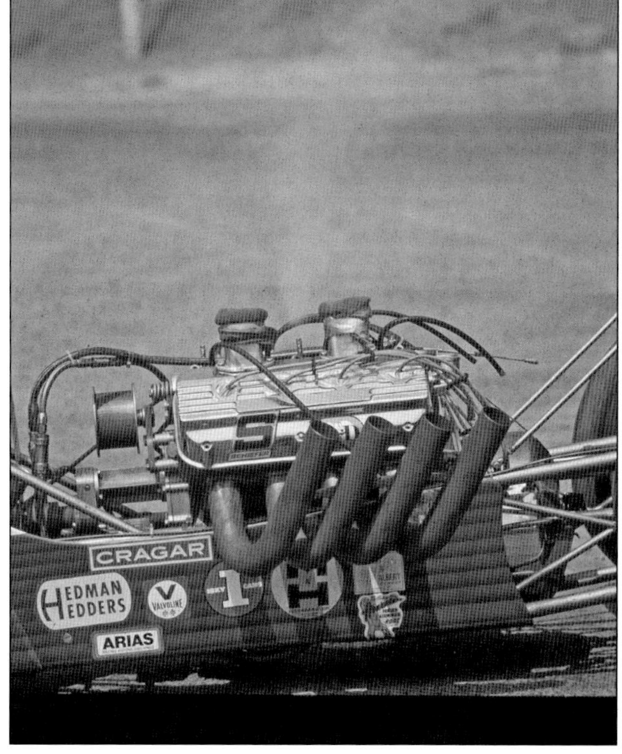

Bill Carter, a master race car painter, tried going top fuel dragster racing at OCIR. Carter had a blower and injectors when he left the starting line, but a little too much nitro—or maybe not enough—sent his blower and injectors into the Orange County skies. Luckily, by the end of his run at OCIR, Carter was not hurt by his kaboom. Only his wallet took a beating.

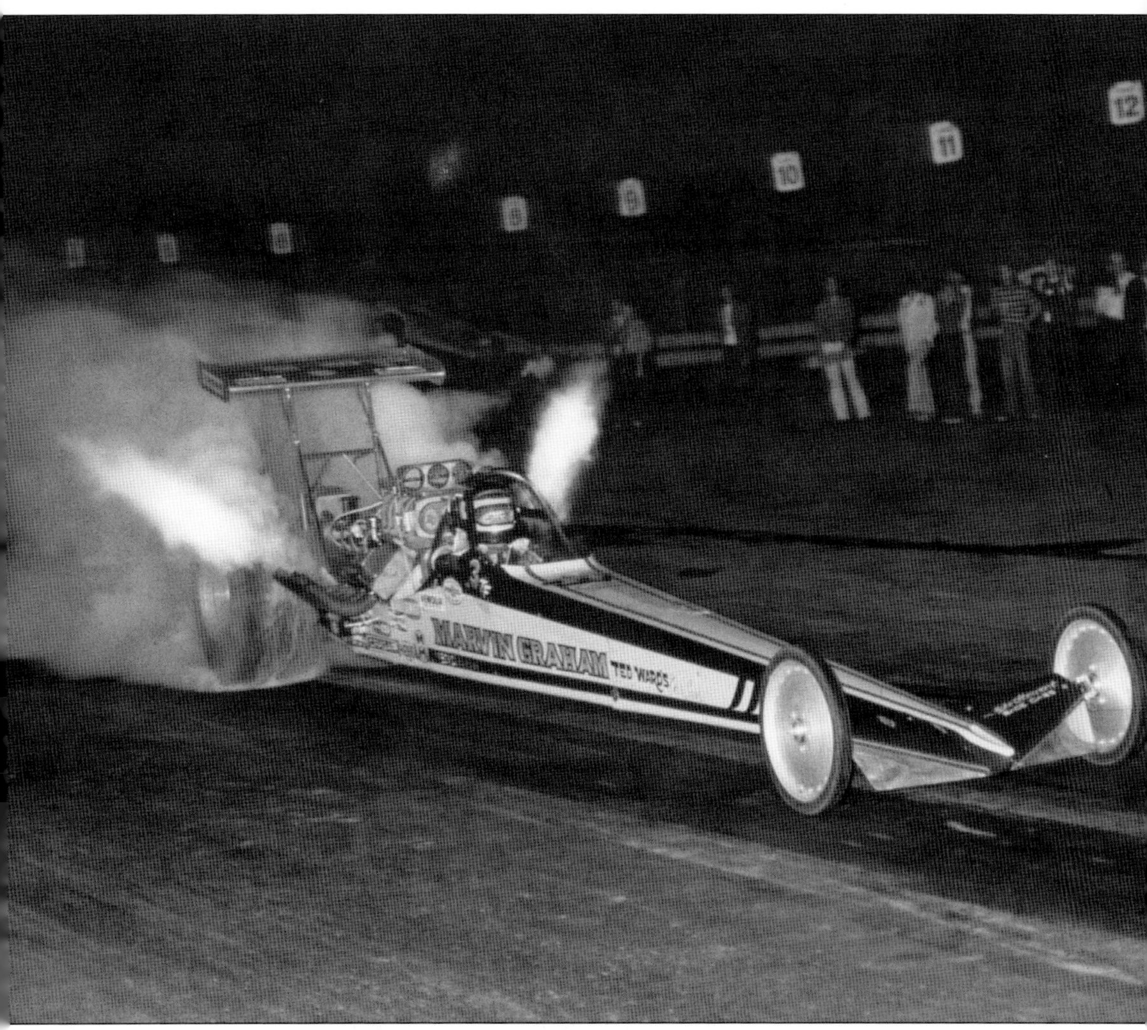

Pictured is Oklahoma's fastest and quickest television repair man, Marvin Graham, at OCIR. Ol' Marvin did well at OCIR's 1975 PDA race when he won top fuel eliminator. Graham was not done with the PDA races yet, though; he ventured to the Seattle PDA race in 1976 and won top fuel there too. In between his PDA wins, he went to the 1975 NHRA US Nationals and won top fuel eliminator there.

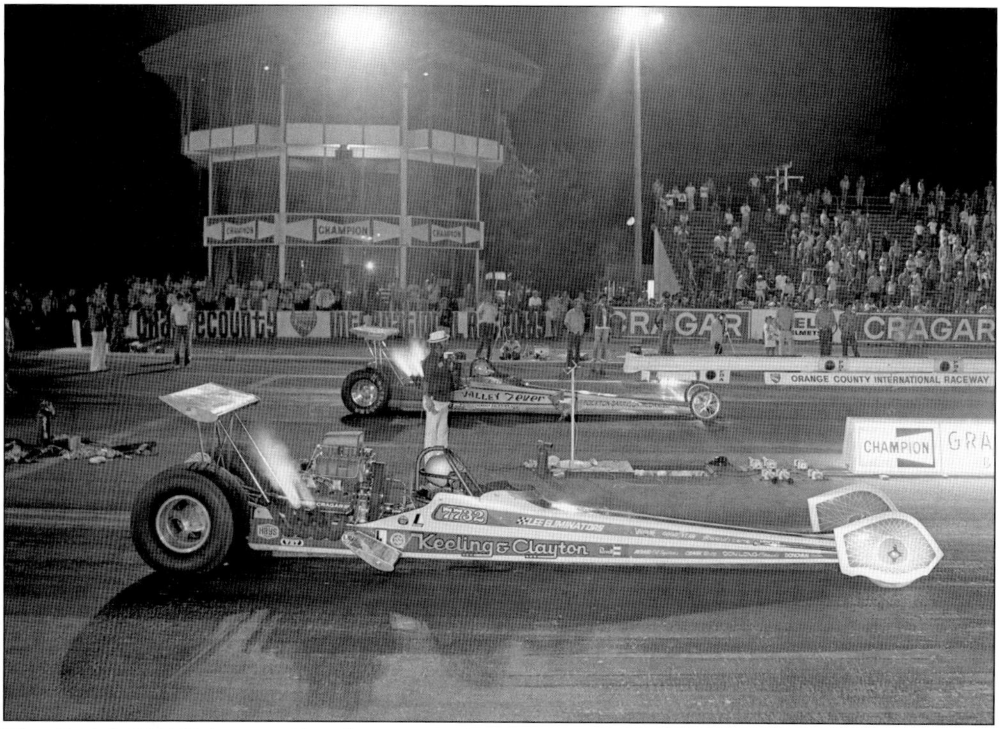

The 1974 OCIR PDA was a Chrysler versus Chevy affair, a real David against Goliath battle. Only this time Goliath was victorious at OCIR. The Keeling and Clayton California Charger top fuel dragster driven by Jake Johnston put away Rance McDaniel driving the Stockton, Garrison, and McDaniel "Valley Fever" top fuel dragster in the final. The winner's circle was complete mayhem with, from left to right, John Keeling, driver Jake Johnston, race queen Barbara Roufs, Jerry Clayton, and PDA promoter Doug Kruse.

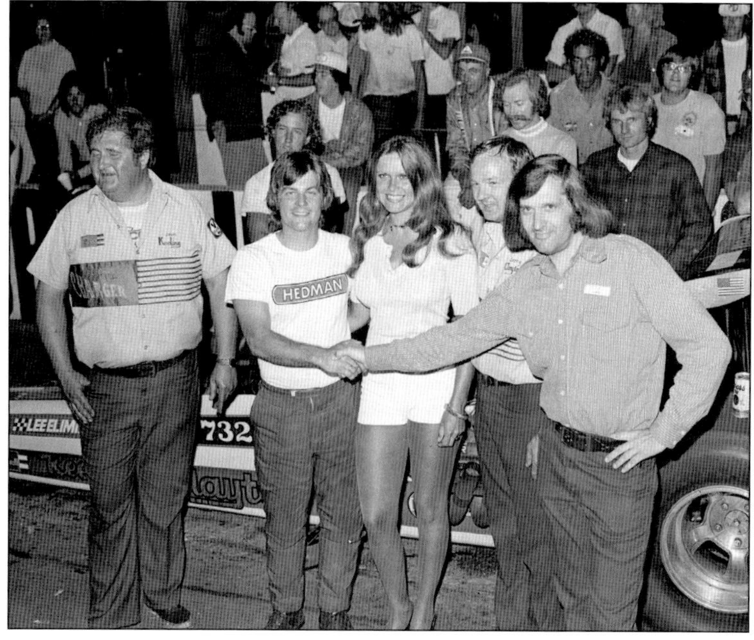

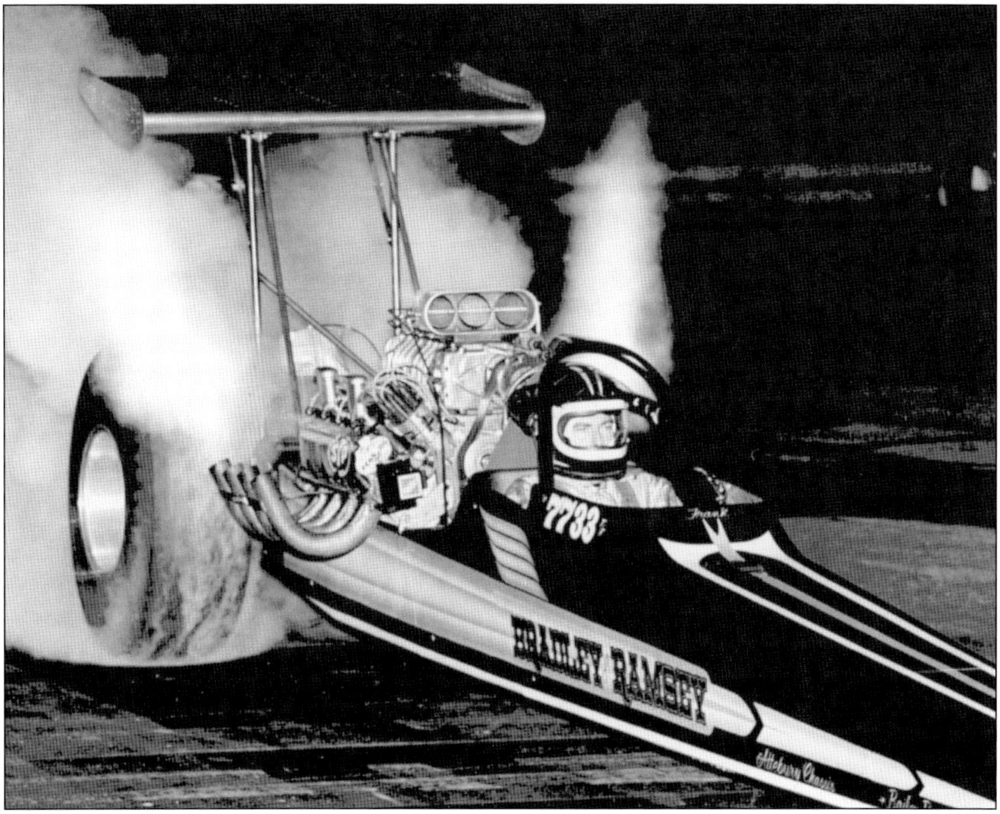

Northern California–based top fuel racer Frank Bradley guided his top fuel dragster to a 5.96 at OCIR on June 29, 1974, to become the 16th and final member of the Cragar five-second club. Bradley was also one of the first members of the four-second club when he ran 4.99 at Pomona in October 1989.

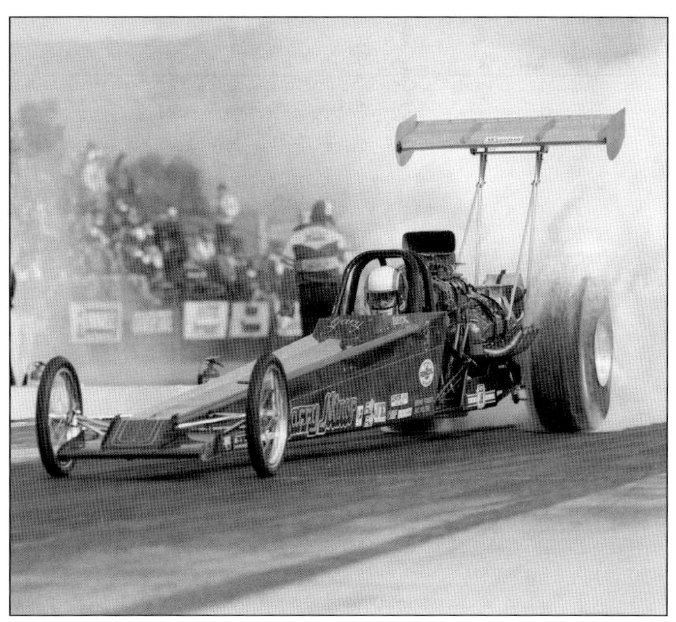

The Canadian and the potato farmer made their mark in OCIR history by winning the 1981 NHRA World Finals held at OCIR. Gary Beck, driving for Larry Minor, put away Dwight Salisbury driving "Fisher's Fever" top fuel dragster. Beck had a 5.57 at 245.23 miles per hour to a losing 6.15 at 219.51 miles per hour. Beck would also win the NHRA World Finals top fuel title in 1983 driving for Larry Minor at OCIR's last drag race.

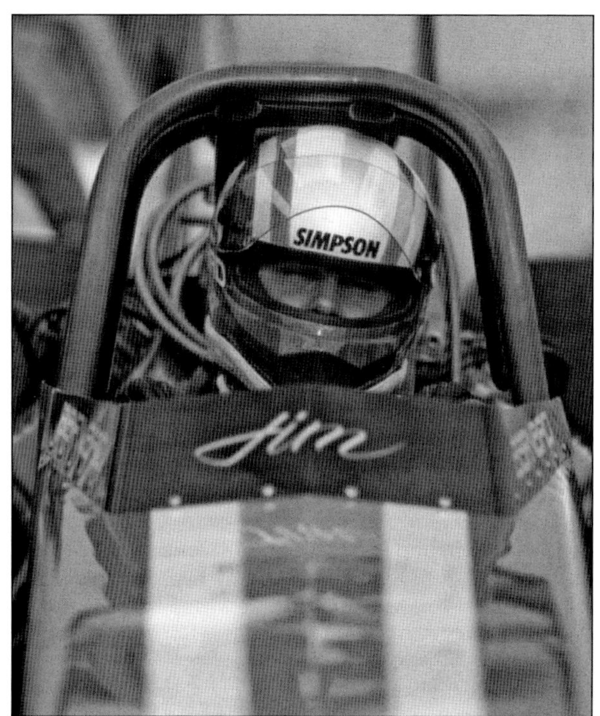

Jim Barnard made the trek from the great Northwest to OCIR in 1982 and won top fuel honors. Barnard ended up facing Gary Beck in the final round. Barnard defeated the Beck and Minor top fuel dragster with 5.92 at 233.16 miles per hour while Beck shut off with a 7.28 at 179.86 miles per hour. It was the biggest win for Barnard in his top fuel career; he was a huge underdog when going into the final round to face Gary Beck.

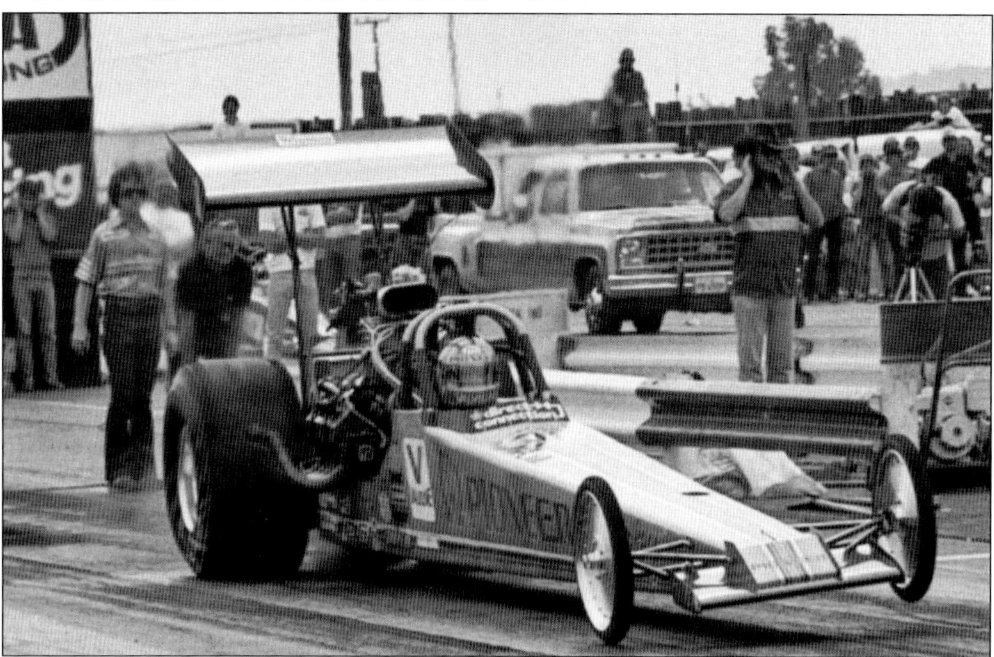

The first lady of top fuel dragster racing, Shirley Muldowney, came to OCIR in 1983 with one goal—to win the 1983 NHRA World Finals at OCIR. She achieved her goal when she faced Joe Amato in the final and beat him with a 5.63 at 246.57 miles per hour to Amato's shutting off 11.75 at 67.93 miles per hour. Muldowney's big win at OCIR was the next to the last hurrah for the racetrack; it would close its doors for good on October 29, 1983, a few weeks after the NHRA World Finals. Gary Beck would win the final race at OCIR driving for Larry Minor.

Two

OCIR Funny Car Racing

Controlled Chaos

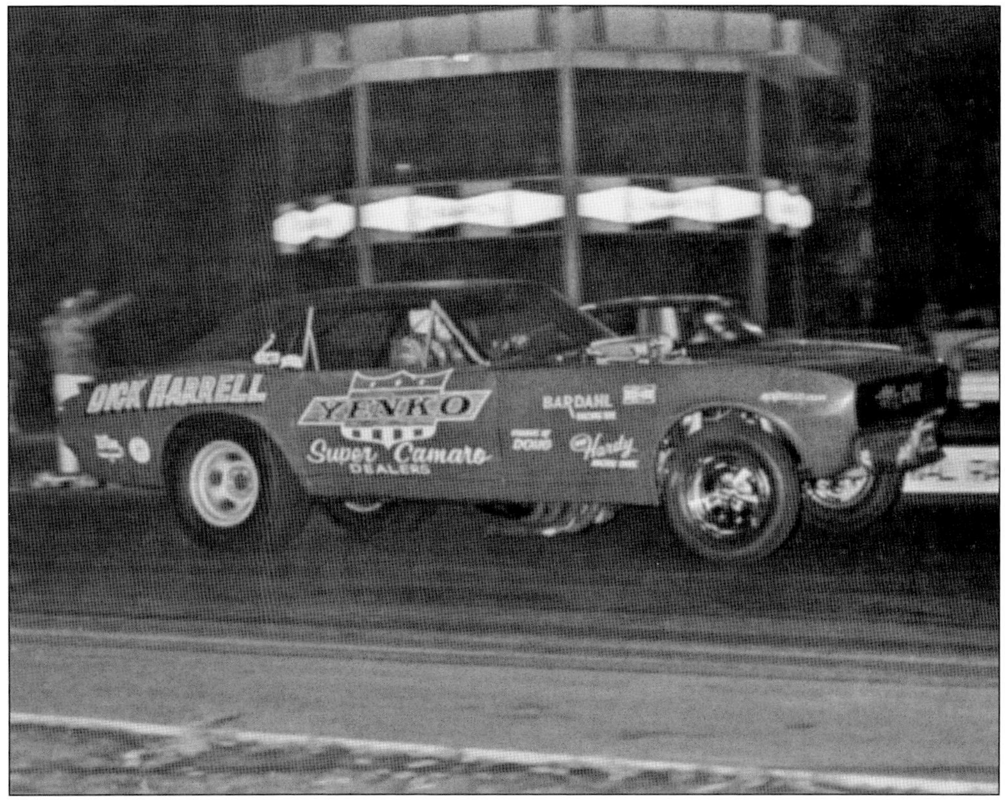

"Mr. Chevrolet" Dickie Harrell brought his 427-cubic-inch-powered Camaro to OCIR's first manufacturers meet in 1967. Harrell had just traded up from his fuel-injected Chevy Nova to the nitro-burning blown Camaro. He would become one of the cornerstones of AHRA funny car racing with his line of Chevrolet-powered funny cars. All that came to a tragic end when he was killed in a racing accident in Canada on September 12, 1971.

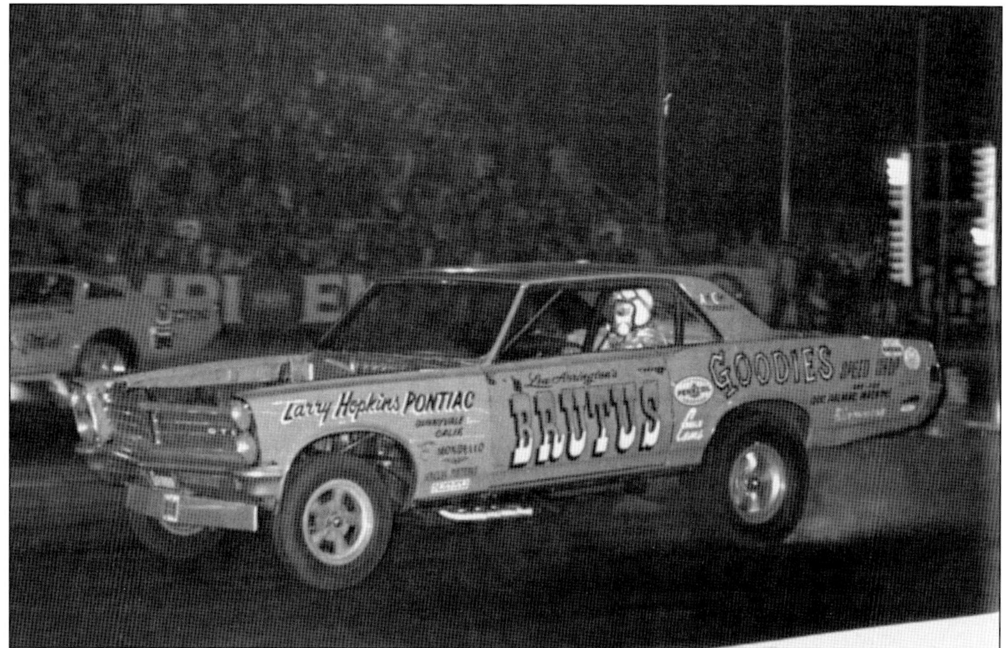

"Jungle Jim" Liberman was at the controls of Lew Arrington's Brutus GTO funny car at the 1967 OCIR Manufacturers Meet. At the same time, Lew Arrington was busy sorting out his new Brutus Pontiac Firebird funny car at the same event. Arrington was the first and only owner/driver who had two entries at that race.

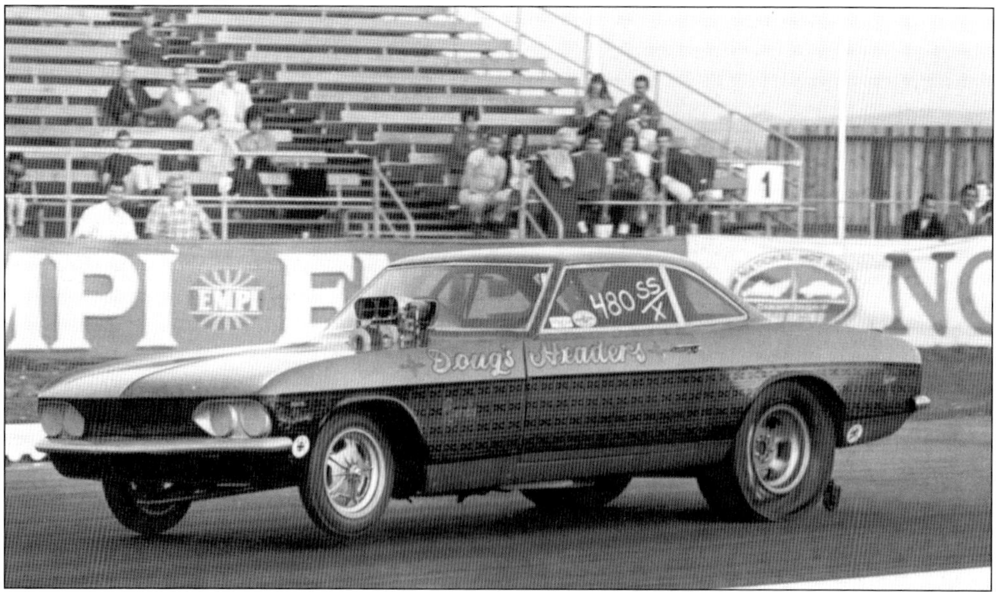

"Doug's Headers," a Chevrolet Corvair, cranked out 191.88 miles per hour for the best speed at the 1967 OCIR Manufacturers Meet. The Pat Foster–built Corvair had its owner Doug Thorley at the controls. Thorley had just returned from the NHRA US Nationals in Indianapolis where he won the S/XS class and ran an unheard of 7.69 ET. Chevrolet won the team honors at the manufacturers meet. The team members were Thorley, Terry Hedrick, Dickie Harrell, Kelly Chadwick, and Ron O'Donnell driving the Chapman Automotive Camaro funny car.

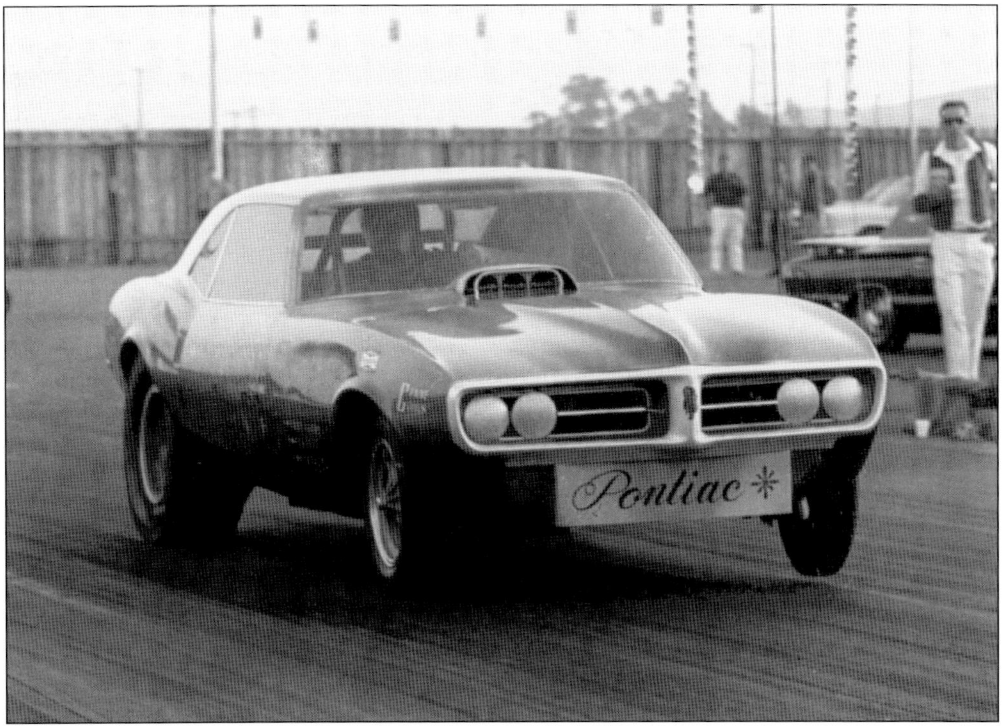

Roy and Don Gay's Pontiac Firebird funny car was one of team Pontiac's strongest cars at the 1967 OCIR Manufacturers Meet. At 1:00 a.m. in the morning, Roy Gay squared off with "Fast" Eddie Schartman for top honors. "Fast" Eddie outran Gay to win the first-ever OCIR Manufacturers Meet. The Gays would soon replace the Firebird body with a GTO one. Sadly, Roy Gay died in a motorcycle accident, and the Gay family withdrew from racing.

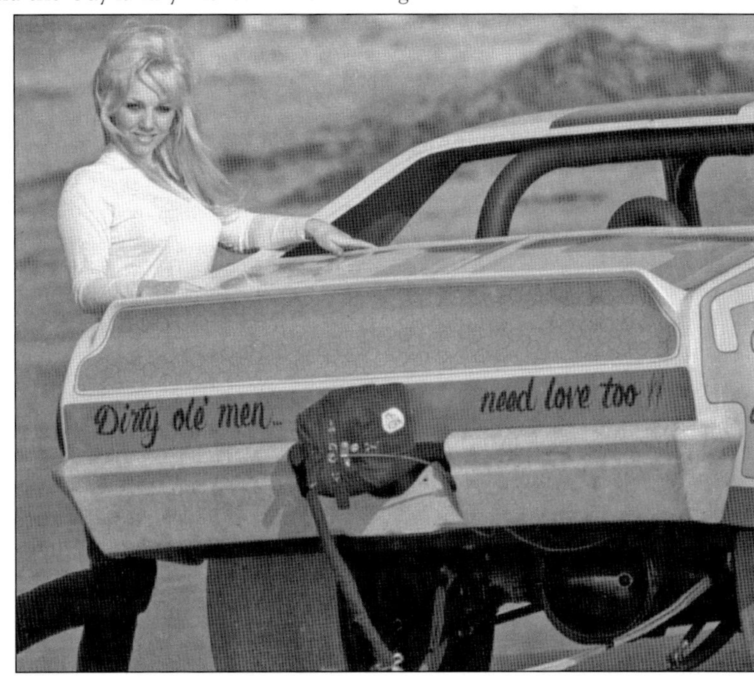

Way before there was "Jungle Pam" Hardy, there was Cheri Walls. Walls was the official backup girl for her then husband, Randy Walls, and their Super Nova funny car in the late 1960s. The husband-and-wife team mainly raced on the West Coast and were regulars at funny car events in Northern California and Southern California. Their home base was El Cajon, California, just down the road from San Diego.

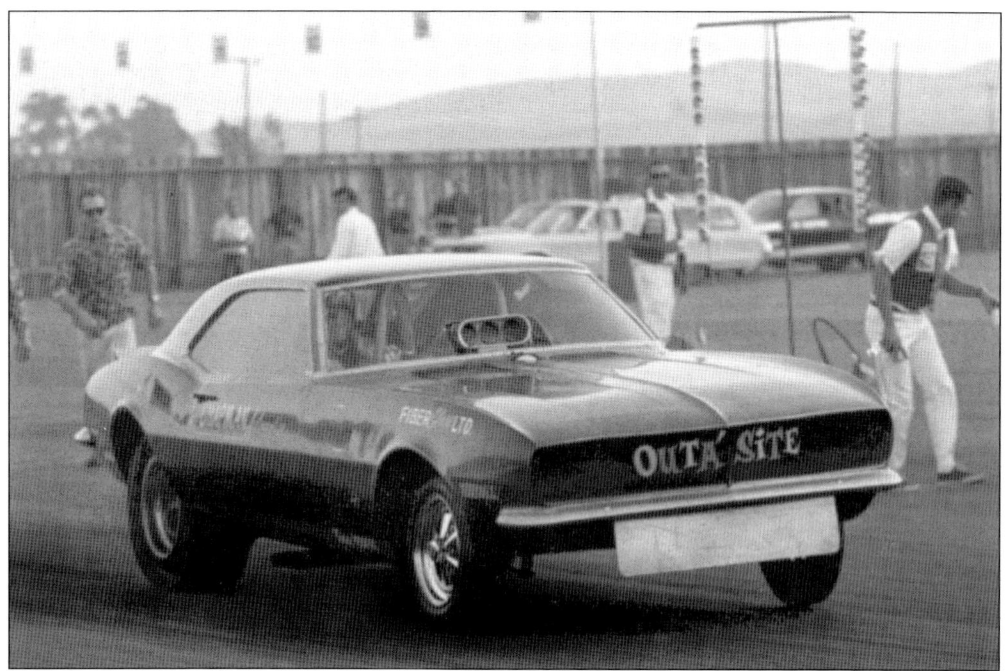

The big noise from Illinois was one Ron "Snag" O'Donnell, the driver and caretaker of the Chapman Automotive Camaro funny car. "Snag" was on the Chevrolet winning team at the 1967 OCIR Manufacturers Meet. He stayed and raced on the West Coast to escape the freezing weather at his home base in Chicago. When spring rolled around, "Snag" headed for the Midwest and racing on the East Coast.

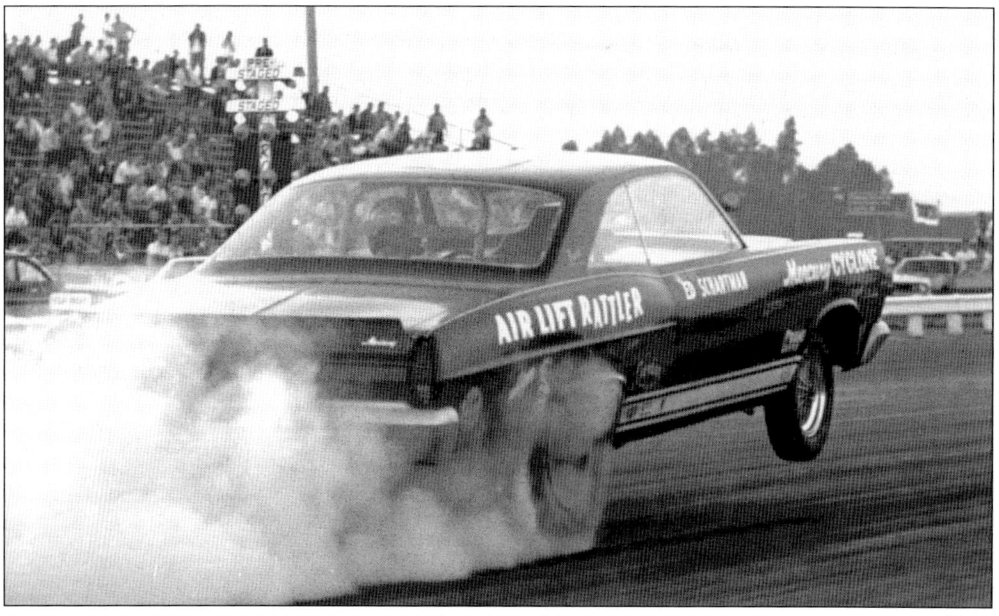

Factory-backed "Fast" Eddie Schartman flexed his Mercury muscle with a victory at the 1967 OCIR Manufacturers Meet. "Fast" Eddie ran a low ET at 7.85 and beat Roy Gay in the final for the overall win. Schartman was one of four Ford/Mercury–backed funny car racers; the others were Don Nicholson, Jack Chrisman, and the Colorado team of Kenz and Leslie.

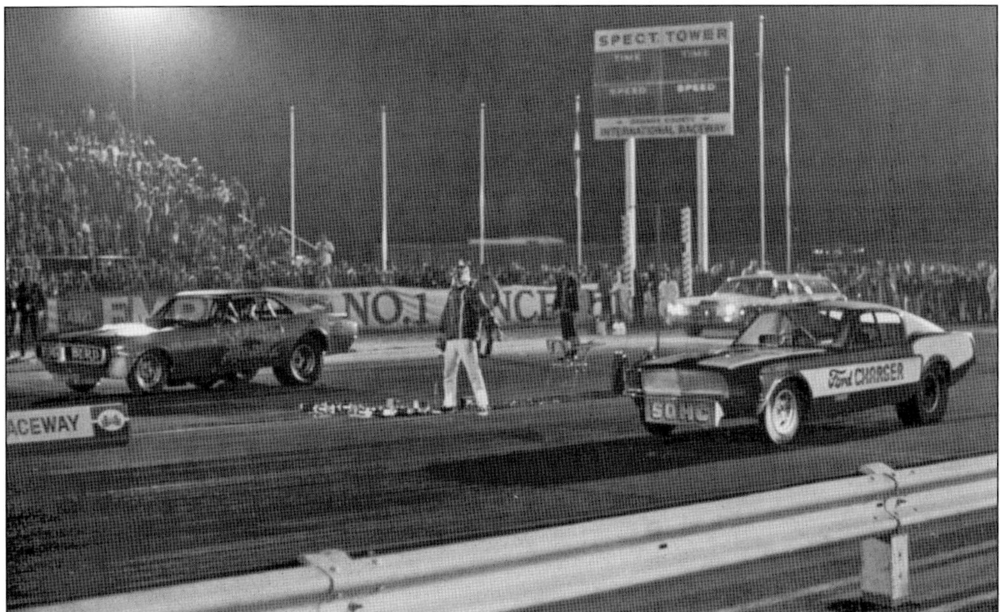

The air was thick with nitro fumes as Phoenix, Arizona's Don Sappington (left) took on "Mr. Ford" Tommy Grove at the 1968 OCIR Manufacturers Meet. This Pontiac versus Ford battle was won by Grove. Grove had to be a happy winner because at the same race the year before Grove blew the roof off his car, and this time his roof stayed on the car.

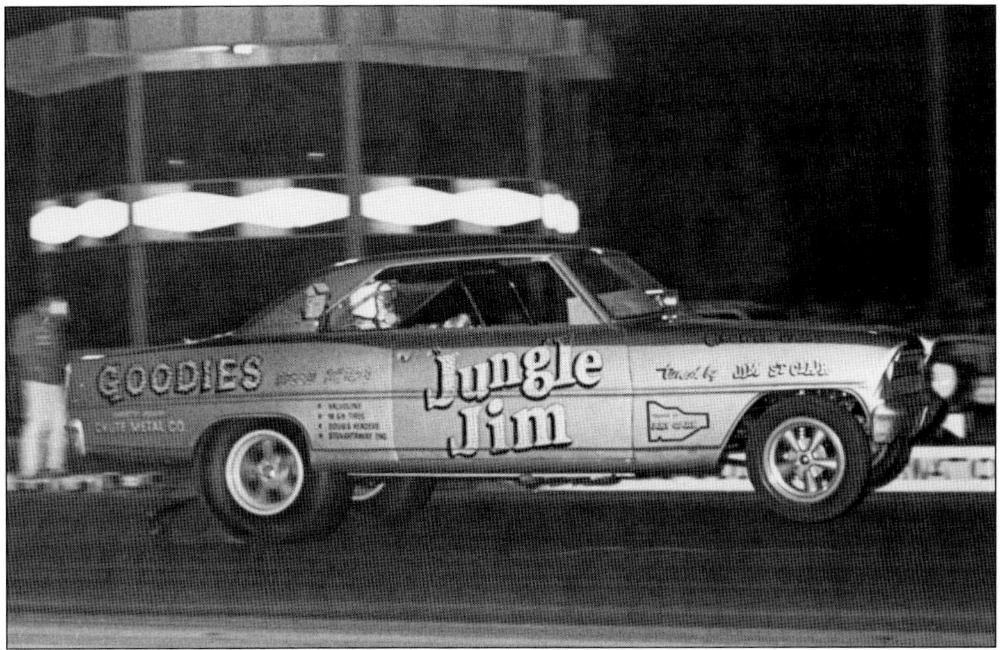

"Jungle Jim" Liberman and his Chevrolet Nova funny car were having a great 1968. Liberman started the year by winning the AHRA's largest funny car event ever held at Lions Drag Strip. Jungle then went to OCIR and won its first-ever All Pro Series race, beating the unbeatable Don Schumacher in the final round. And at the 1968 OCIR Manufacturers Meet, he was part of the winning Team Chevrolet.

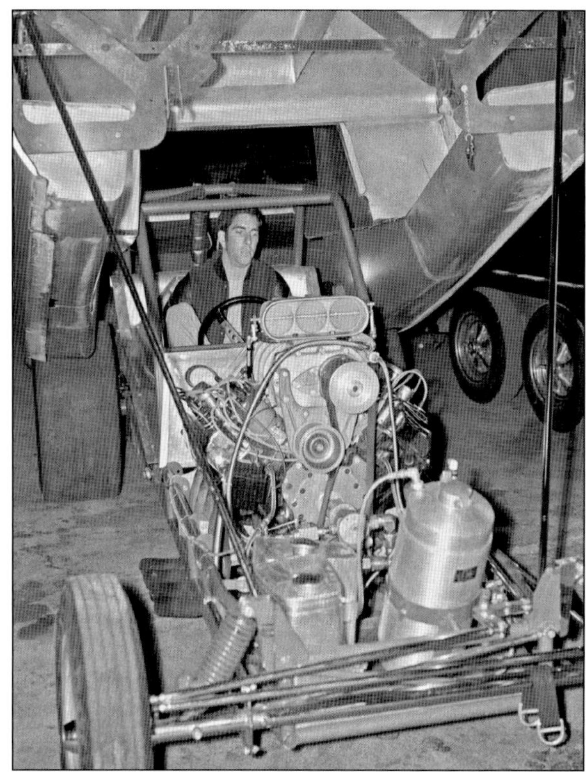

The OCIR Big Four Funny Car Championships were held on May 4, 1968, and OCIR saw the "All American Boy," Charlie Allen, take home low ET honors at 7.84; he was runner-up to Michigan's Dick Loehr for top honors. Also in 1968, Allen won the OCIR Funny Car 500, beating Gas Ronda in the final. Fast forward 22 years into the future and Charlie Allen was the last manager for OCIR from 1980 to 1983. Allen had the dubious honor of padlocking OCIR for a final time on October 29, 1983.

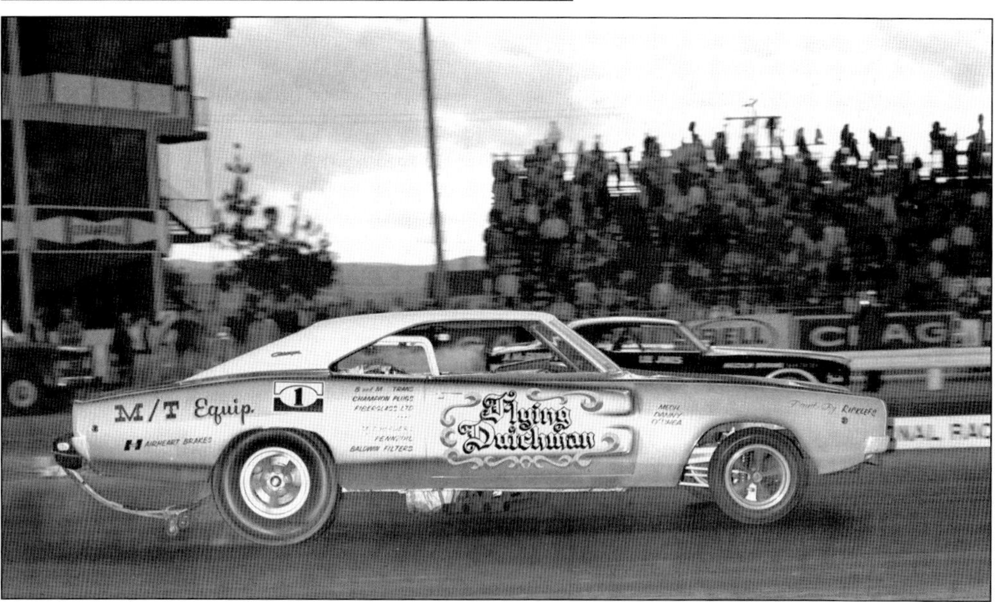

"Flying Dutchman" Al Vander Woude was a very popular early funny car racer in SoCal. Woude raced some of the strangest Mopar-bodied funny cars, that this Dodge Charger seems almost normal for him. On the other side of the track is Lee Jones and his Washington, DC–based funny car. After this event in 1968, Woude went on tour and relocated to the Kansas City area. Jones went east and partnered with Malcom Durham in a two-car team. Lee Jones would lose his life in a horrific funny car accident at an East Coast track.

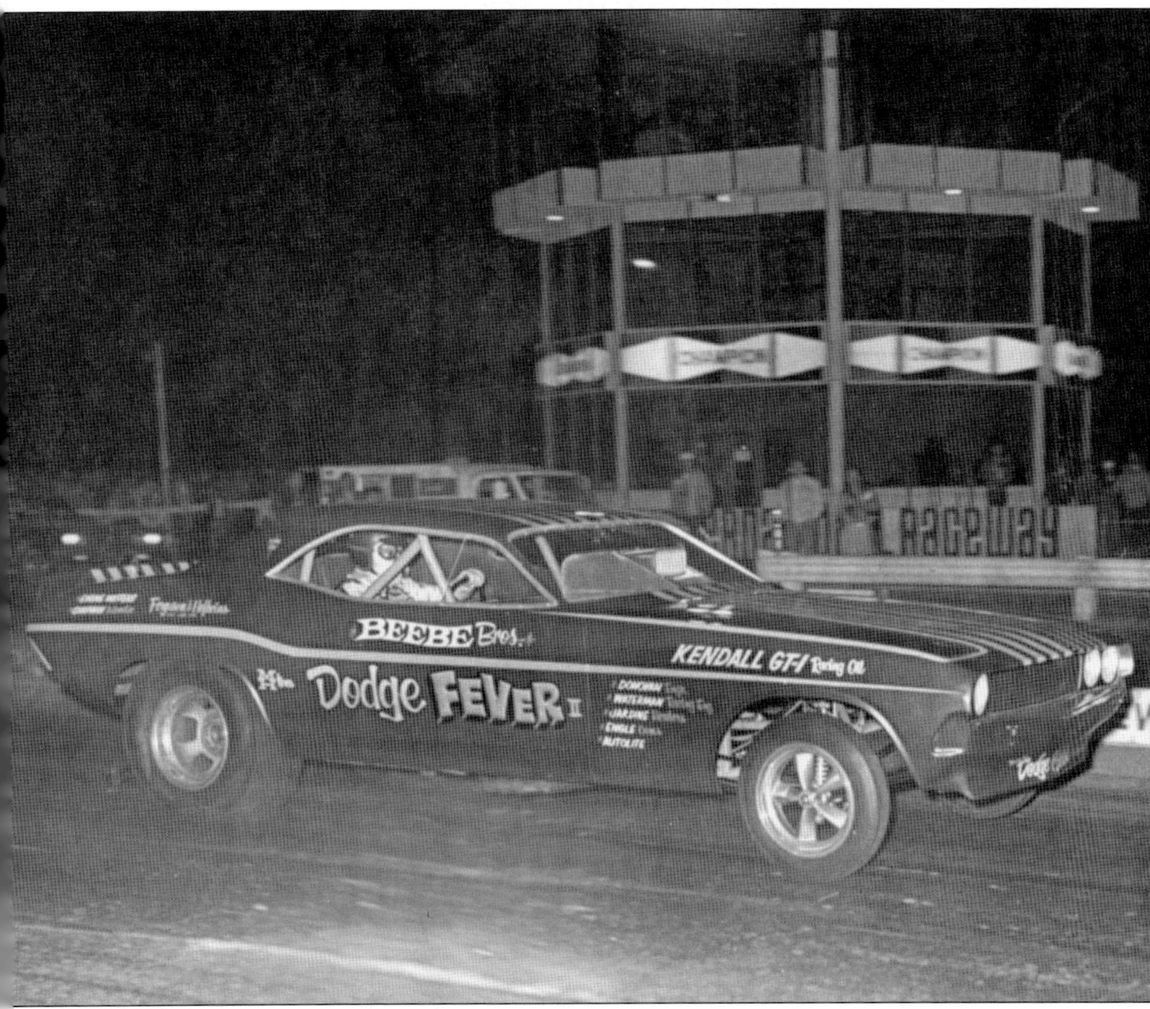

The "Dodge Fever" funny car was owned by Dallas Ferguson and Dean Hofheins out of Utah. But the car was based and run out of Garden Grove, California. The Beebe Bros., Tim and Dave, maintained it in 1969–1970. Brother Dave drove the Tim Beebe–tuned funny car to an OCIR record 6.99 ET at 210 miles per hour in 1970. Also at OCIR in 1970, Dave won the Big Four Funny Car Championships, beating Manuel Herrera in the final.

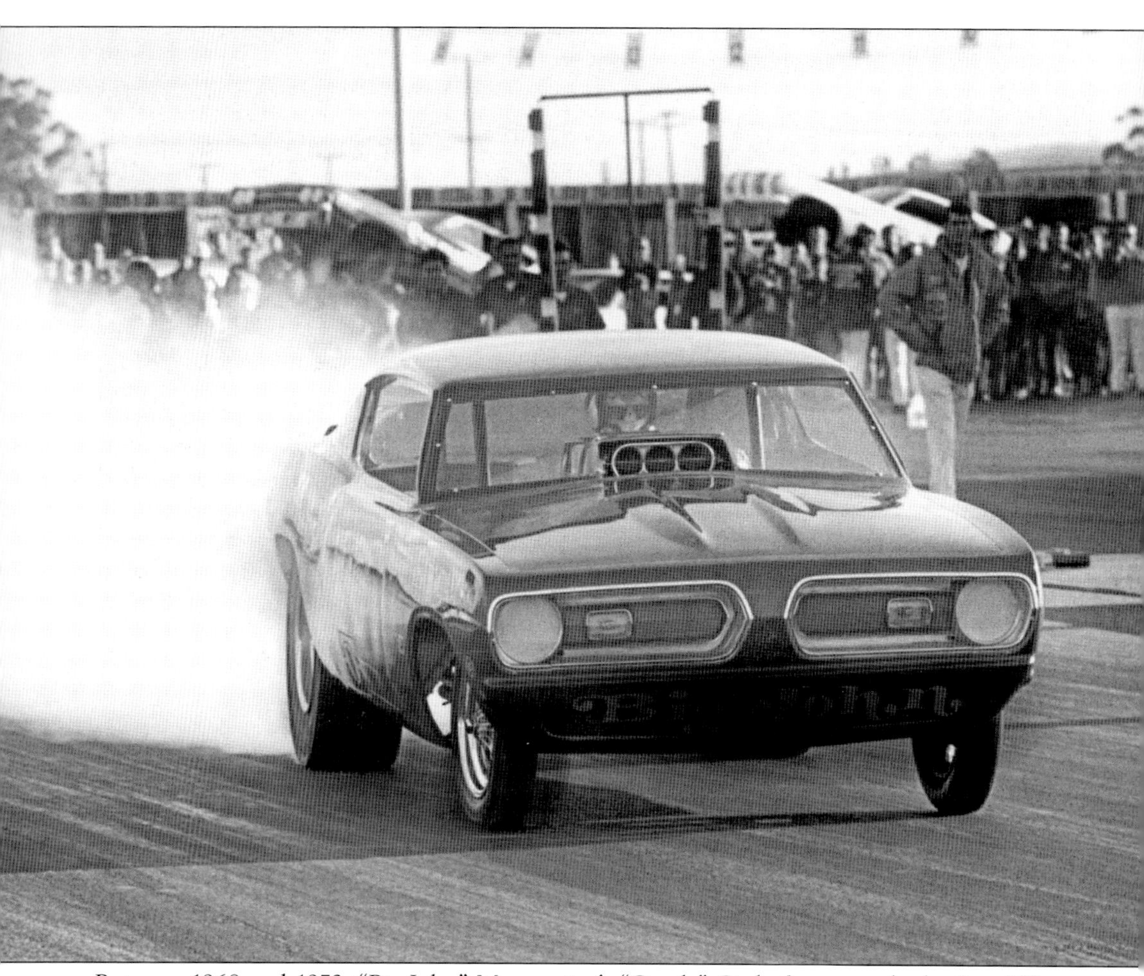

Between 1968 and 1972, "Big John" Mazmanian's "Candy" Cuda funny car had a few different drivers—Dave Beebe, Richard Sirooinian, Arnie Behling, Wendell Shipman, Larry Reyes, Mike Snively, and Danny Ongais. Sirooinian won the 1968 OCIR Manufacturers Meet on November 23, 1968. Beebe won the 1969 OCIR PDA race on July 19, 1969. Sirooinian won the 1970 OCIR NHRA Division 7 race, and Danny Ongais won the OCIR East/West Funny Car Championships on October 14, 1972. At the end of 1972, Mazmanian sold his entire funny car operation to Vel Miletich and Rufus "Parnelli" Jones.

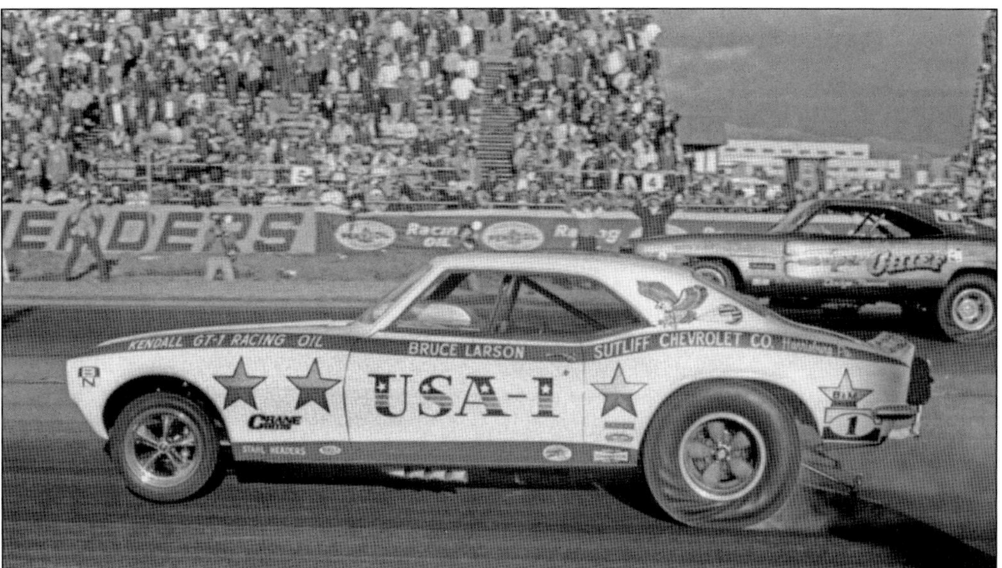

Bruce Larson traveled all the way from Camp Hill, Pennsylvania, to compete at the 1969 OCIR Manufacturers Meet. Larson was having a standout year with his all-Chevrolet Camaro funny car; he had just won the Super Stock Magazine Nationals at York, Pennsylvania. Larson also set a new NHRA record ET for funny cars at 7.41 with his USA-1 Camaro funny car.

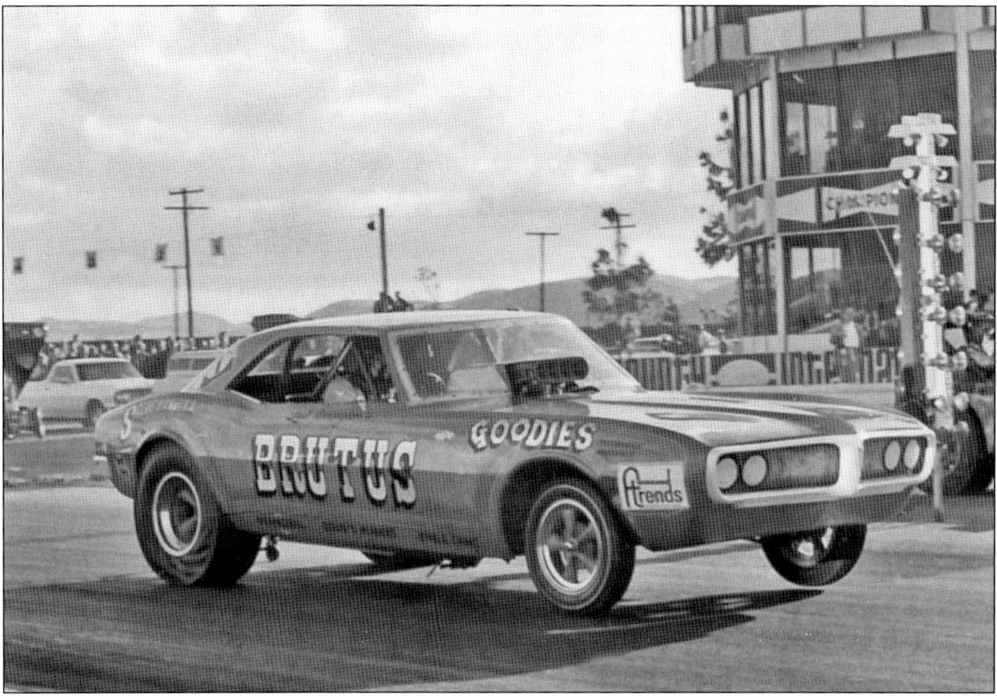

San Jose's Lew Arrington was a Pontiac dealership mechanic before the funny car bug bit him in 1965. First, it was his Brutus GTO funny car, then he was at the controls of his third Firebird-bodied funny car at the 1969 OCIR Manufacturers Meet. He gave an unknown kid named Jim Liberman his first ride in a funny car when he allowed Liberman to drive his Brutus GTO in late 1965 and 1966. Arrington became one of the full-time touring funny car pros in the 1970s.

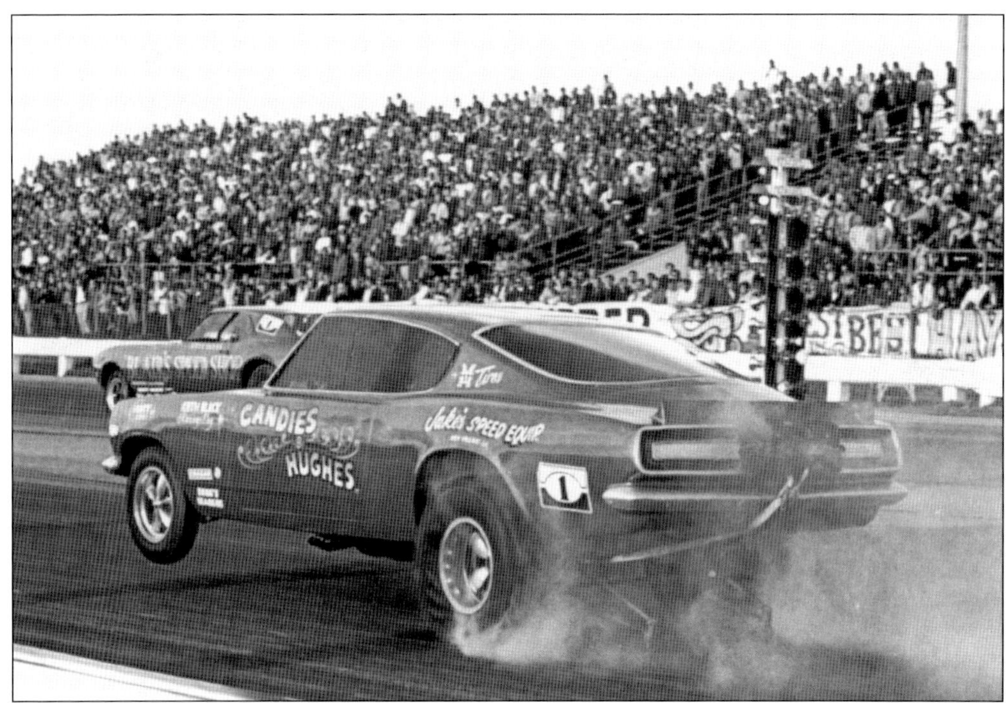

Playing catch-up is Leonard Hughes in the Candies and Hughes Cuda. Out in the distance is Steve Bovan and the Blair's Speed Shop Camaro funny car; Bovan won this round at the OCIR Manufacturers Meet. On May 15, 1968, Bovan set both ends of the OCIR track records for funny cars with 7.68 at 185.64 miles per hour in his Blair's Speed Shop Camaro.

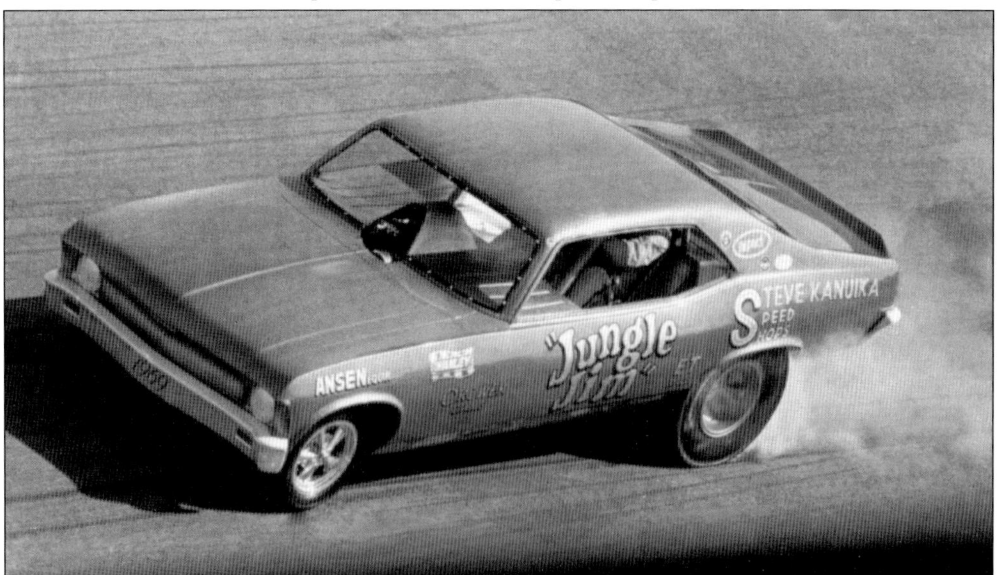

Team Jungle Jim made an appearance at the 1969 OCIR Manufacturers Meet. This is "Jungle Clare" Sanders driving Jim Liberman's No. 2 Chevrolet Nova funny car. Earlier in the year, Sanders drove the Liberman-owned Nova into the winner's circle at the NHRA Winternationals in Pomona, California. That made funny car history because it was the first time NHRA included a funny car eliminator bracket at an NHRA national event.

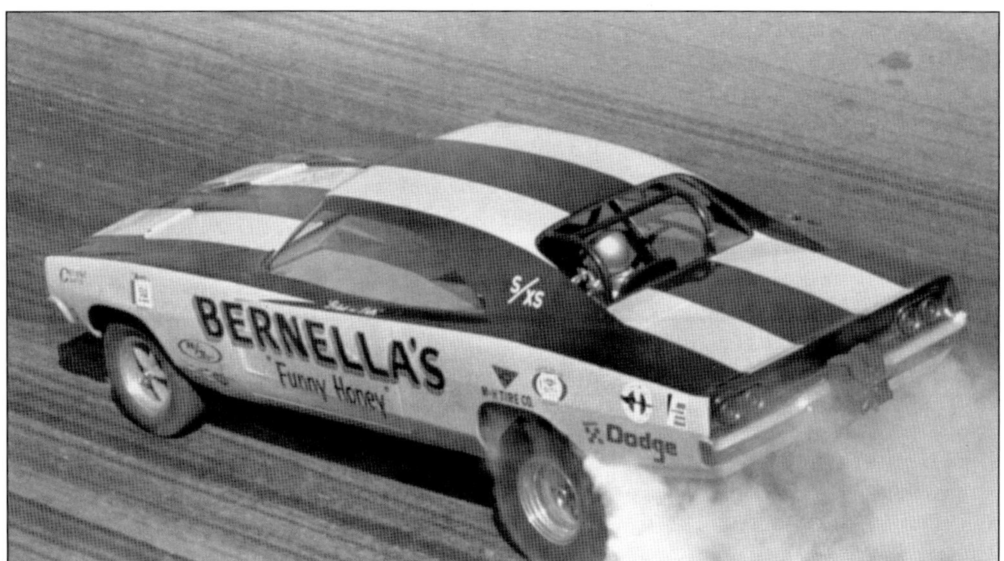

Making a rare West Coast appearance at OCIR in 1969 was Michigan's Della Woods and her "Funny Honey" Dodge-bodied funny car. Woods was one of the first female funny car drivers in the United States in the 1960s. Woods and her brother Bernie mainly raced in Michigan and the Midwest, but she made funny car history of sorts when she became the first woman to enter a pro class at an NHRA national event, the 1969 NHRA Winternationals in Pomona, California.

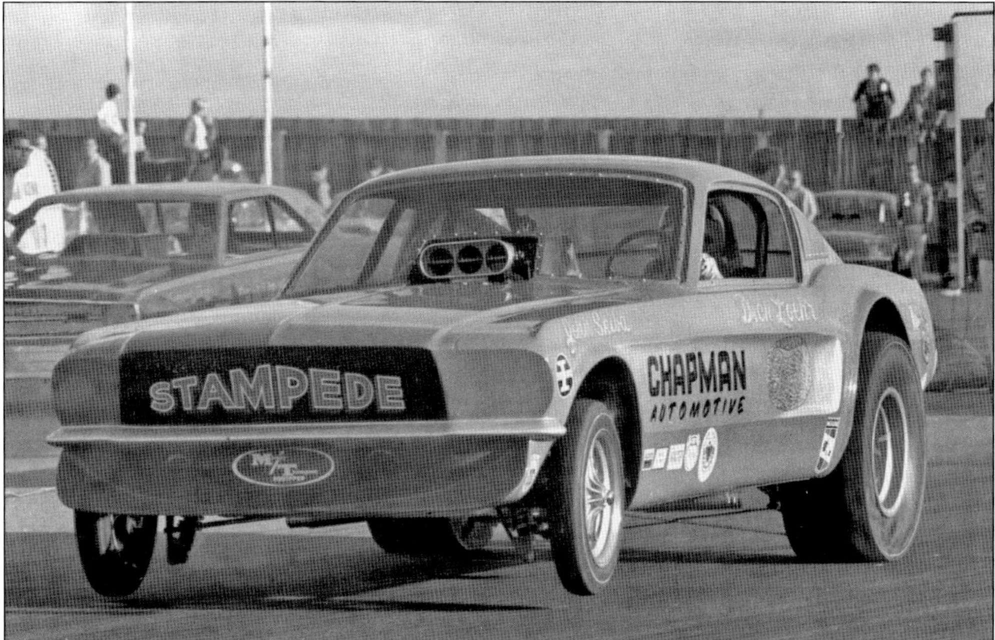

The pride of Kalamazoo, Michigan, Dick Loehr made his mark in OCIR funny car history in 1968. Loehr came to the West Coast and first raced in Northern California at Fremont and then headed south to sunny Southern California. Loehr and his Ford-backed "Stampede" Mustang funny car won the Big Four Funny Car Championships on May 4, 1968, with a final round victory over local hero Charlie Allen. In 1970, Loehr traded in his funny car for a brand-new Ford Maverick pro stock and went NHRA pro stock racing until Ford suddenly dropped out of racing.

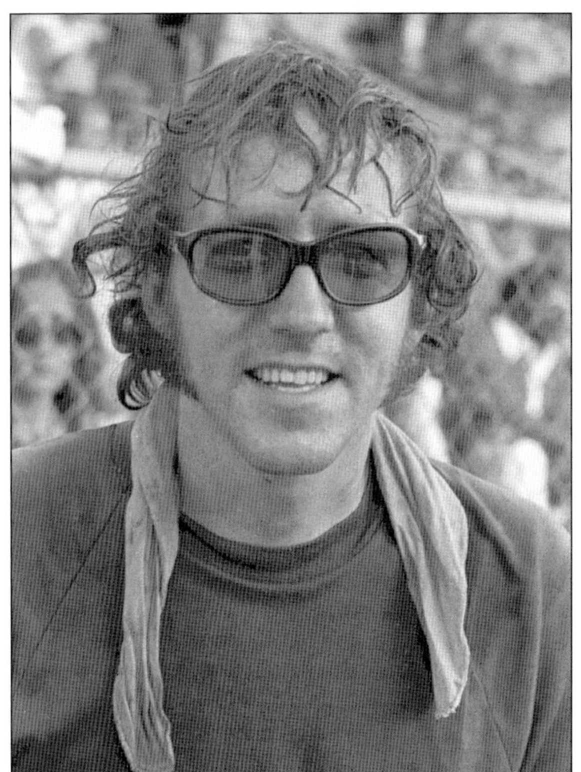

Chicagoland businessman and racer Don Schumacher won the first season All Pro Series race title at OCIR in March 1969. Just prior to that he was runner-up to Rich Sirooinian at the 1968 OCIR Manufacturers Meet. On August 29, 1970, Schumacher and his "Stardust" Cuda ran a 6.93 ET to capture OCIR's funny car ET record. He backed it up with a 7.02 at 210.28 miles per hour for the record, and OCIR rewarded Schumacher with $1,000 cash for setting that record. Schumacher rounded out 1970 when he won the OCIR East/West Funny Car Championships, defeating Gene Snow in the final with a 6.99 ET to a losing 7.02 ET.

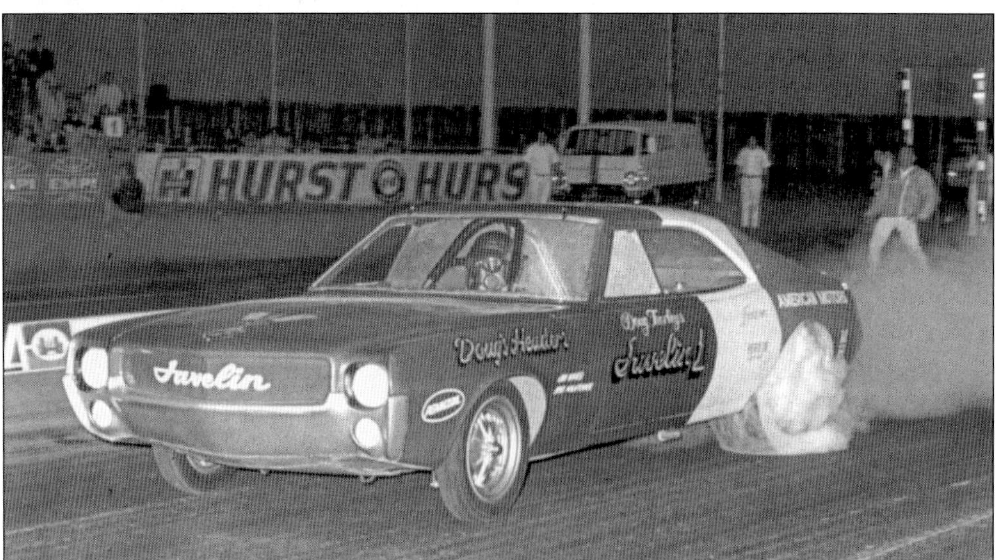

Doug Thorley went with AMC for 1969 with this one-of-a-kind Woody Gilmore chassis, rear-engine "Javelin" funny car. Thorley hired top fuel driver Bobby Hightower to drive his back-motored creation. The car was not around a long time in 1969 because at Irwindale, it took flight at the finish line. The car landed upside down, spinning on its roof, then struck the guardrail, knocking the body off and up righting the car. Amazingly, Hightower, who luckily was not hurt, kept his cool and drove the bent race car to a stop in the shutdown area at Irwindale. Thorley did not rebuild the flying Javelin.

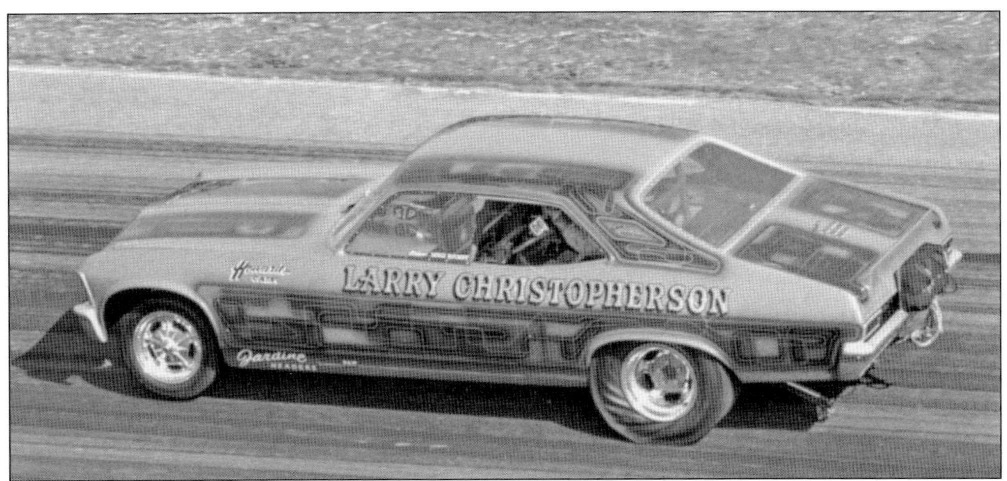

Arizona racers Mike Hamby and Larry Christofherson combined forces to field this psychedelic-painted Chevrolet Nova funny car at OCIR in 1969. Christofherson owned the car, and ex gas coupe star Mike Hamby drove the Chevrolet Nova. In the next three years, Christofherson partnered with Dickie Harrell in a Vega-bodied funny car and then Randy Efros in another Vega-bodied funny car. Christofherson did drive both of these cars. Hamby returned to drive Christofherson's last funny car in 1974, the "Arizona Wildcat" Vega.

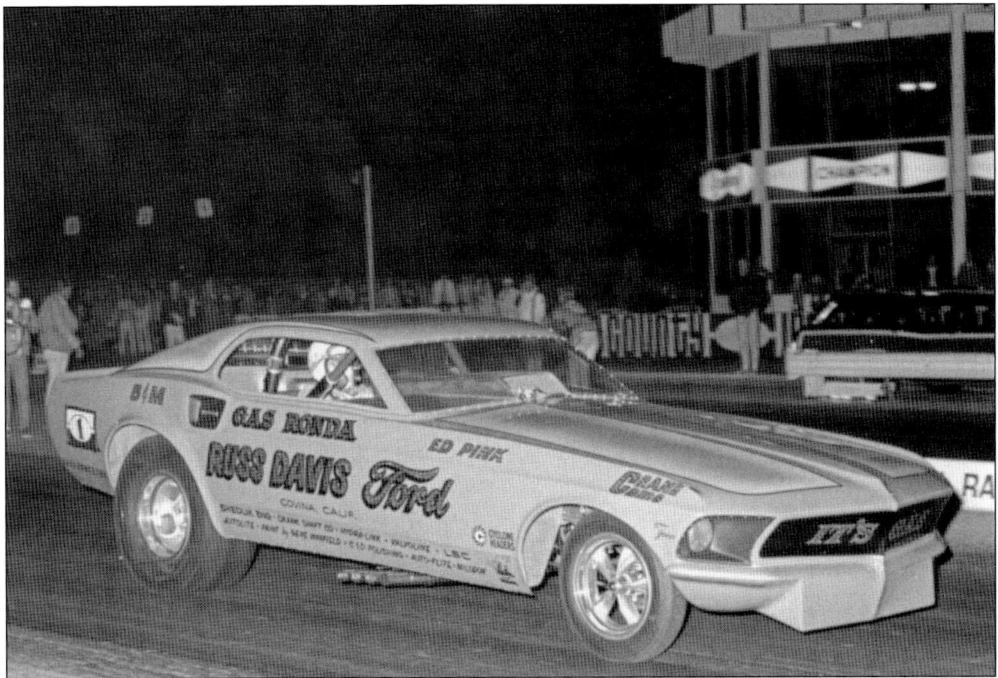

The dapper dance instructor Gasper Ronda cha-cha'd his way into the 1968 OCIR Manufacturers Meet winners circle on November 16, 1969. Ronda defeated Pat Minick in the "Chi-Town Hustler" in the final round. Gasper also ran low ET for the event at 7.26. This would be Ronda's biggest and final win in his Ford Mustang. At the first event of 1970, the AHRA Winternationals in Scottsdale, Arizona, Ronda's hands were severely burned from a transmission failure at the finish line. He retired from driving, and Dick Poll became the driver of Ronda's Mustang. After a few outings with Poll driving, Ronda sold the car to fuel altered owner Dave Bowman.

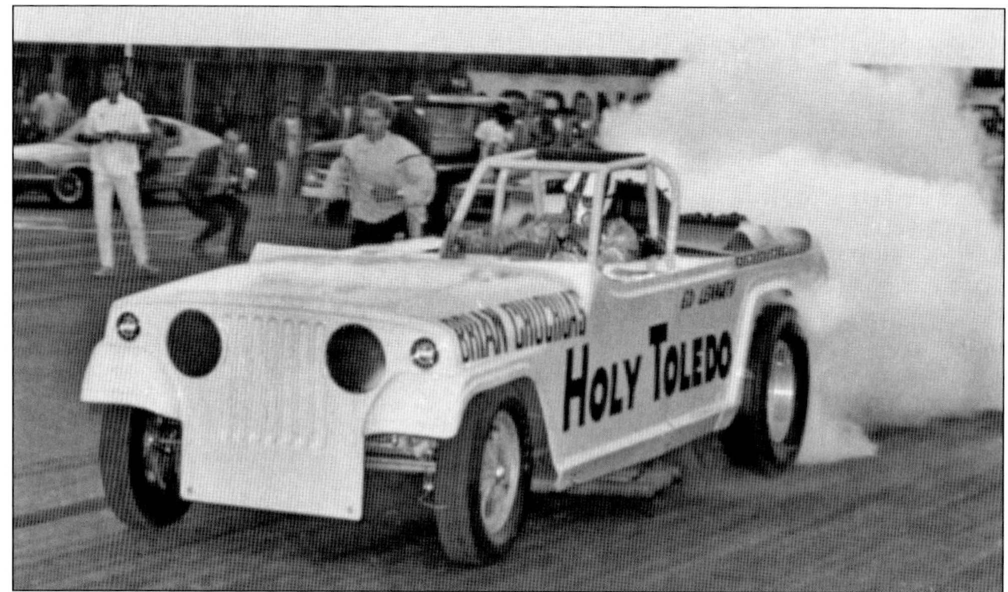

The big yellow brick, also known as the "Holy Toledo" funny jeep, was a big favorite with fans at OCIR in 1969. Even though the body style had been banned by the NHRA, owner/driver Ed Lenarth was able to race his big yellow brick at local funny car events at OCIR, Lions, or Irwindale. Lenarth was not going to break any ET or speed records with his Holy Toledo brick, but he did manage to get a best of 7.37 at 197 miles per hour at OCIR.

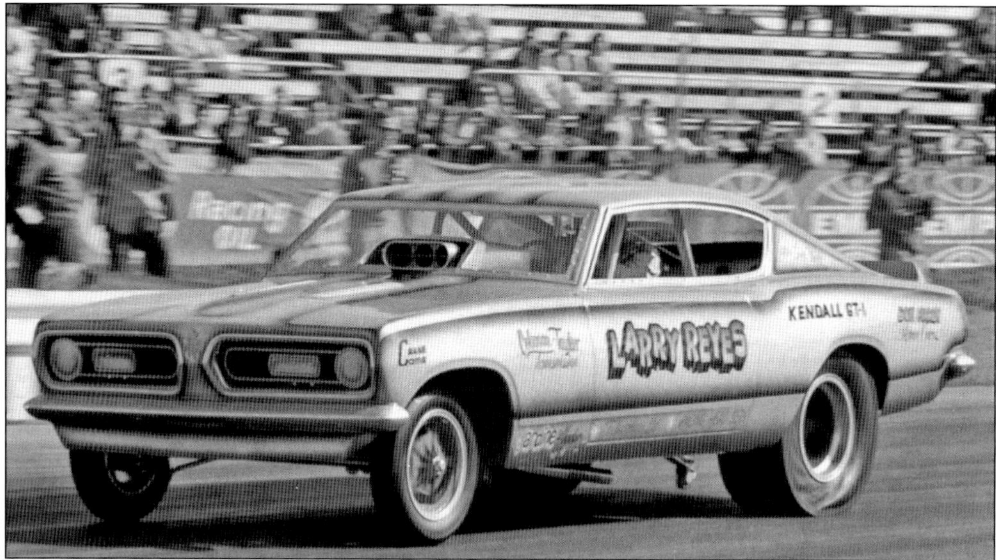

This is one of those funny cars that OCIR race fans only saw once, and then it disappeared. Memphis, Tennessee-based Larry Reyes debuted his all new Cuda funny car at OCIR in late 1968. But only after a few runs, Reyes sold his Cuda to Paula Murphy. Reyes was not without a ride for long as he was named the driver for Roland Leong's all new Dodge Charger funny car for 1969. At the 1969 NHRA Winternationals in Pomona, California, Leong and Reyes debuted the full-size Charger in grand style when the car flew at the finish line on its first full run down the quarter mile. The car landed upright but the chassis was bent and the body destroyed. Reyes had a rather sore back from the flight. A new mini Charger was assembled and debuted at OCIR just a few weeks later.

The winning team at the 1970 OCIR Manufacturers Meet was Team Plymouth. Pictured are, from left to right, Larry Reyes (Super Duster), Don Schumacher (Stardust Cuda), race queen Sue Monroe, Larry Arnold (The Kingfish Cuda), Leonard Hughes (Candies and Hughes Cuda), and Richard Sirooinian (Big John Mazmanian Cuda). Don Prudhomme and one other team member were shy and did not show for the team photograph.

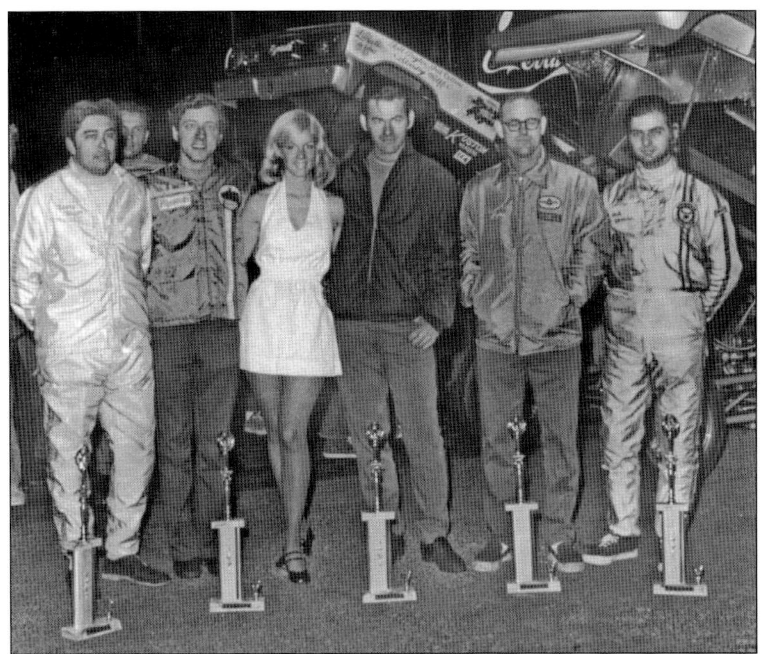

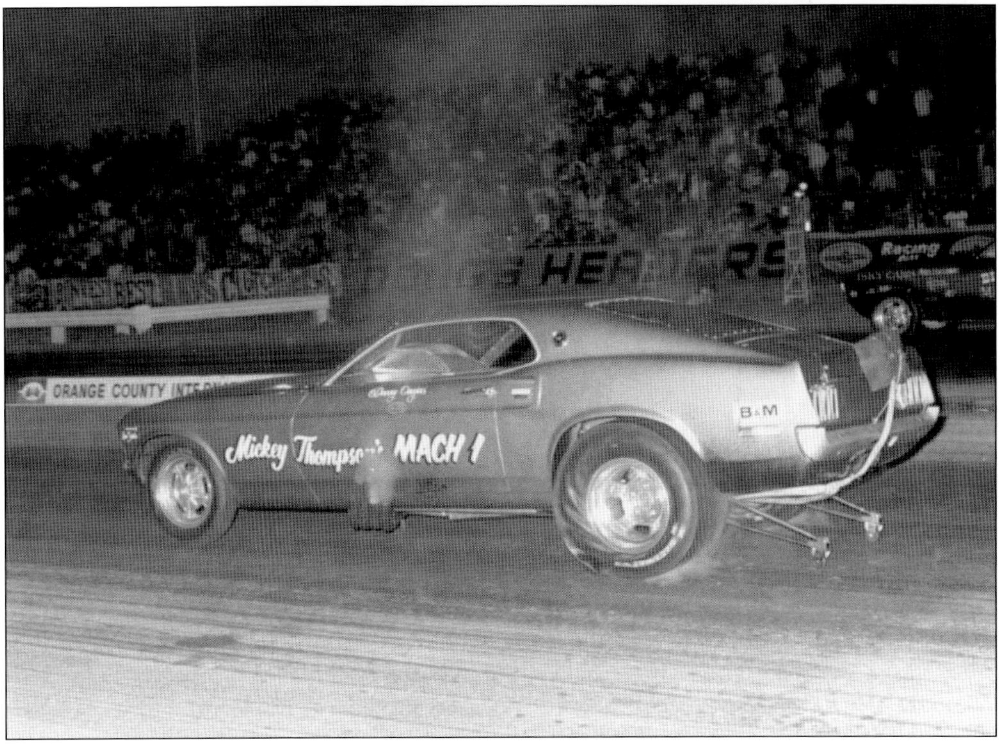

The killer car in funny car racing in 1969 was the Mickey Thompson–owned Ford "Mach 1" Mustang driven by the "Flyin' Hawaiian" Danny Ongais. On July 5, 1969, Ongais won the OCIR Nitro Championships, beating Larry Fullerton in the final. He also set low ET at 7.35 for a new OCIR track record. Then on July 19, he was runner-up to Dave Beebe, who was driving Big John Mazmanian's Cuda at the 1969 OCIR PDA race.

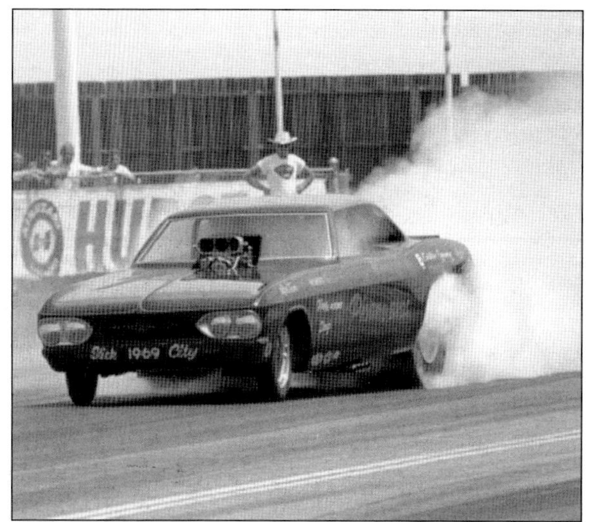

The Pisano Bros., Joe and Frankie, were regular participants at OCIR funny car events. This is their Chevrolet Corvair funny car that they just purchased from Doug Thorley. The Pisanos won the first-ever funny car eliminator at OCIR in 1967 with their Camaro funny car. But that car was lost in a two-car crash at Irwindale with Randy Walls in early 1968. A quick deal with Thorley, and the Pisanos were back in business. Their Thorley Corvair was not around for long, though, as it was stuffed into the OCIR guardrail by Sush Matsubara. Of course, the Pisanos came back once more with a repaired funny car.

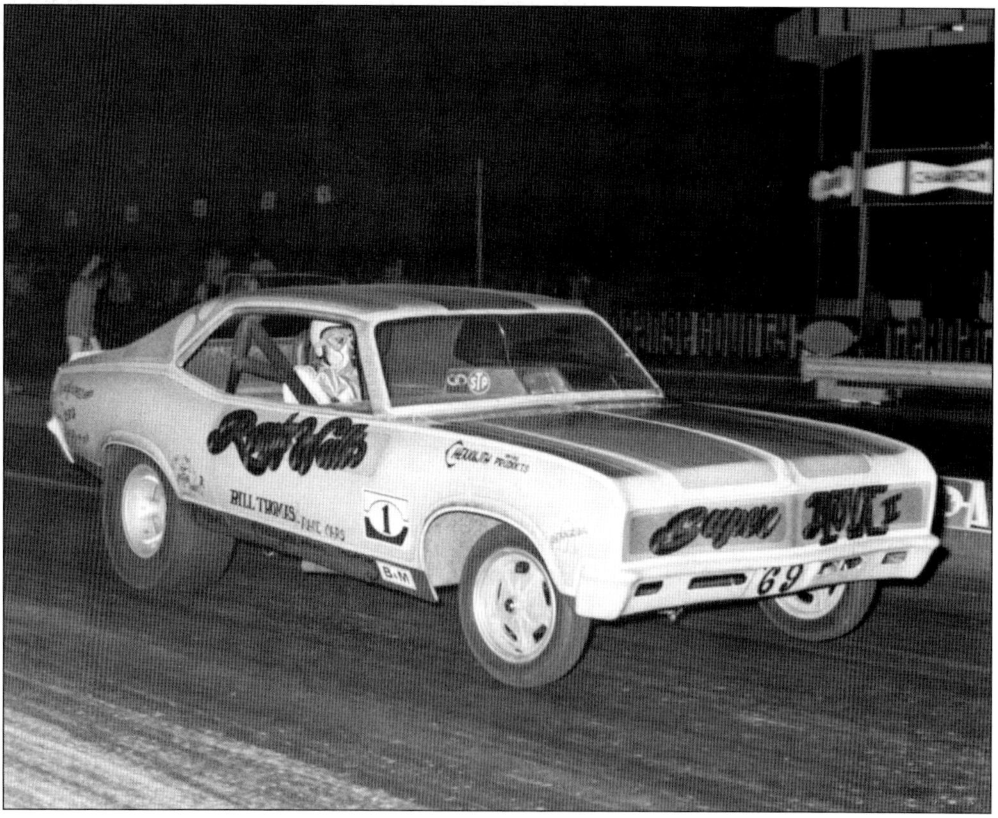

El Cajon's Randy Walls and his "Super Nova" were regularly competing at OCIR and other tracks in Southern and Northern California from late 1966 into the 1970s. Walls's first Super Nova was a 1965 Chevrolet Nova; it was lost in a two-car crash with the Pisano Bros. at Irwindale in 1968. Needing a car to finish his commitments, Walls bought a slightly used Corvair funny car from Hayden Proffitt. Then at the beginning of 1969, he debuted an all-new Bill Thomas–built Super Nova funny car. On May 31, 1969, Walls was runner-up to Larry Reyes driving Roland Leong's Dodge Charger at OCIR's Funny Car 500.

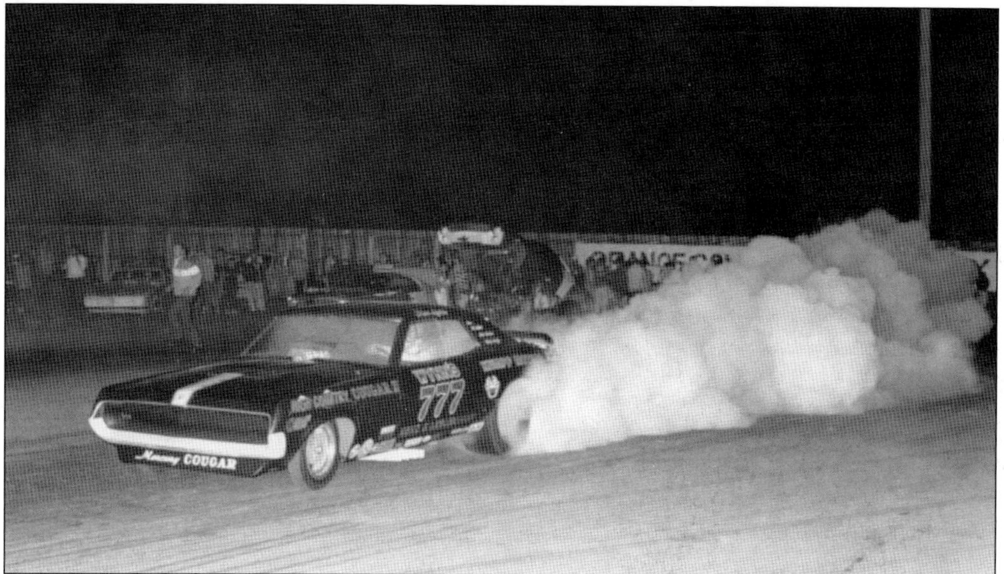

Kenz and Leslie's "High-Country" Mercury Cougar was state of the art in funny cars from Colorado in 1969. Ex-top fuel dragster pilot Ron Leslie was at the controls of the mighty 429 Ford SOHC–powered Cougar. The team not only participated in drag racing but also was well known by land speed record (LSR) racers at Bonneville. The team had a sleek streamliner that it ran at Bonneville every season.

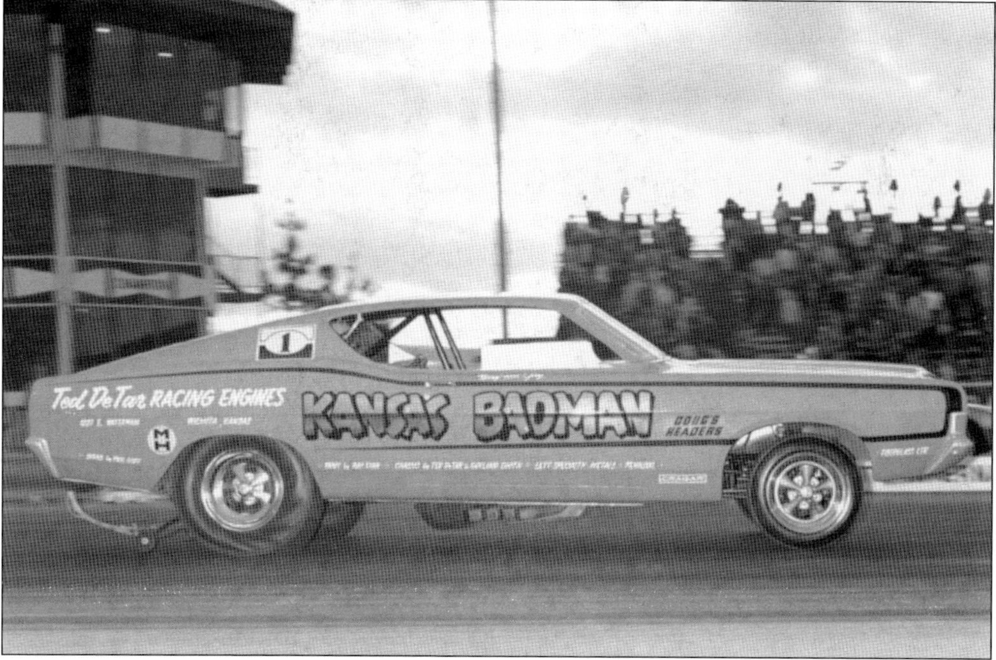

Joplin, Missouri–based Terry Ivey came to OCIR in 1969 with an all-new Ford Torino GT–bodied funny car built by Ted Detar. Ivey purchased the car from Detar just weeks before Detar was killed in a racing accident in Florida. Ivey would soon replace the heavy Torino body with a Ford Maverick body. Then, in 1971, Ivey went Mopar with a Duster body on his funny car. Ivey was a regular on the AHRA funny car circuit.

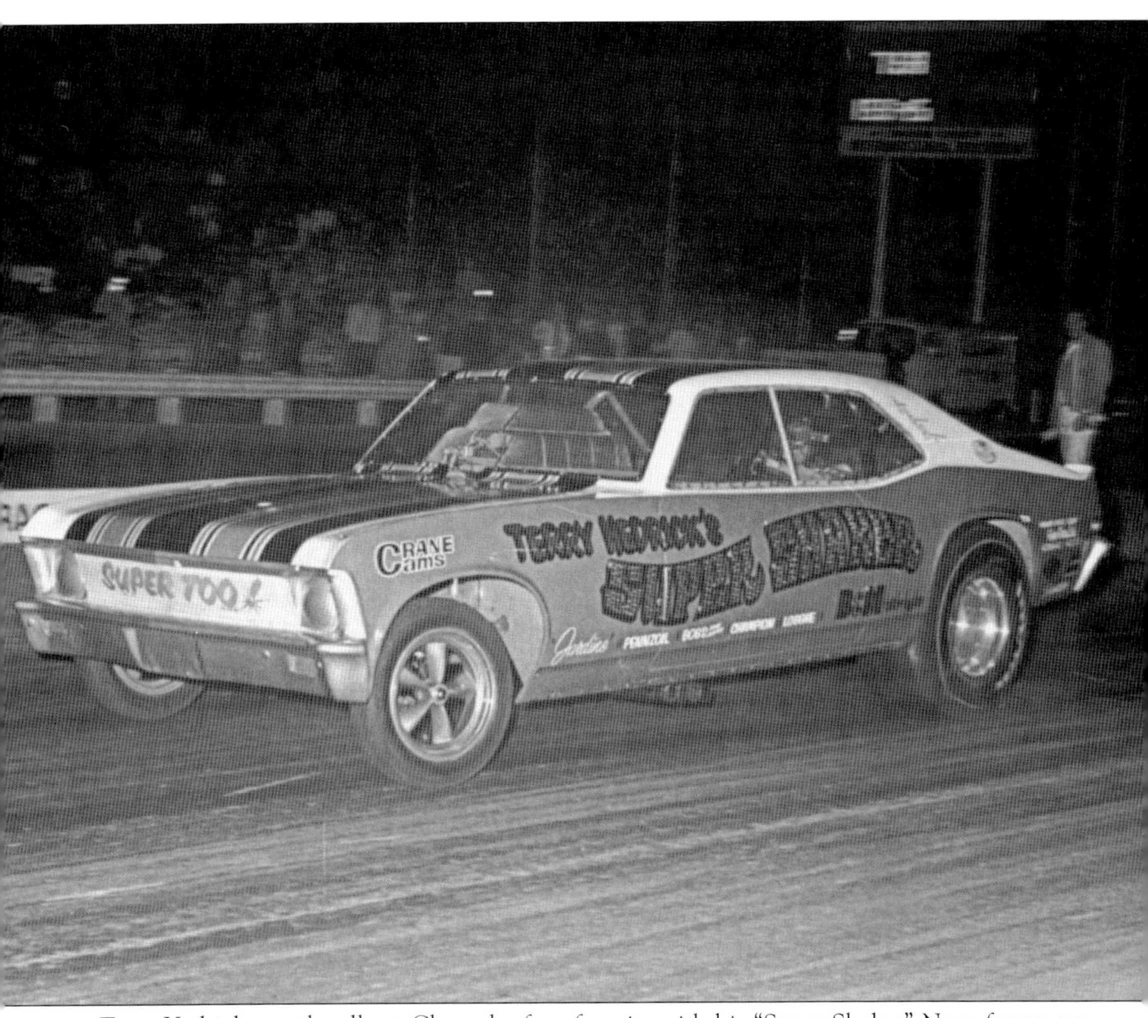

Terry Hedrick was the all-out Chevrolet fans favorite with his "Super Shaker" Nova funny car. Hedrick had the first all-Chevrolet funny car to run in the 6.00 ETs at 200 miles per hour. To say Hedrick loved to race was a vast understatement. When he toured the United States, it was common for him to run 80 to 85 dates a year. Sometimes racing five times a week, Hedrick's Nova was a welcomed sight on the AHRA funny car circuit in 1969.

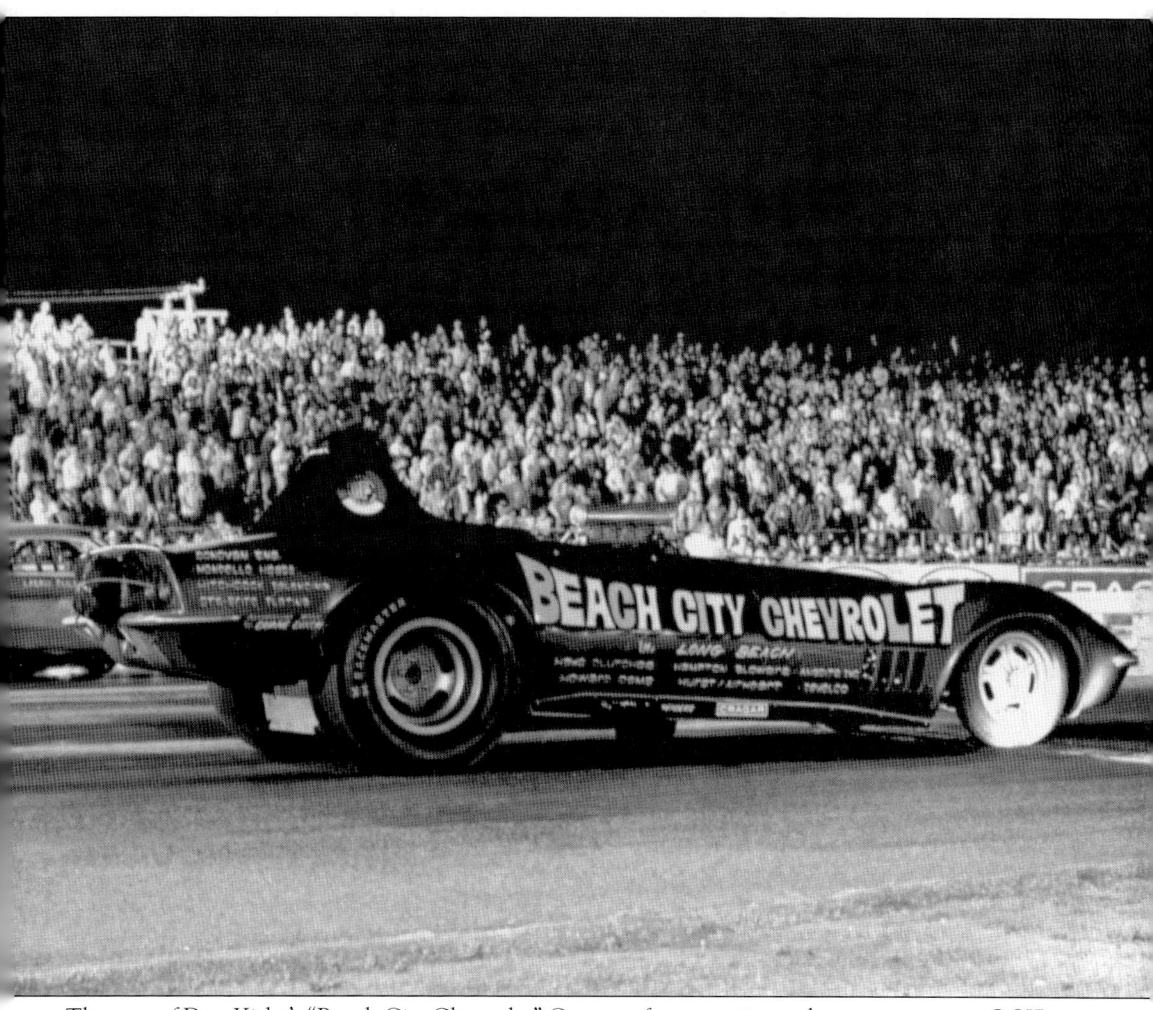

The saga of Don Kirby's "Beach City Chevrolet" Corvette funny car is a rather strange one at OCIR. His first Beach City Corvette burned to the ground at Irwindale in 1969. Driver Gary Gabelich escaped the inferno and was not injured in the blaze. About a year later at OCIR, Ronnie Goodsell was driving the roadster-style Corvette funny car. During a single run in the evening at OCIR, the car exploded into a huge ball of fire at the finish line. Goodsell was trying everything to get the blaze out and get the car stopped. He spun the car out in the OCIR shutdown area, but now it was going backwards through the trees that were on the left side. Goodsell missed the trees and nailed the eight-foot chain-link fence. Then, still on fire and backwards, the car climbed the hill that separated the racetrack from the freeway, vaulting over the hill and into the slow lane. Still on fire, Goodsell scrambled out of the burning mess as a truck driver stopped and tried to put out the fire with a fire extinguisher. The fire finally burned itself out, and Kirby was given a ticket by the California Highway patrol for littering.

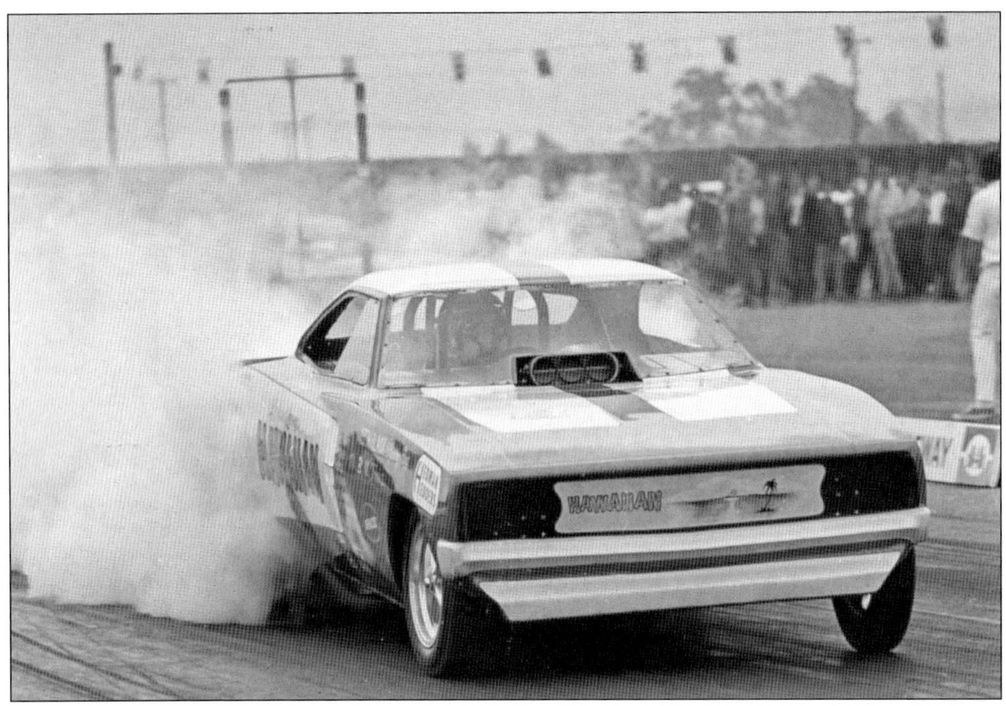

Roland Leong replaced his high-flying, full-size Dodge Charger funny car with this all-new, non-flying Dodge Mini-Charger funny car in mid-1969. Larry Reyes was still the pilot (pun intended) of Leong's first venture into the world of funny car racing. Leong and Reyes won the first three races that they entered, including the May 31, 1969, OCIR Funny Car 500, beating Randy Walls in the final. Reyes also ran low ET and the top speed of the event—7.38 at 200.07 miles per hour.

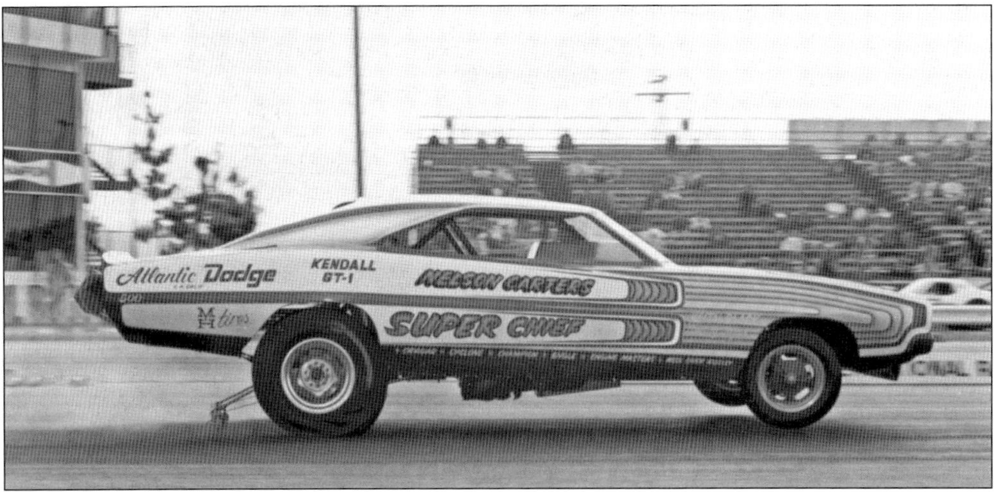

OCIR manager Mike Jones, on September 1968 at the NHRA Division 7 World Championship Series race, offered to pay a $2,000 bounty on any funny car that set the S/XS ET record at OCIR. Dave Beebe driving Nelson Carter's "Super Chief" claimed the bounty with runs of 7.77, 7.79, 7.68, and 7.70; his best speed was 197.36 miles per hour. The record was set at 7.68 for the S/XS class. The Oklahoma-based Carter had other drivers for his line of Super Chief funny cars, including Rod Peru, Byan Teal, Steve Bovan, Dave Beebe, Tim Grose, Bob Pickett, and Steve Bernard, who crashed the final version of the Super Chief at OCIR.

Boat racer "Diamond" Jim Annin and Mike Snively teamed up in 1970 and went funny car racing. Their Dodge Challenger had the best that money could buy in 1970. A Pat Foster dragster-style chassis and a Keith Black Hemi were under the Dodge Challenger shell. The duo won the NHRA Division 7 funny car title for 1970 and garnered top honors at the OCIR Funny Car 500. The big win at OCIR came on Annin's birthday.

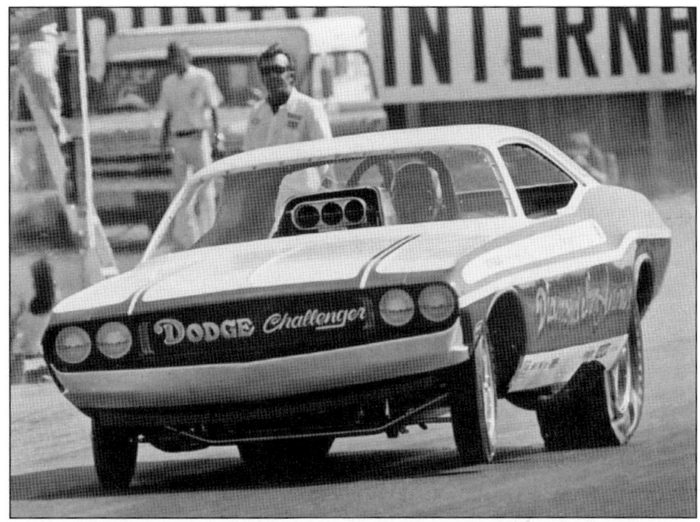

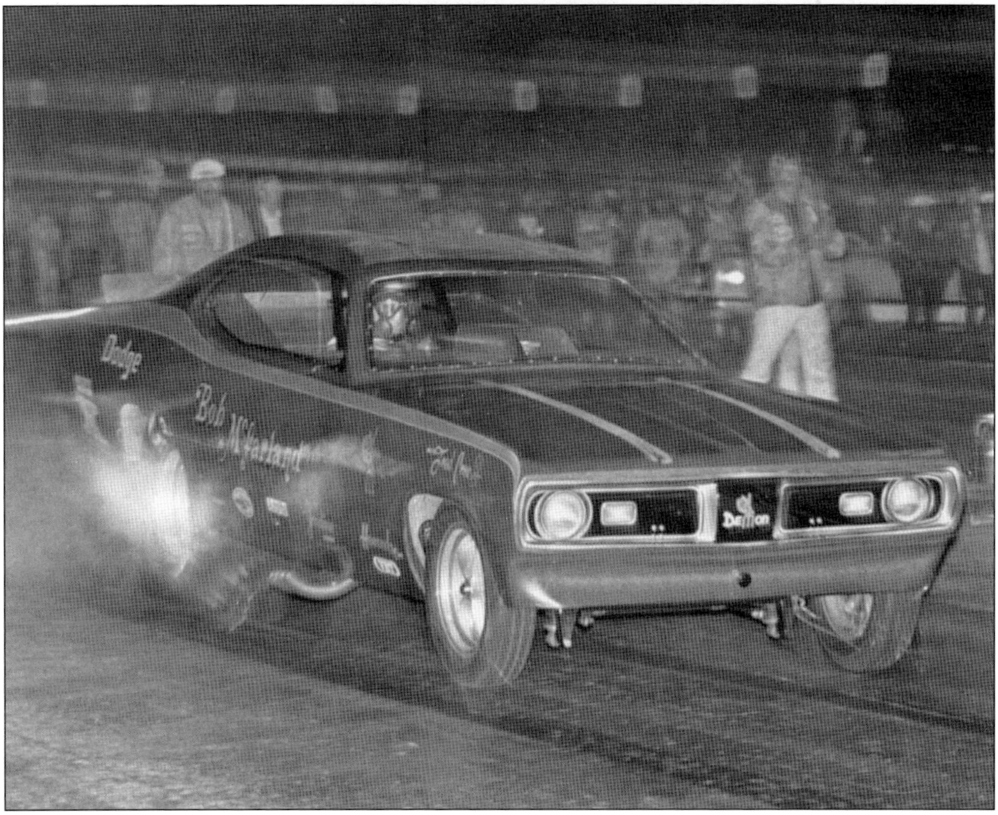

Arizona fertilizer farmer Bob McFarland experienced the highs and lows of funny car racing in 1971. First, on May 1, 1971, McFarland and his rather outdated Chevy Nova funny car upset Big John Mazmanian's Cuda to win OCIR's Big Four Funny Car Championships. Also in 1971, McFarland was driving his all-new Dodge Demon funny car at Lions when he had a huge explosion and fire in his Demon. McFarland got the inferno stopped and was trying to get out of the burning funny car. Funny car owner Mickey Thompson was on the scene and pulled McFarland from the fire. The Demon burned to the ground, thus ending McFarland's 1968 to 1971 funny car career.

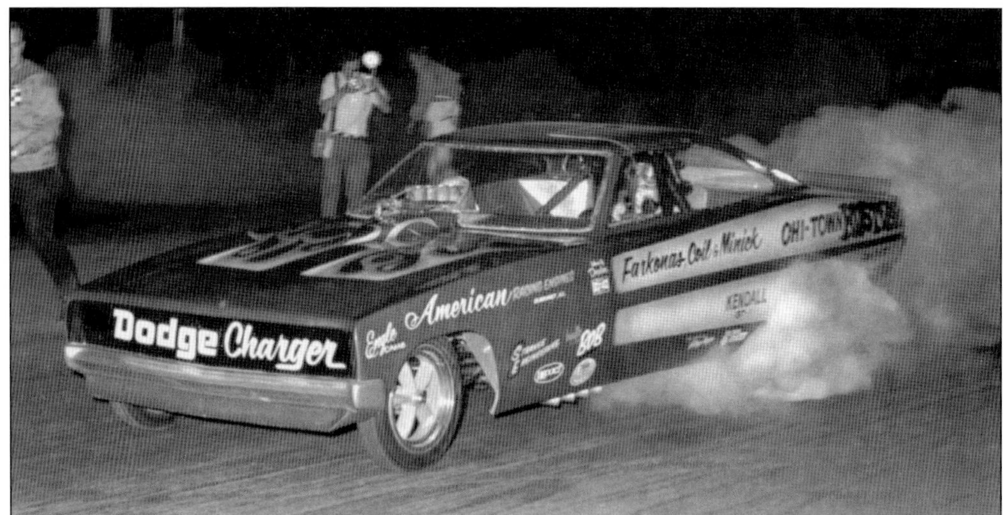

Another funny car that came to the West Coast to escape the Chicagoland winters was the team of John Farkonas, Austin Coil, and Pat Minick with their Chi-Town Hustler Dodge Charger. Always the showman, driver Pat Minick showed how Midwest funny cars do burnouts, and the OCIR fans loved it. The boys from Chicago won the 1969 OCIR East/West Funny Car Championships and then in the same year were runners-up to Gaspar Ronda at the OCIR Manufacturers Meet. They had low 7.27 ET at the event. They proved that they could race with the best in the west in 1969.

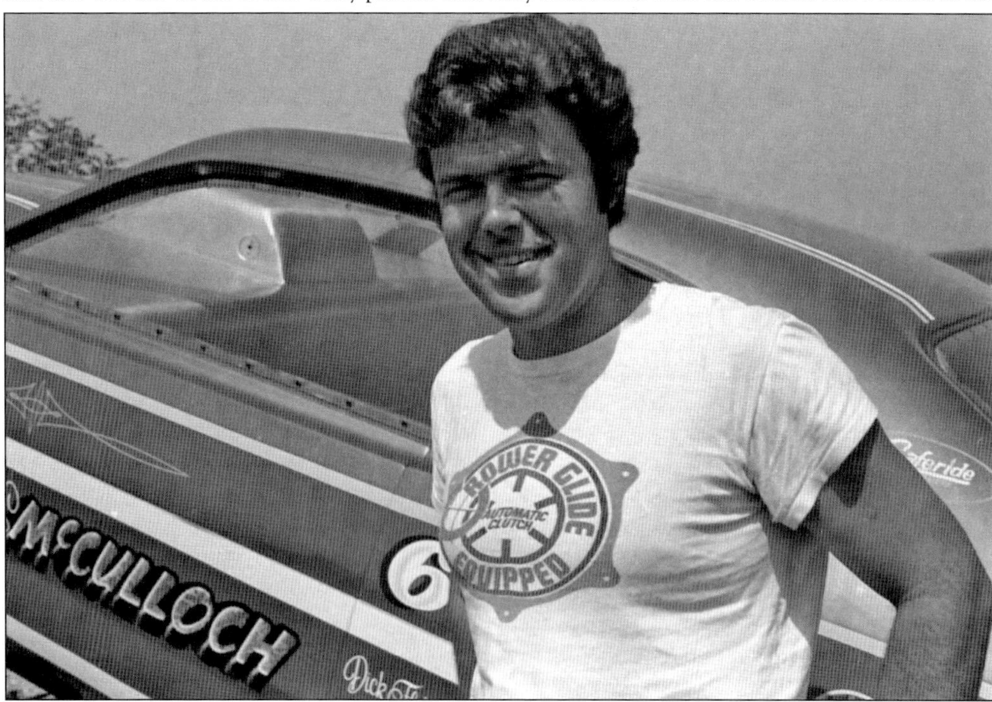

Washington State's Ed "the Ace" McCullouch enjoyed his time racing at OCIR in the 1970s. McCullouch and then partner Art Whipple posted a 7.11 ET at 205.46 miles per hour at the 1970 OCIR PDA meet. Then on his own, McCullouch won the 1972 OCIR East/West Funny Car Championships over Jim Dunn. At the 1975 OCIR Manufacturers Meet, McCullouch defeated Jake Johnston, driving for Joe Pisano, to take top honors at the event. Not bad for an old Northwest top fuel dragster driver.

Dallas, Texas, furniture store owner Harry Schimdt and driver Jake Johnston did all the right things at the 1970 OCIR Manufacturers Meet and took home top honors with Schimdt's "Blue Max" Ford Mustang-bodied funny car. The talented Johnston ran a 6.72 ET at 217.91 miles per hour, defeating Big John Mazmanian's Cuda in the final round. Pictured are Blue Max driver Jake Johnston with race queen Sue Monroe.

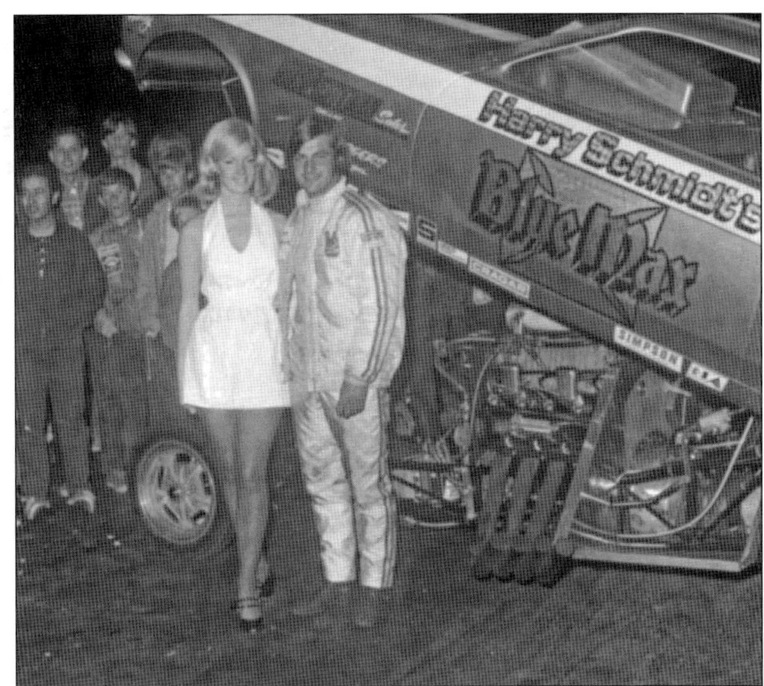

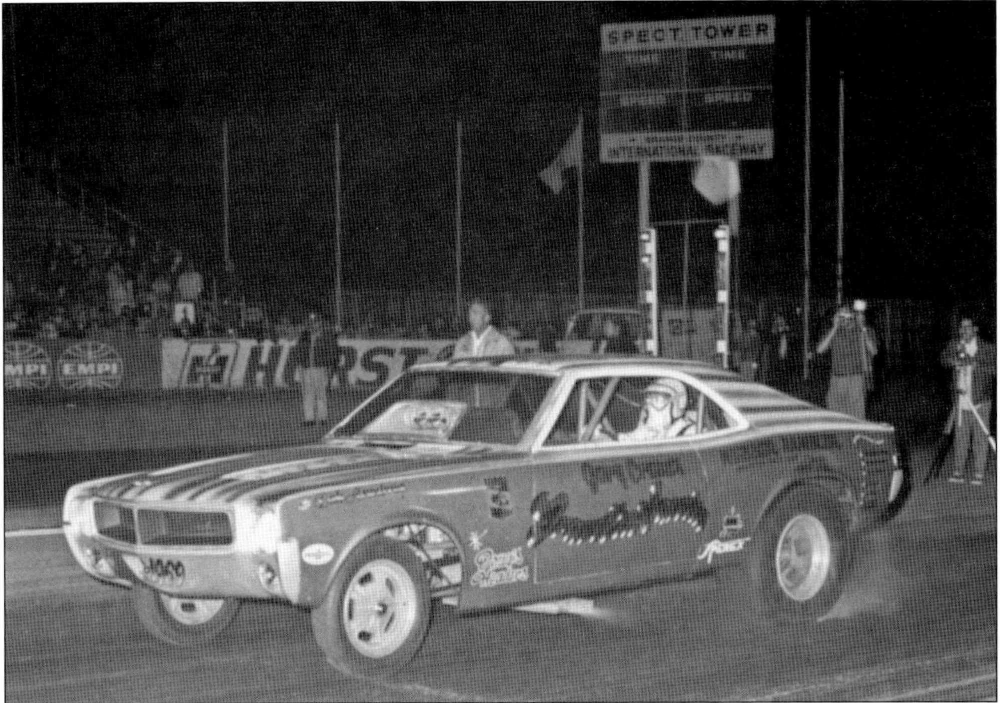

Canada's Gary Crane made the very long tow from Alberta to race his "Travelin Javelin" funny car at OCIR in 1970. Crane's Javelin-bodied funny car was one of a few that raced with that style body. Javelin's multicolored paint scheme made it standout at the OCIR events that Crane attended in 1970. Sometimes a fellow Canadian could be found behind the wheel of Crane's Javelin and that was Dale Armstrong.

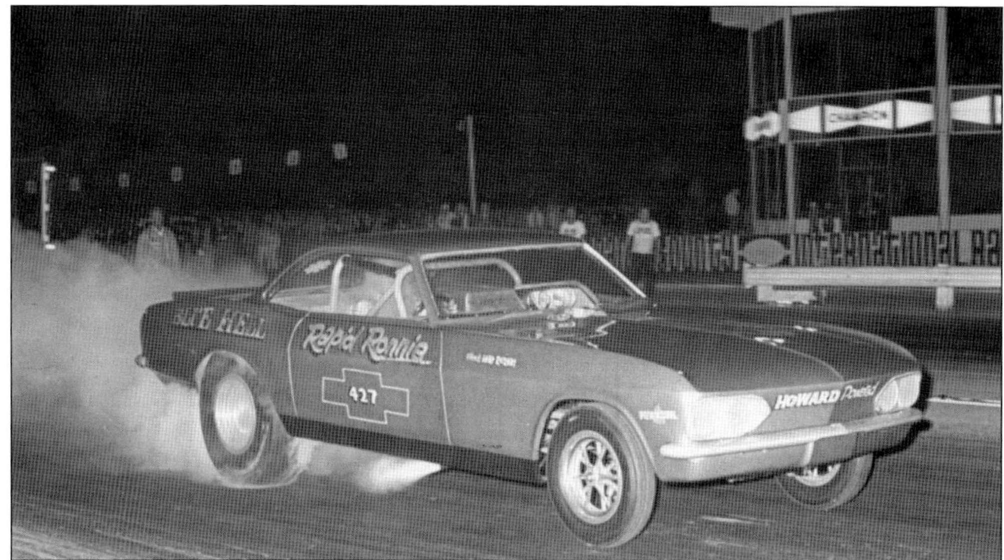

"Rapid" Ronnie Runyan raced his Chevrolet Corvair bodied funny car for three years, from 1968 to 1971. If the brothers Runyan, Ronnie and Mike, were not on tour, they could be found racing at one of the funny car events in Southern California. When AHRA held their Mr. Chevrolet event at Scottsdale, Arizona, in 1970, Ronnie was there and took home the Mr. Chevrolet title. Ronnie also held the AHRA ET record for the one-eighth mile at 5.08 at 168 miles per hour. In 1971, Ronnie debuted an all-new Chevrolet Vega-bodied funny car and moved his base to the Midwest to be closer to the AHRA funny car circuit.

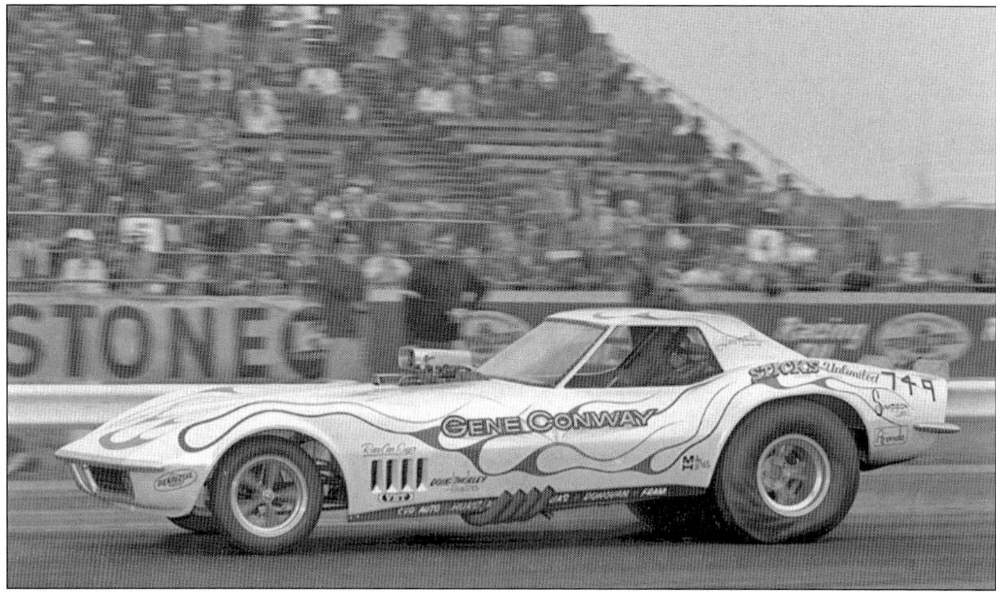

With his Destroyer funny Jeep outlawed by NHRA, Gene Conway first went to a Pontiac Firebird–bodied funny car, then to the roadster-style Chevrolet Corvette. Then after NHRA outlawed the roadster-style funny cars, he built this hardtop Corvette funny car. Conway won back-to-back OCIR PDA races in 1970 and 1971; at both events he defeated Ray Alley in the final round. Also in 1970, Conway was runner-up to Don Schumacher at the OCIR East/West Funny Car Championships held on October 10, 1970.

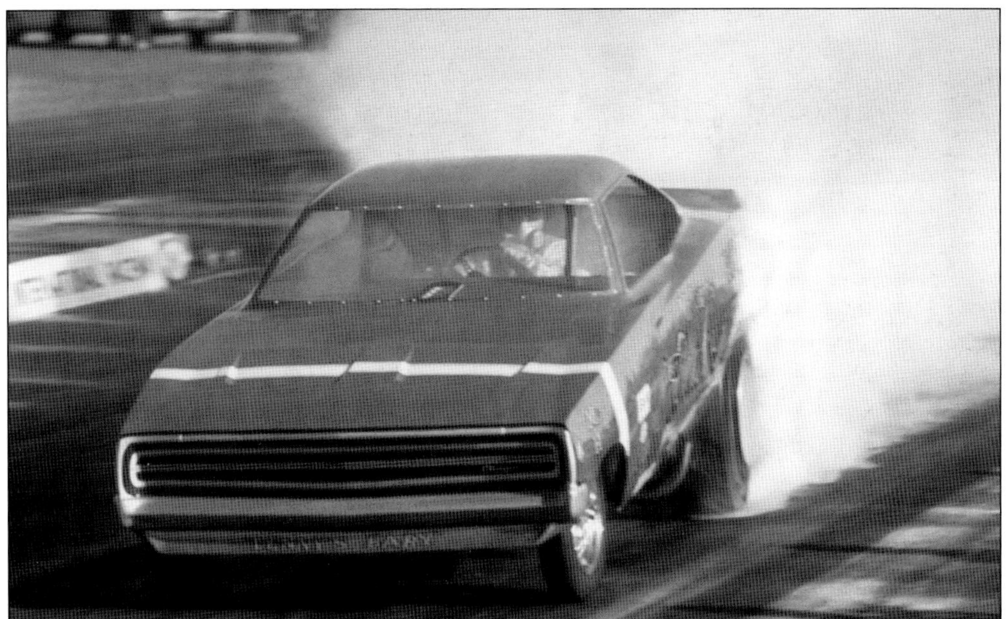

Another Chicagoland funny car racer escaping the bitter cold of the Midwest was Gary Dyer and Mr. Norm's Super Charger funny car. (Norm Klaus was known as "Mr. Norm.") Dyer was no stranger to touring as he raced year-round and kept very busy with his blower building service for race cars. Dyer retired from driving when Mr. Norm sold his entire funny car operation to Kenny Safford. No worries for Dyer, though, because his blower business was booming.

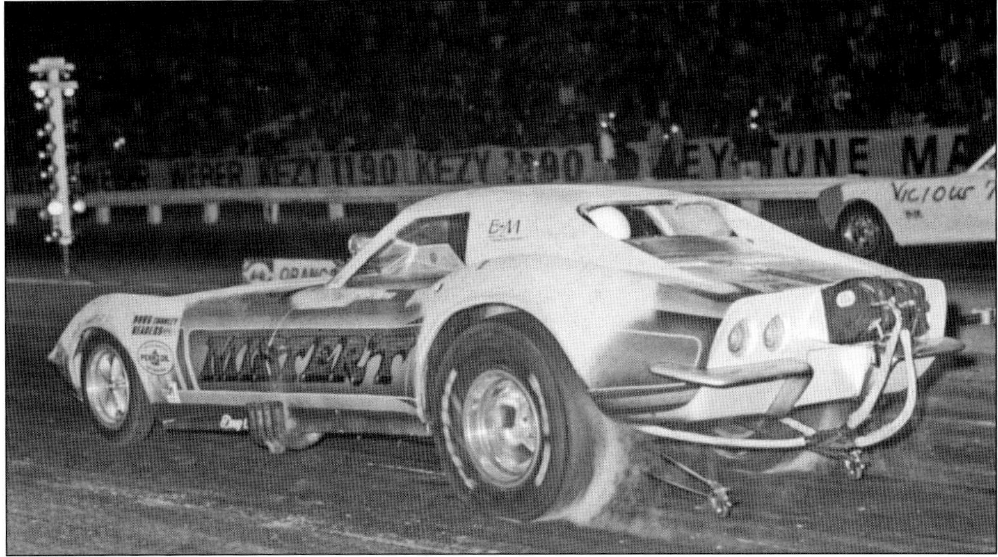

Pictured at OCIR in May 1970, the "Mister T" Corvette funny car sports scars from its spectacular debut at Bakersfield in March 1970. Driver Vic "Flipper" Morse went for quite a ride when the wayward funny car flipped upside down at the Bakersfield finish line. Amazingly, the car only suffered body damage and one very embarrassing moment for Morse in the mishap. Morse would vacate the driver's seat to Rusty Delling later in the year. Delling crashed and destroyed the car at Lions Drag Strip when the cars transmission exploded at the finish line. Delling was seriously injured but did recover, the car was not rebuilt, and Delling never drove again.

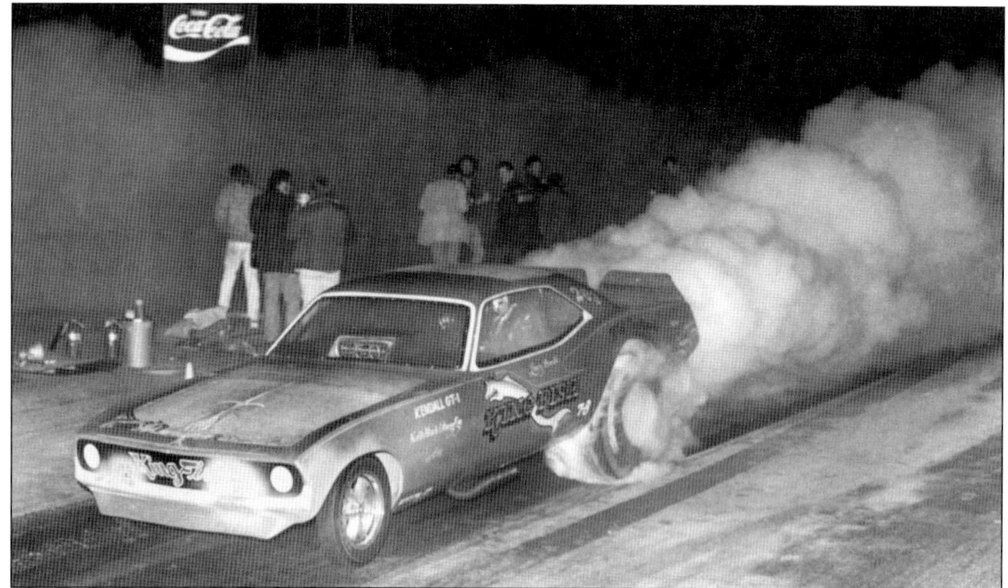

At OCIR in 1970, T.B. Smallwood's "Kingfish" Cuda sports a few scars from a tangle with a Christmas tree at an Eastern racetrack. Driver Larry Arnold and the Kingfish Cuda were part of the winning team at the 1970 OCIR Manufacturers Meet, Team Plymouth. At the 1970 NHRA Supernationals in Ontario, California, Arnold was runner-up to Gene Snow in the funny car eliminator. By 1971, Arnold owned the Kingfish Cuda. He returned to the Supernationals and won funny car eliminator.

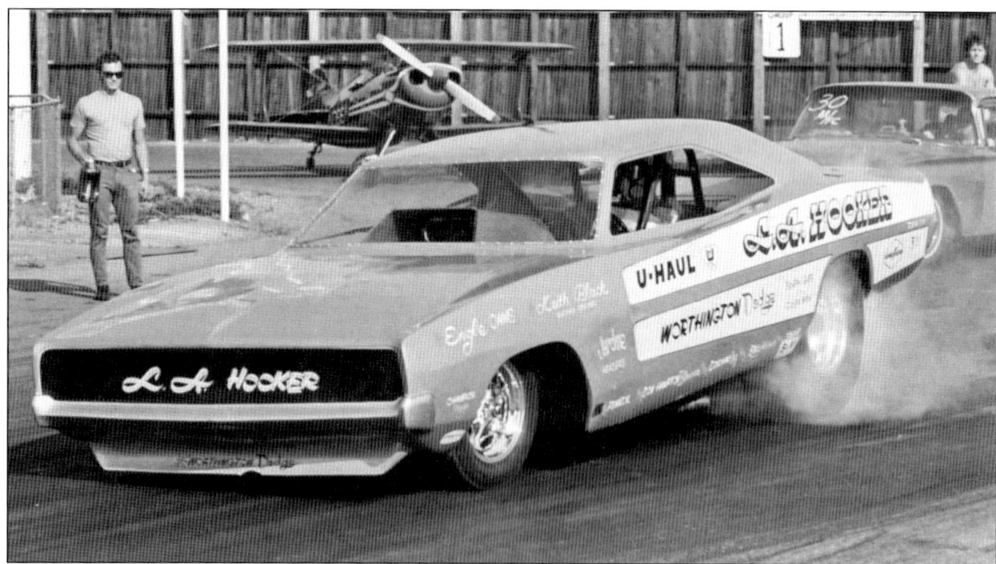

Gene Beaver and the Condit brothers, Bill, Dave, and Steve, parked their top fuel dragster and went funny car racing with a slightly used Dodge Charger purchased from Oklahoma's Nelson Carter in 1970. The former "Super Chief" now became the "L.A. Hooker" with Dave Condit driving and brothers Steve and Bill crewing. Gene Beaver did the tune-ups on the blown nitro-burning Hemi. The team mainly match raced in the summer months in the Midwest and returned home to SoCal in the fall to race. Gene Beaver had a nephew who he sometime brought out to the races in SoCal. John Force was that nephew.

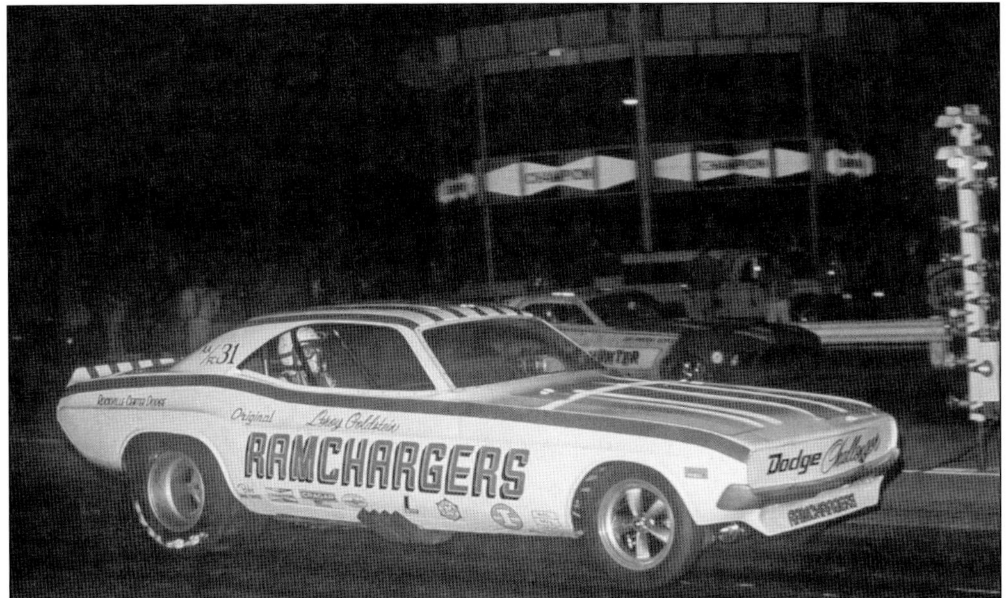

All new for 1970 was Michigan's "Ramchargers" Dodge Challenger funny car. It replaced their mighty candy-striped top fuel dragster. But there was no change of drivers as Leroy "the Israeli Rocket" Goldstein was at the helm of the candy-striped Challenger. The Ramchargers funny car with Goldstein driving is credited with the first six second runs in a funny car eliminator. This took place at New York National Speedway in 1970. The Ramchargers car club's crew chief was Phil Goulet.

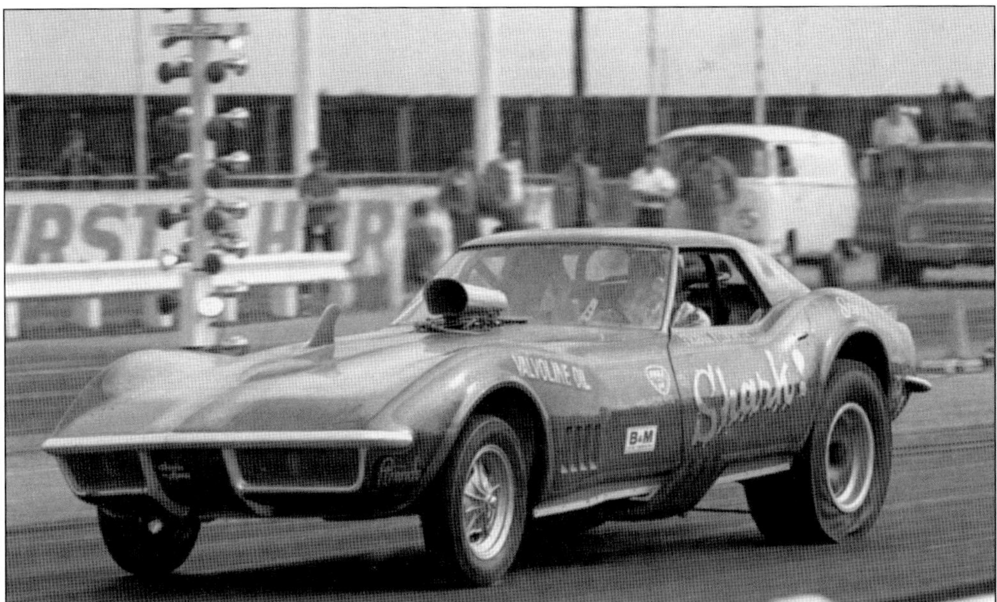

Rhode Island's Frank "the Beard" Federici had the first Corvette-bodied funny car on the East Coast in 1967. Here in 1970 at OCIR, "Jungle Clare" Sanders is piloting Federici's "the Shark" Corvette funny car. Federici's Corvette had a 426 Hemi on nitro for power, and either Sanders or Federici drove in 1970. Federici raced his Shark at Suffolk, Virginia, in 1971 and crashed and totaled the car. It is believed Federici retired after the accident.

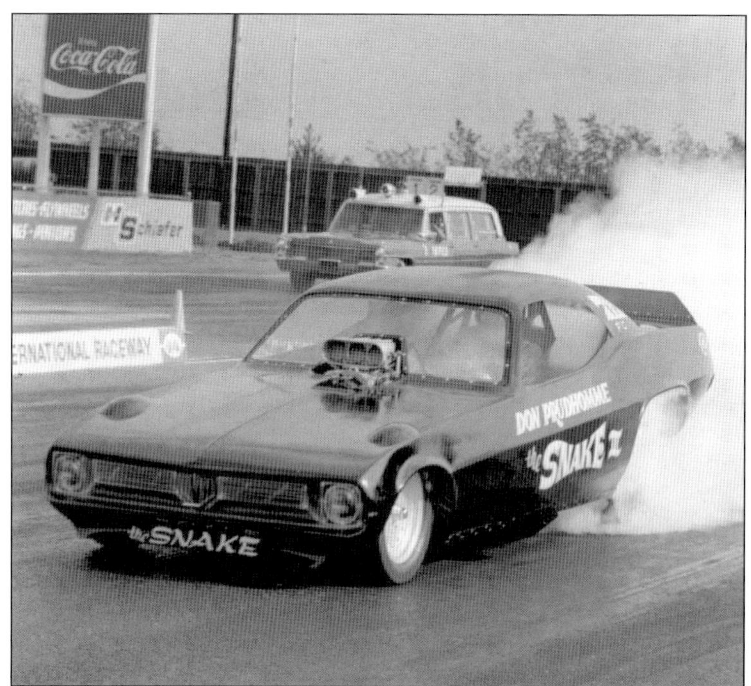

Don "the Snake" Prudhomme and his "Hot Wheels II" Cuda raced in season three of the All-Pro Series at OCIR in 1971. The Snake clicked off a 6.70 ET in the second race of the series. But he did not back it up, so it was not recognized as an OCIR track record. Undaunted, he returned to race at the third part of the series on March 27, 1971, and won the event. He also posted both ends of the OCIR funny car track records at 6.63 at 226.13 miles per hour.

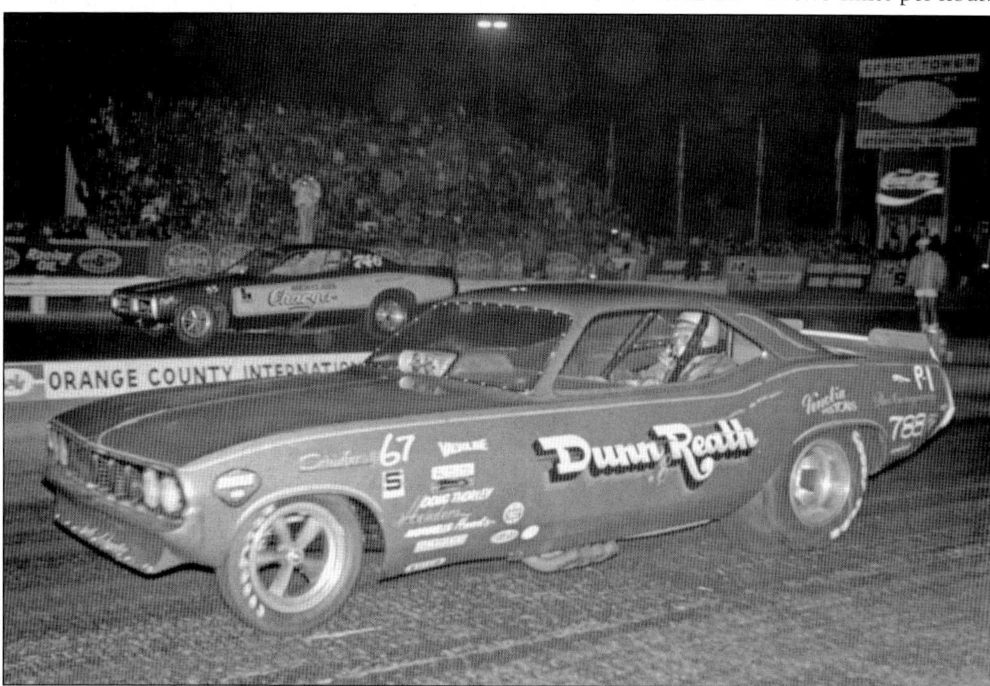

The new no frills Cuda funny car of Dunn and Reath took on the big money funny cars at the 1971 OCIR Manufacturers Meet on November 6, 1971. Driver Jim Dunn waded through a huge field of funny cars to come up one round short of winning the event. Dunn lost the final round to Pat Foster driving Barry Setzer's big-money Vega funny car. Dunn did have a low ET of the event at 6.70. Dunn and Reath proved that they could run with the best of the funny car class with their no-frill, economy-built Cuda funny car.

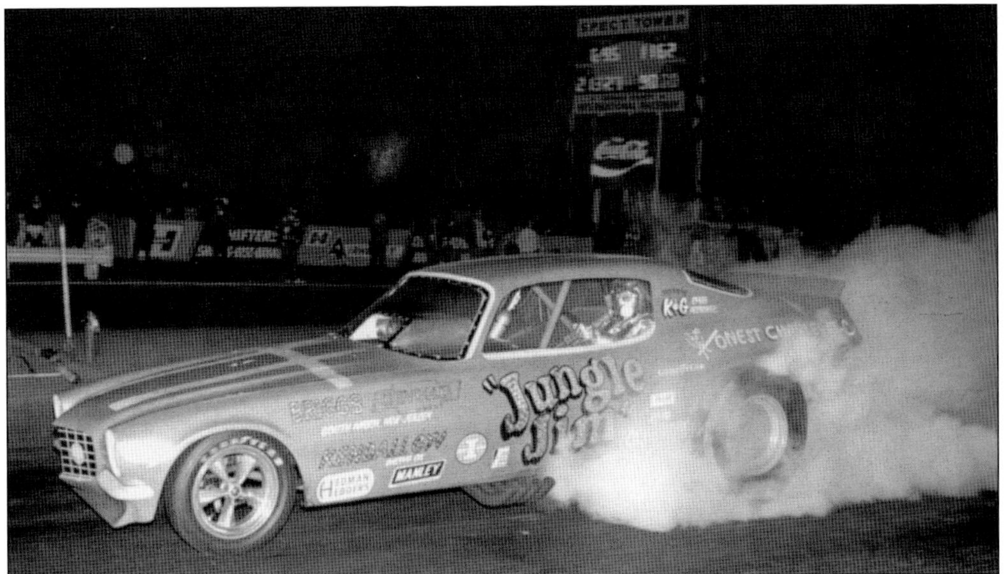

In 1971, Jim Liberman changed body styles for his funny cars, from Nova to Camaro. He was also now running a Chrysler Hemi for power in his Camaro-bodied funny car. Liberman was a regular at the OCIR Manufacturers Meets since the first race in 1967. He headquartered in California in the winter because West Chester, Pennsylvania, was his home base to race in the East in the summer. Besides being a very popular funny car driver, Liberman was a wheeler dealer of used funny cars. It is said that he bought or sold 37 funny cars from 1967 to 1977, and at his high point in popularity, he had four Jungle Jim funny cars racing all over the United States.

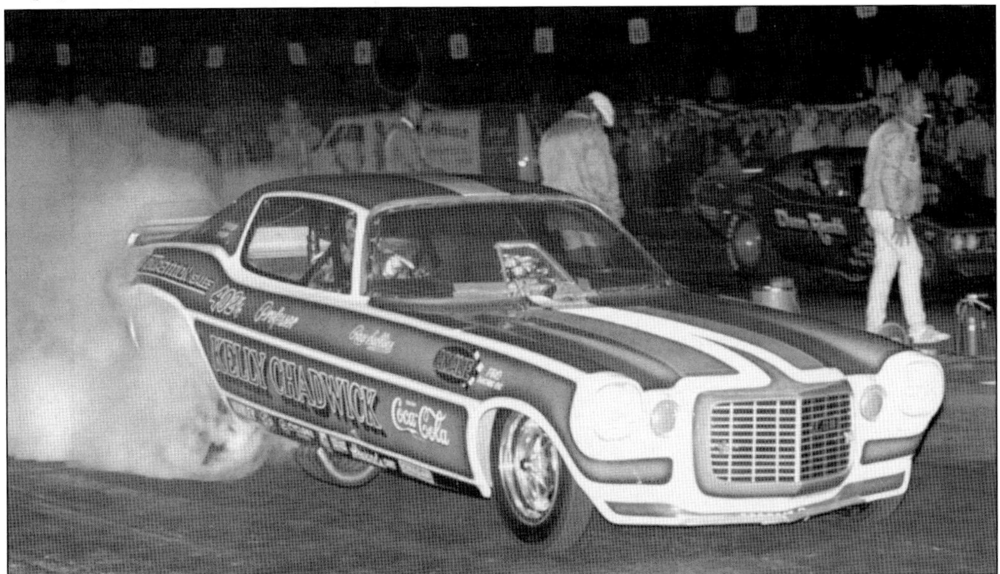

Texan Kelly Chadwick was a full-time high school teacher who turned into a full-time funny car racer in the late 1960s into the 1970s. Chadwick toured the country with his all-Chevrolet Camaro funny car in 1971 and could be found match racing and running at AHRA major events. His trip to OCIR in 1971 was a great moment for him and his legion of Chevy fans. At the 1971 OCIR Manufacturers Meet, Chadwick did not disappoint his fans. He blasted out a 6.73 ET, making him the quickest Chevrolet-powered funny car in the country on November 6, 1971.

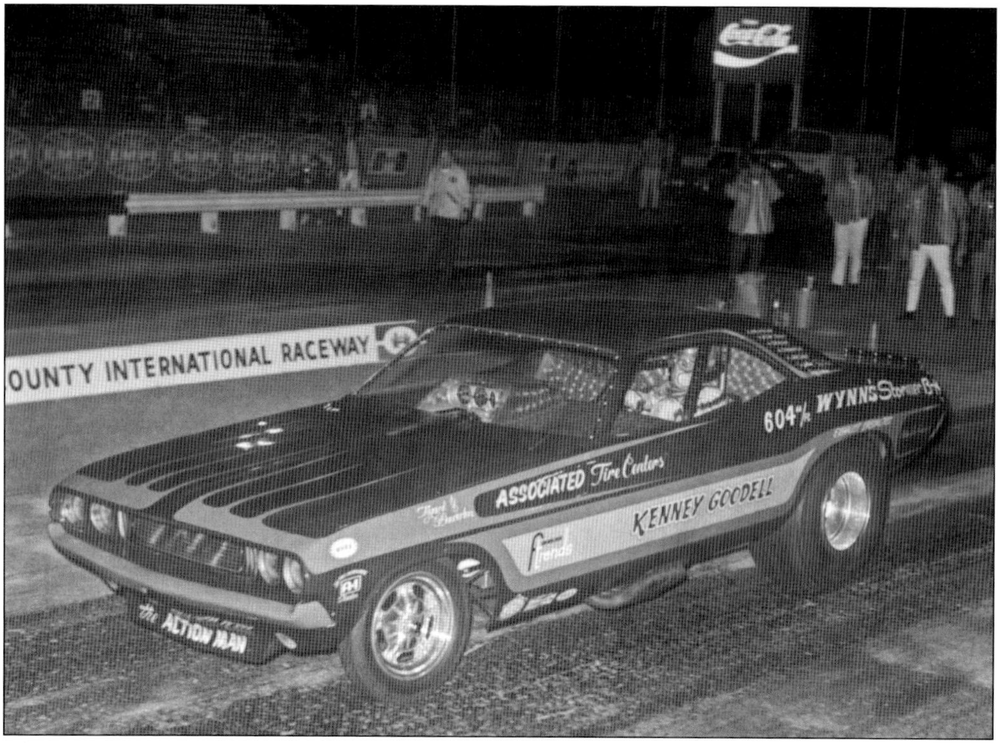

The great Northwest's self-proclaimed "Action Man "was Kenney Goodell. Goodell was one of the first funny car racers in the Northwest to run a blower on his Mustang funny car in 1967. He was also the first to have a major sponsor with Wynn's Oil Company on the side of his Mopar-bodied funny cars. Goodell added a top fuel dragster to his race team in 1972, also sponsored by Wynn's. Goodell was considered one of the big four funny car racers from the great Northwest; the others were Whipple and McCullough, Jim Green, and the always humble Jerry "the King" Ruth.

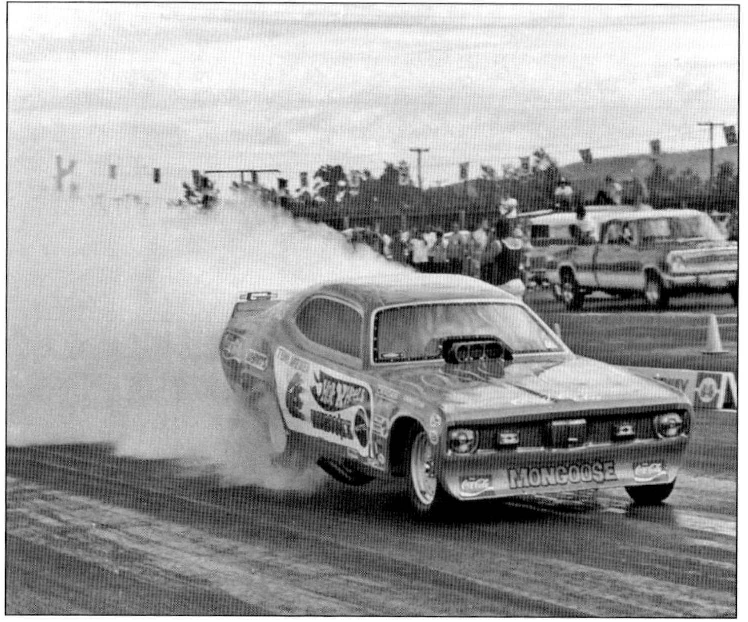

Poor ol' "Mongoose," also known as Tom McEwen, could not seem to get a win at OCIR with his top fuel dragster. But his Hot Wheels Duster funny car was a different story. Season five of OCIR's 1972 All Pro Series had McEwen winning three of the four races in the series to claim the overall title. And at the 1973 OCIR Manufacturers Meet, he was runner-up to Pisano and Matsubara's Revell-backed Vega funny car.

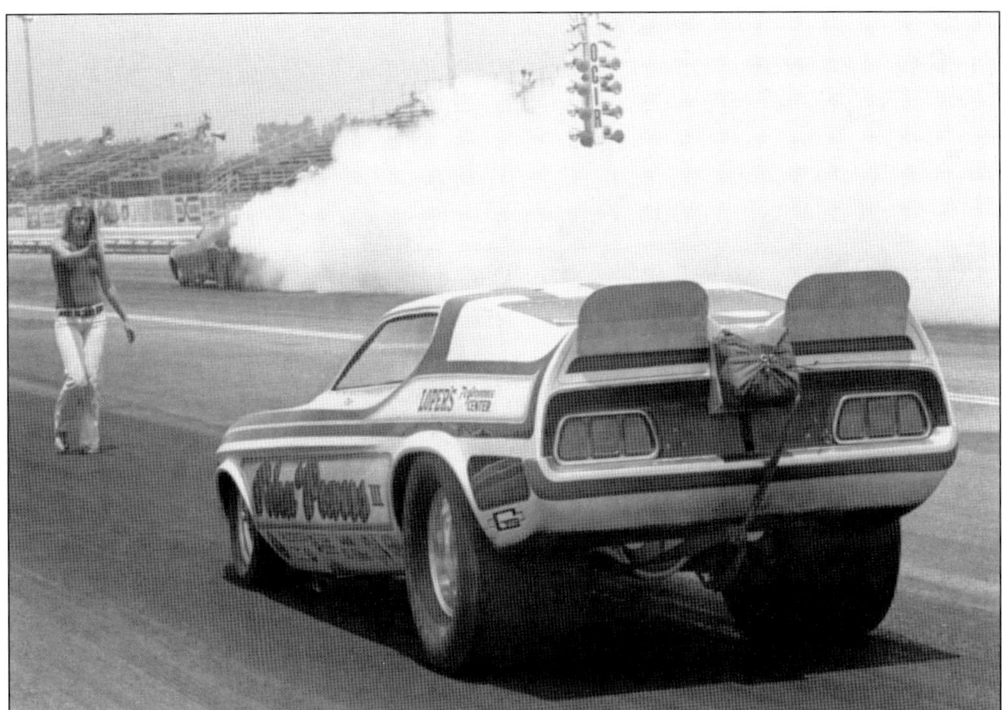

The unsung heroes of funny car racing are women like Suzie Shumake, wife of driver Tripp Shumake. Here at OCIR in 1971 or 1972, she backs her husband up while he is driving the Arizona-based, John Powers–owned Mustang funny car. Tripp had many funny car rides in the 1970s and 1980s, and Suzie was there for him to get through good and bad times in funny car racing.

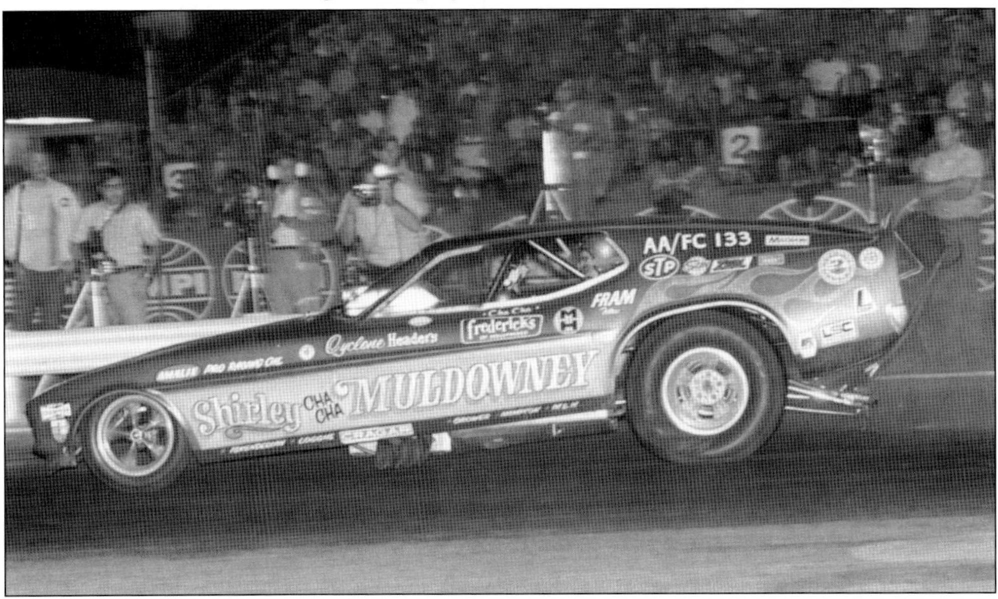

The year 1971, at the OCIR Manufacturers Meet, saw the first appearance of Shirley Muldowney and her "Bounty Huntress" Ford Mustang funny car on the West Coast. Muldowney gave female funny car fans something to cheer about that long ago evening at OCIR. She did not win, but she showed that she was no fluke when it came to driving a nitro-burning funny car.

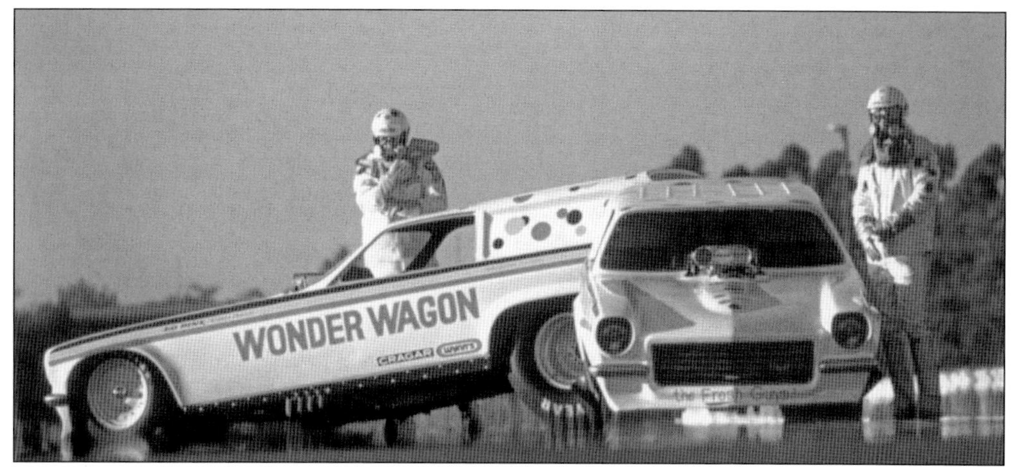

Another big company that entered the wacky world of funny car racing was ITT Continental Bakeries, also known as Wonder Bread. The company's two-car team featured Chevrolet Vega panel bodies painted like a loaf of Wonder Bread. The "Wonder Wagons" also featured a John Buttera chassis and 426 Hemi power. Kelly "the Controller" Brown and Glen Way were chosen as drivers. Not all went well at OCIR during testing of the Wonder Wagons, though. Glen Way's car was crashed and totaled, leaving only one loaf of bread to race in funny car.

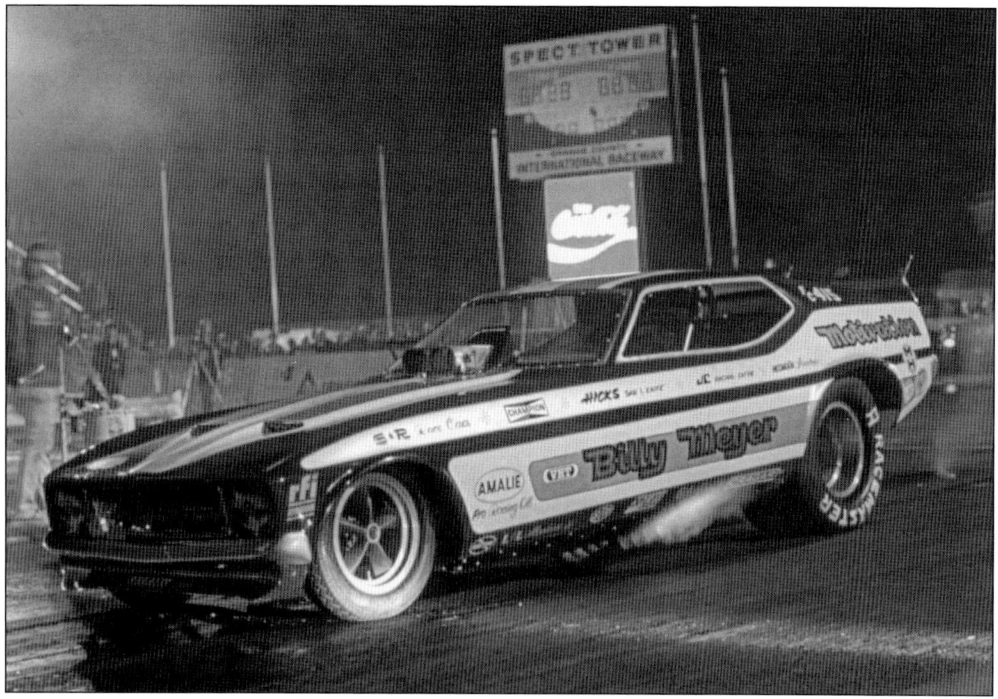

"Waco Willie," also known as 16-year-old Billy Meyer, stunned the OCIR funny car crowd at the 1972 OCIR Manufacturers Meet by taking his former Grover Rogers Ford Mustang funny car and beating Ron Colson in the Chi-Town Hustler for the funny car title. At 16 years old, Meyer was the youngest funny car event winner ever at OCIR. He also had the low ET of the event at 6.51. Fast forward to 1981, and Meyer was runner-up to Craig Epperly at the OCIR Manufacturers Meet. Meyer came back to OCIR in 1982 and won the Manufacturers Meet over Kenny Bernstein. He also set top speed and low ET of the event at 5.90 at 245.23 miles per hour.

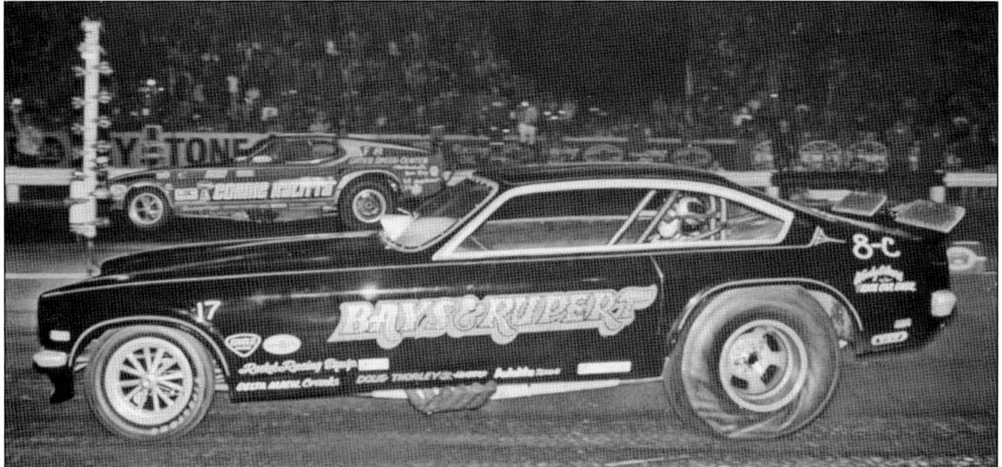

Former SoCal top fuel racers Richard Bays and Frank Rupert went funny car racing in 1971.The duo's funny car was the first to feature a Chevrolet Vega body in Southern California. The pair mainly raced in California because of their commitment to their real jobs. Here at the 1972 OCIR Manufacturers Meet, they square off with Michigan's Connie Kalitta and his Ford Mustang funny car. Bays and Rupert won the Ford versus Chevy matchup. Frank Rupert, an ex-top fuel dragster pilot, was the driver of the black Vega funny car.

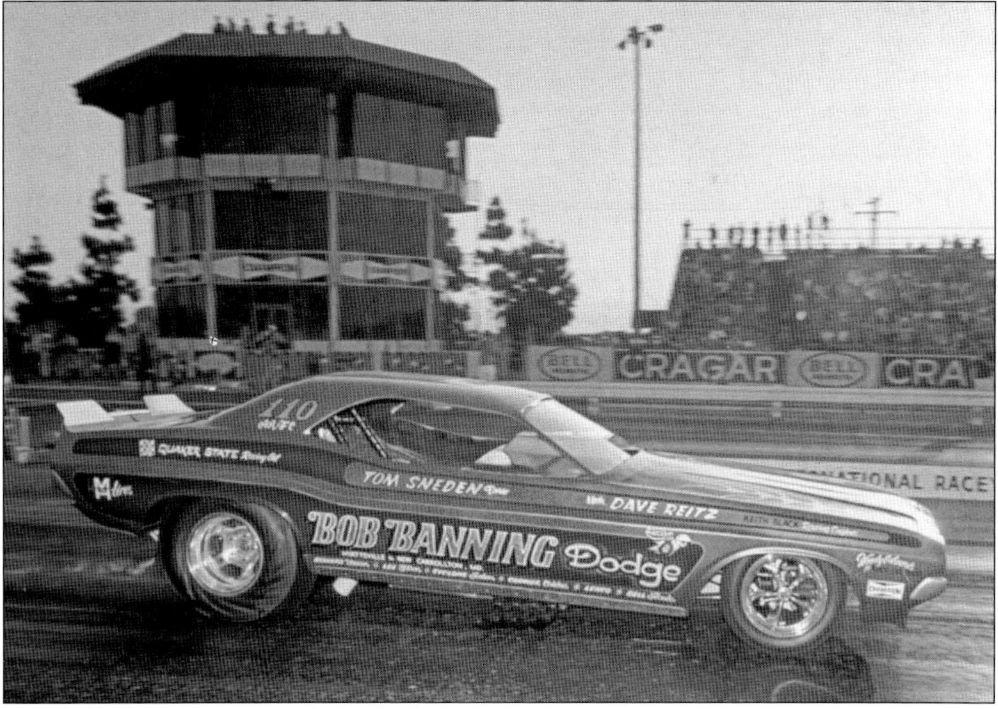

At the October 1971 OCIR East/West Funny Car Championships, the Maryland-based funny car of Tom Sneden and Dave Reitz came all the way to the raceway to try out the guardrail. The car was damaged, so they had a long sad tow back to Hyattsville, Maryland. Things got better for the pair as they won the eighth annual 1972 Cars Magazine Championships in Atco, New Jersey. Tom Sneden was the driver, and Dave Reitz turned the wrenches on the beautiful lime green Bob Banning-backed Dodge funny car.

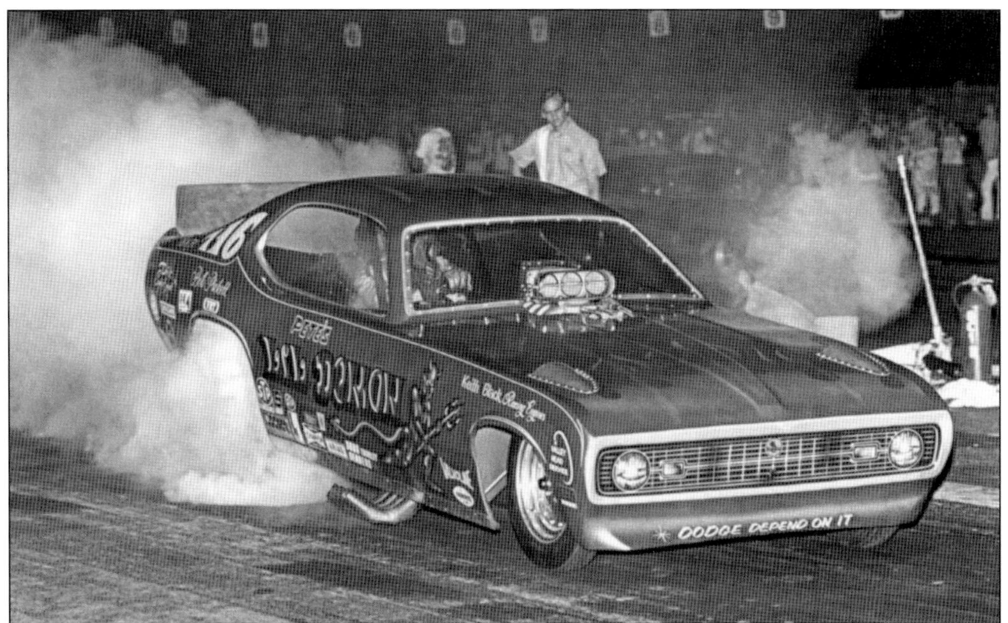

"Pete's Lil Demon," driven by Bob Pickett, was one of the 70 funny cars that attended the November 3, 1972, OCIR Manufacturers Meet. The event featured 49 separate races plus fireworks, a marching band, and 25,000 fans in the stands for the OCIR funny car extravaganza. In 1974, Pickett would win the OCIR PDA race over Dave Condit in the Plueger and Gyger Mustang funny car.

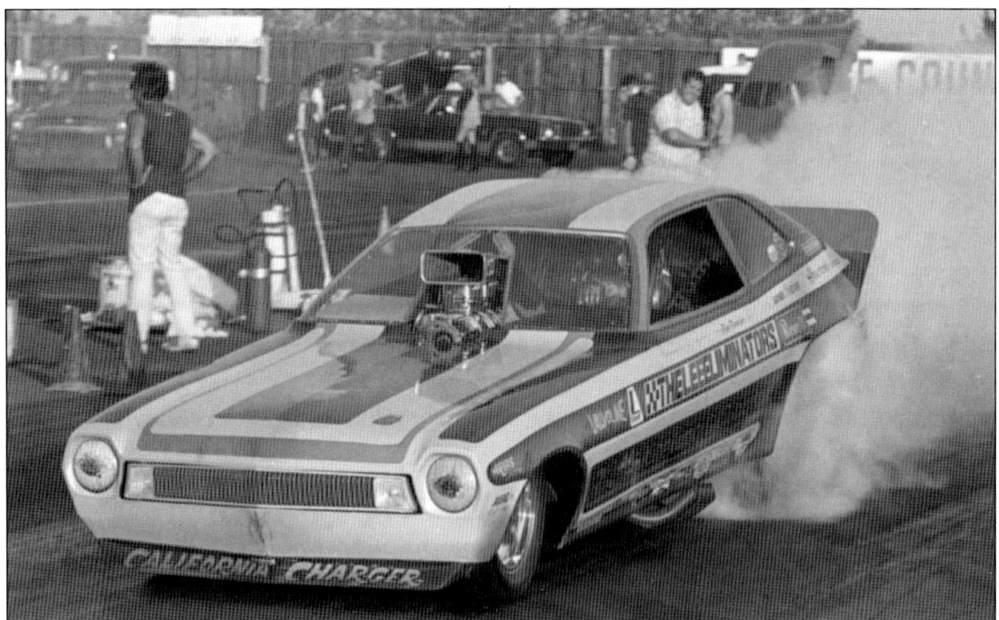

After their "California Charger" top fuel dragster won top fuel eliminator at the 1970 NHRA Supernationals in Ontario, California, the team of John Keeling and Jerry Clayton decided to go funny car racing. In late 1971, they added a Ford Pinto–bodied funny car to their California Charger racing stable. In the first runs on the car, their top fuel dragster driver, Rick Ramsey, drove the Pinto. Ramsey did not like driving the funny car, and Tom Ferraro was soon the new driver for the shiny new blue Pinto.

The Chicagoland invasion at OCIR continued with Dale Creasy and his driver "Animal" Al Marshall with Creasy's Ford Torino–bodied funny car, the "Tyrant." Like all the other Ford Torino funny cars, the body weight was becoming a problem for Creasy in 1971. Being the only Torino got them a lot of attention at OCIR, but attention does not win races, so in 1972, the Torino body was scrapped for a Ford Mustang one.

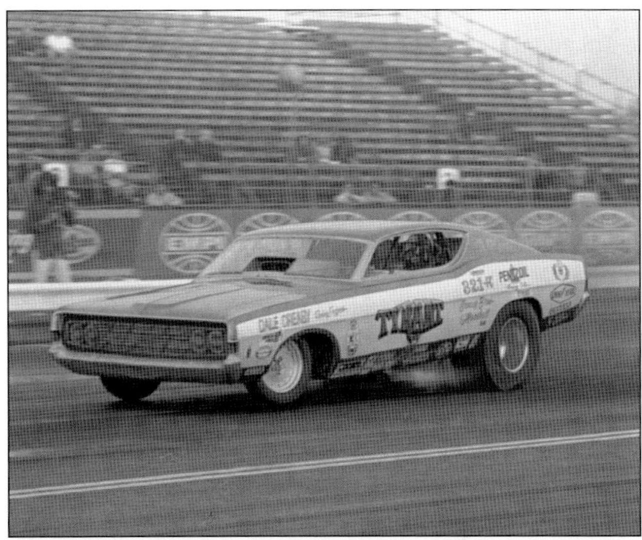

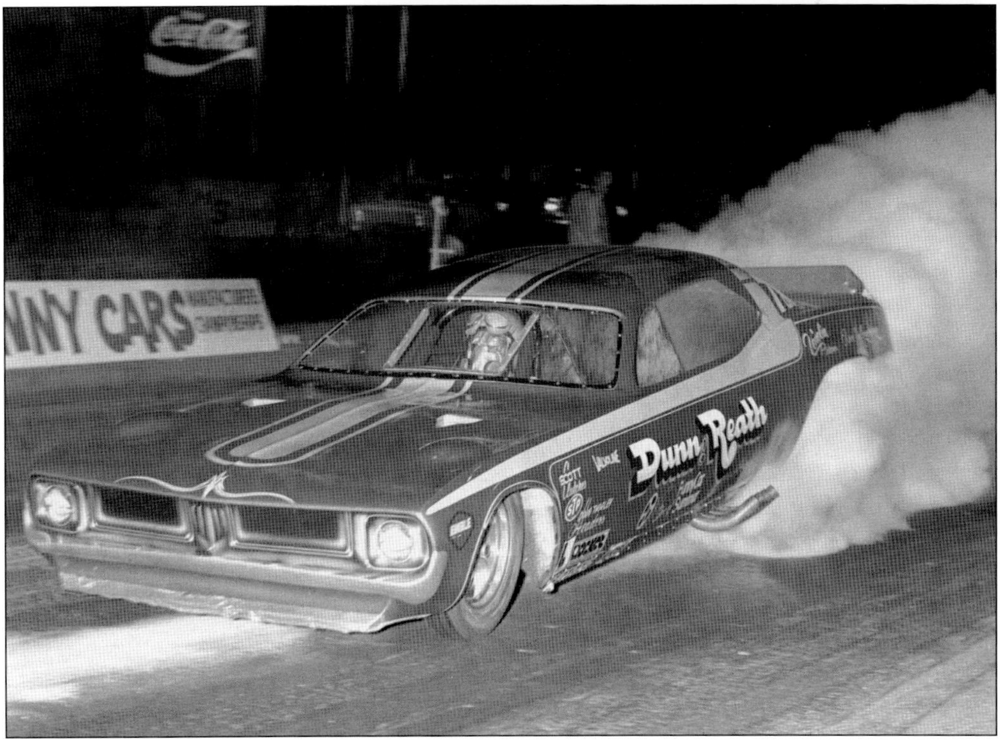

The Dunn and Reath rear-engine funny car was the most successful of the handful of back-motored funny cars that raced in the 1970s. Before winning funny car eliminator at the 1972 NHRA Supernationals in Ontario, California, Dunn was runner-up to Pat Foster in Barry Setzer's Vega funny car at the OCIR Funny Car 500 on May 28, 1972. So, guess who Dunn raced in the final at the NHRA Supernationals? Yes, it was Dunn versus Foster for all the money, with Jim Dunn putting the rear-engine car in the winner's circle for its first major event win. Pictured is the 1973 version of the Dunn and Reath rear-engine funny car, it was longer and lower than the original car. However, the car still had handling issues so the team returned to a basic front-engine funny car at the end of 1973.

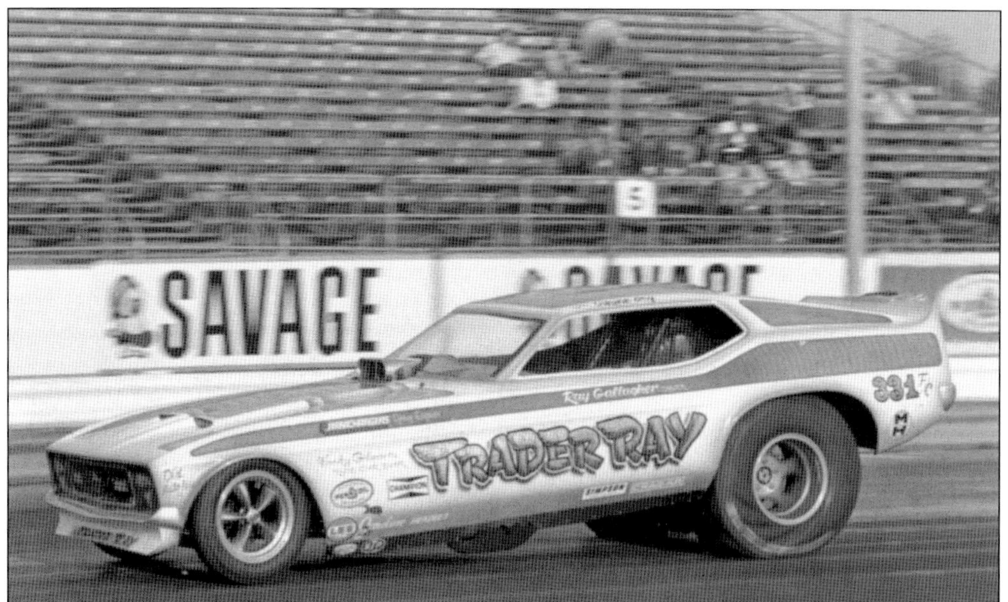

Michigan's Duane Ong raced one of the first successful rear-engine top fuel dragsters in 1971. His "Pawnbroker" top fueler was the first to win a major AHRA or NHRA sanctioned event. But even with his success, the dragster was not getting bookings or making any money. Ong parked the dragster, went into partnership with Ray Gallager, and raced the "Trader Ray" Ford Mustang funny car in 1972. Ong came west in 1972 and raced at OCIR. When winter broke, he headed home to Michigan. Somewhere along the way, the entire funny car rig was stolen. The Trader Ray Mustang was never recovered, putting Duane Ong out of racing.

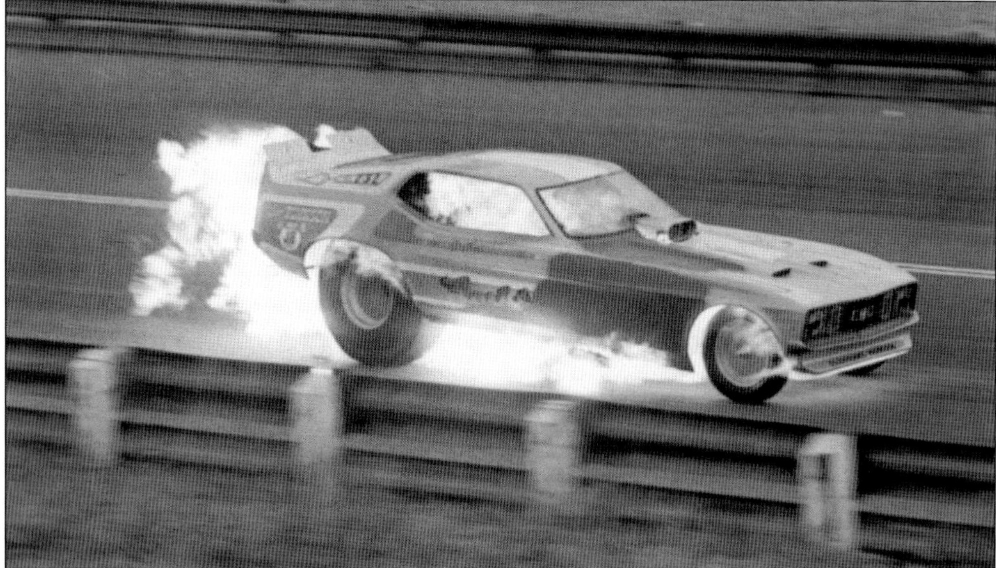
Having a hot time at OCIR in 1972 is Ron Fassl driving the Arizona-based "Elephant Hunter" Ford Mustang–bodied funny car. Fassl is trying his best to get the fire out and the car stopped in the OCIR shutdown area. By the looks of the primer spots on the car, it has had fire issues prior to the OCIR cookout. Fassl was able to get the car stopped, and the OCIR fire crew snuffed the stubborn blaze out, saving the car from burning to the ground.

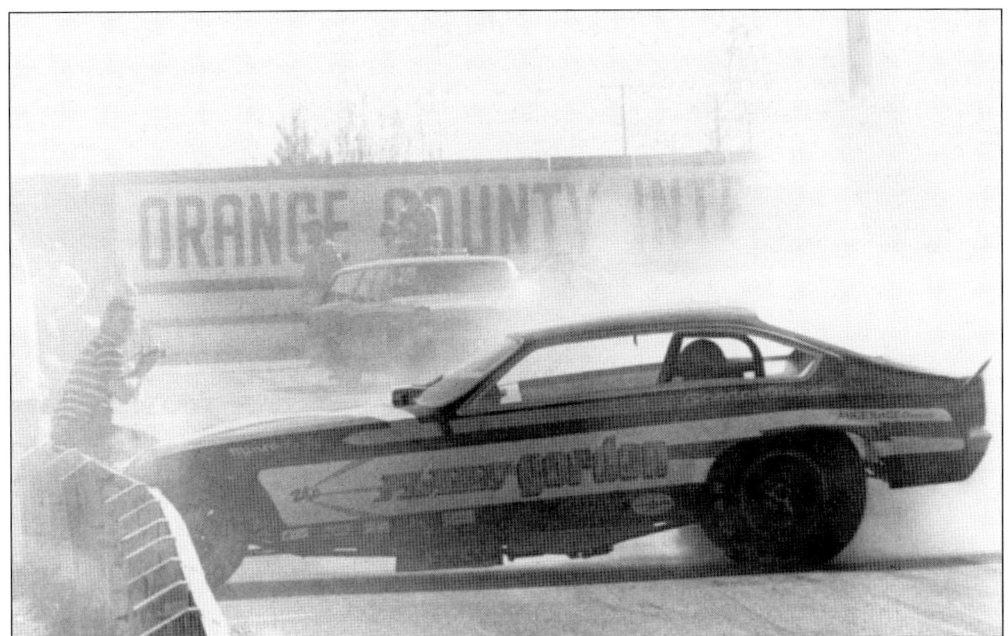

"Flash" Gordon Mineo elected himself the official OCIR guardrail tester in 1972. Mineo had a few handling issues on a burnout and stuffed his Vega-bodied funny car head on into the guardrail. The now shorter Vega funny car was rushed to chassis builder Mike Kase. Kase would make the necessary repairs on the wounded Vega so Mineo could leave on time for his 1972 tour east.

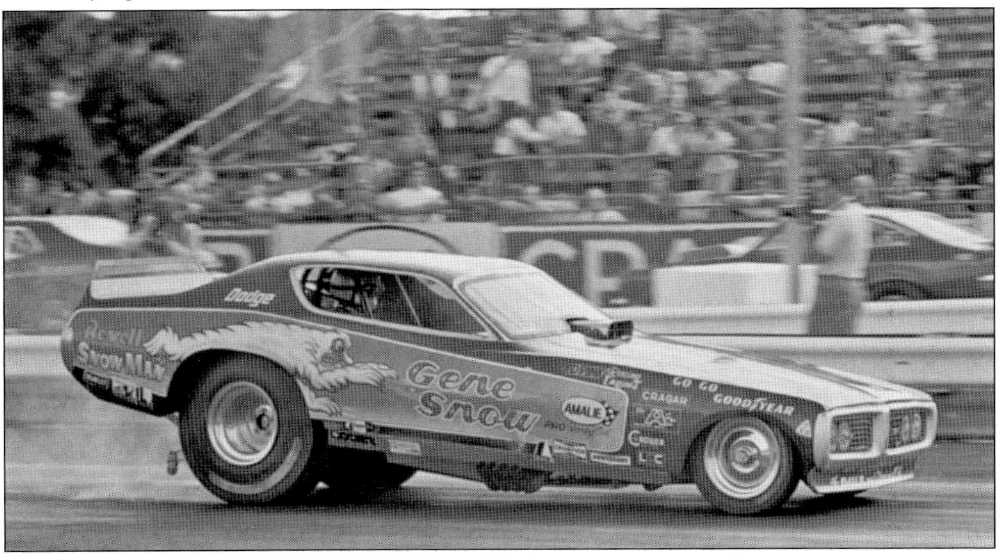

Fort Worth, Texas, was home to Gene Snow and his fleet of funny cars. Snow had a wonderful time at the OCIR All Pro Series season three; he was runner-up to Jim Dunn in the first race. Snow ran a 6.88 at 214.88 miles per hour for low ET and top speed at that event. In the fourth race in series three, he once again raced Jim Dunn in the final; this time the Texan took home top honors and set low ET and top speed 6.83 at 217.39 miles per hour. And he won the overall title in funny car in season three. Season four and Snow is back at it again, this time beating Ray Alley in the season's final race. He once again set low ET and top speed at 6.57 and 223.88 miles per hour. In 1972, Snow was picked by Revell to be its first sponsored drag racer. He became the "Revell Snowman" (pictured).

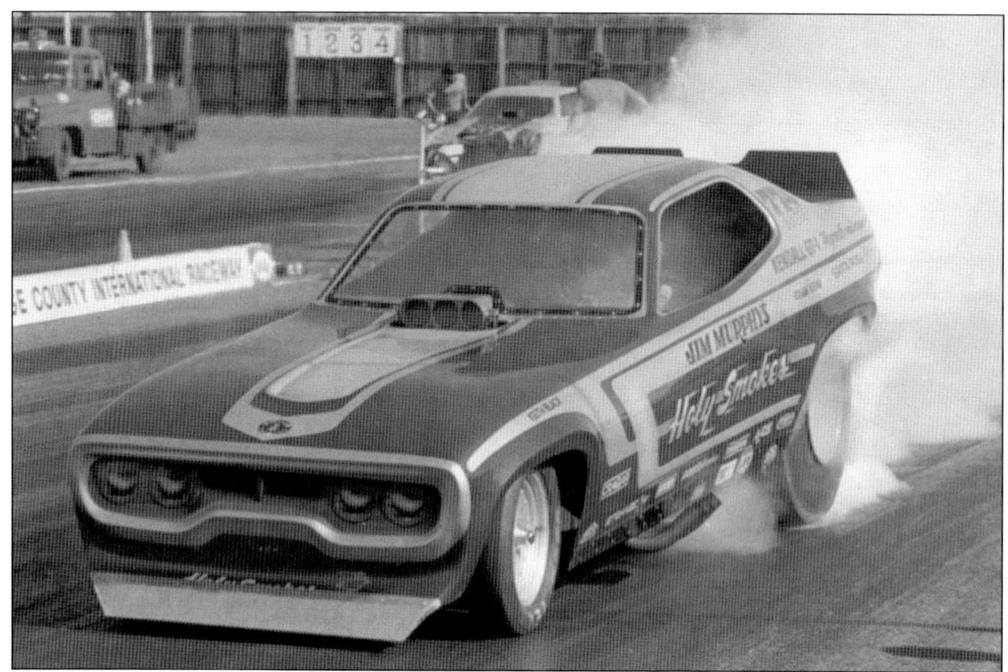

Northern California's Jim Murphy attended just about every big funny car race at OCIR between 1971 and 1972. Murphy was a former boat racer and quickly adapted to land racing with his "Holy Smokes" funny car. His Plymouth Satellite–bodied funny car was the third in the lineup of Holy Smokes funny cars that Murphy raced at OCIR. Murphy went top fuel dragster racing briefly in 1973 with Tim Beebe; he drove their "Fighting Irish" top fueler. Murphy was in a top fuel dragster when in 1980 he won OCIR's Nitro Championships. Murphy is still active today in drag racing; he wheels one of the quickest and fastest nostalgia top fuel dragsters out of his home in Santa Rosa, California.

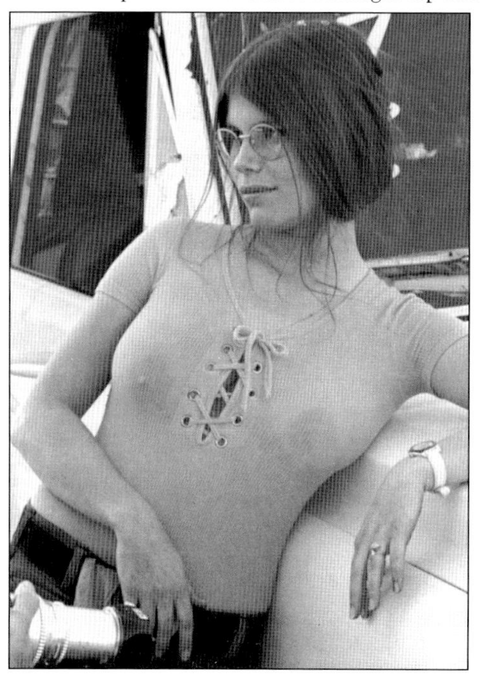

"Jungle Pam" Hardy was the darling and sex symbol to all the male funny car fans in the 1970s. Hardy was a big part of the "Jungle Jim" Liberman funny car circus/show, and the fans loved to watch her jiggle and wiggle backing up Liberman's Vega funny car. Racetrack promoters insisted when they booked Liberman to race at their track that Hardy be with him, as she was part of the show. Hardy became a drag racing icon even though she never drove down a drag strip. Yes, she was a welcome sight at OCIR in 1972 and 1973.

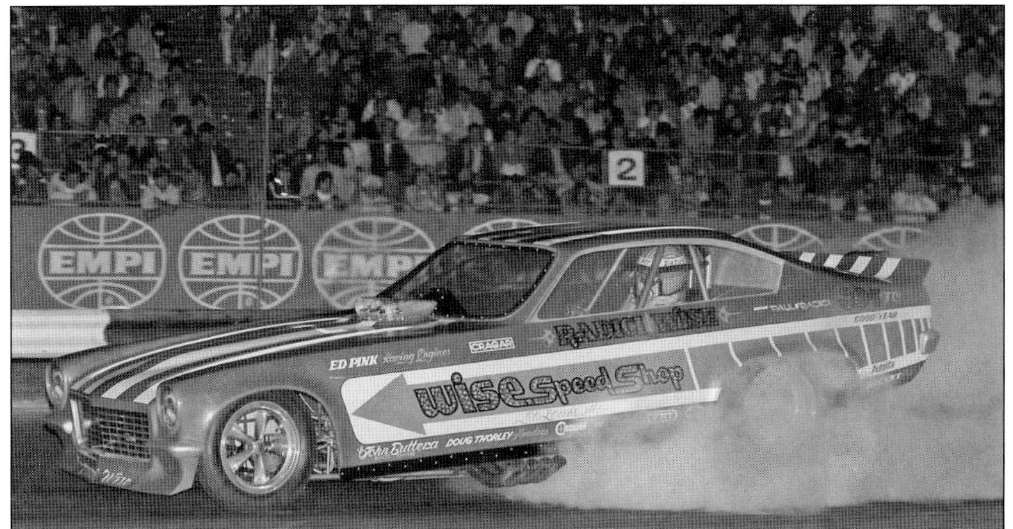

Racing out of the Wise speed shop in St. Louis was the team of Dave Wise and Paul "Wrong Way" Radici. This dynamic duo started funny car racing with a very used Camaro funny car in 1970. In 1972, the Camaro went away for a brand-new John Buttera chassis and Kirby Vega body, which was also painted by Don Kirby. They took their new funny car to Dallas, Texas, to race and blew the body off the car along with the blower. Undaunted by their misfortune, they quickly repaired the very wounded funny car. In the winter months of the 1970s, they raced at OCIR and Irwindale. With Radici at the controls, their Vega set the NHRA one-eighth mile ET and speed record at 4.52 and 176 miles per hour.

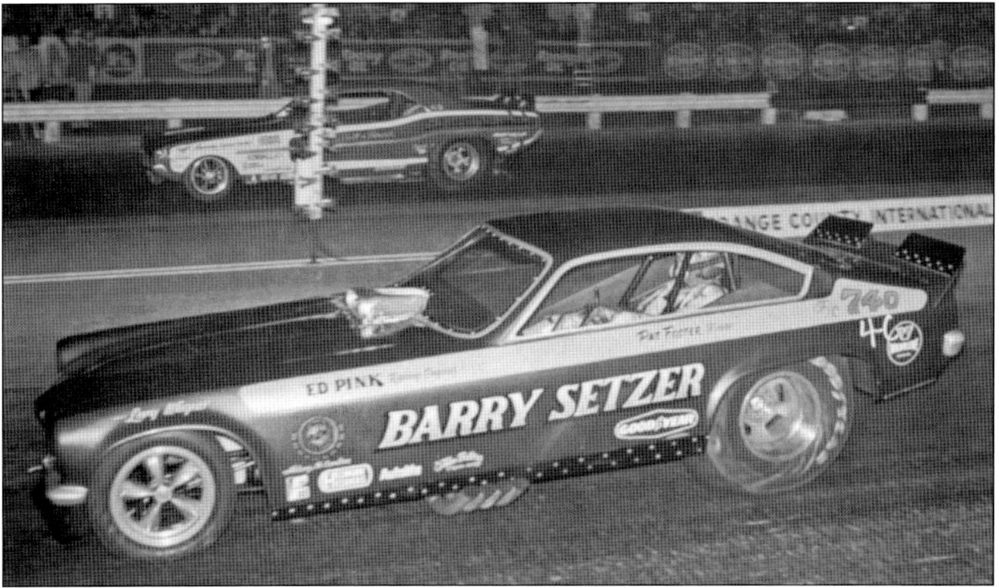

North Carolina's double-knit king Barry Setzer went funny car racing in a big way in 1971. Here, in 1971, Pat Foster is driving the candy-red Chevrolet Vega–bodied funny car at the 1971 OCIR Manufacturers Meet. Foster won the race over Jim Dunn in the final round. In 1972, the Setzer/ Foster Vega won the Nitro Championships. Also in 1972, Foster won the OCIR Funny Car 500 in Setzer's Vega. In 1974, Foster was driving "Lil" John Lombardo's Vega funny car to the OCIR winner's circle at the Nitro Championships. Foster enjoyed racing at OCIR.

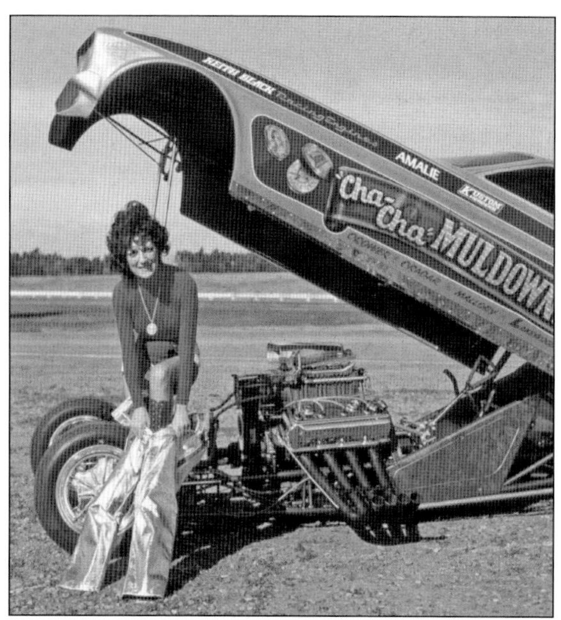

Late in 1971, Shirley Muldowney picked up her all-new Buttera chassis, Kirby-painted, Keith Black Hemi–powered Ford Mustang funny car. This photograph was from a *Drag Racing* magazine feature shoot. The magazine put her on the cover for her first big national exposure. This funny car was only photographed at OCIR but never ran there. Muldowney went on tour with her new toy in 1972. At an International Hot Rod Association race in West Salem, Ohio, she had a huge fire and burned the body off the car. She also burned her hands and around her eyes. Being a true racer, she got her car together quickly and with a borrowed Cuda body from Don Schumacher finished her dates for the year.

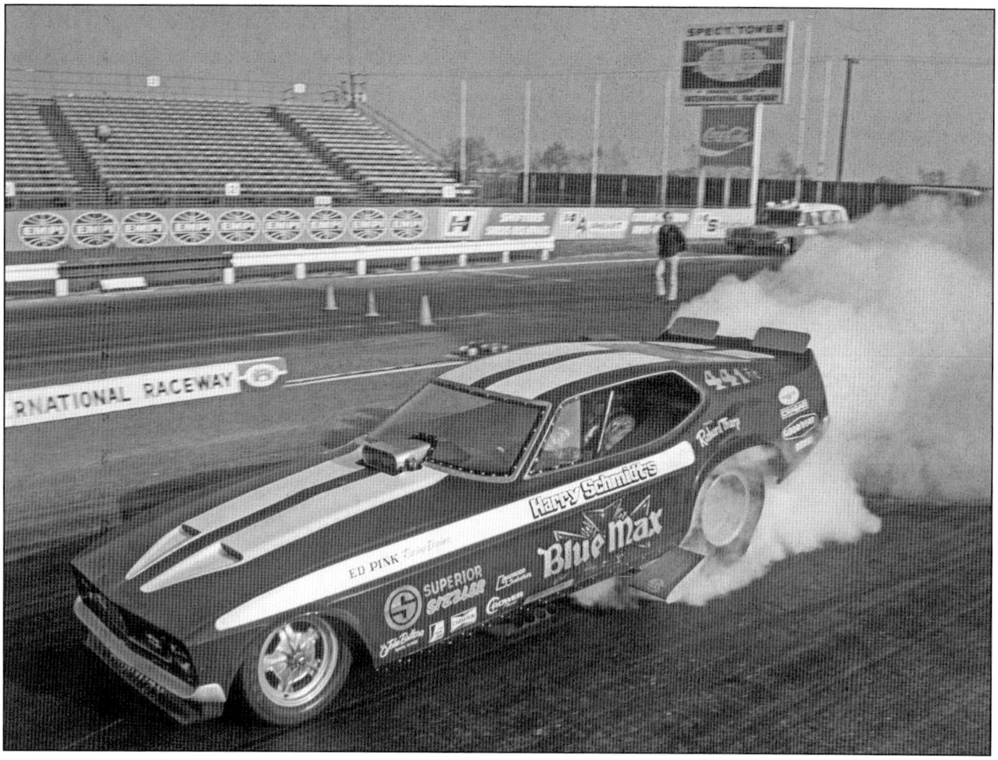

One of the most colorful drivers to ever traverse down the OCIR quarter mile was Texan Richard Tharp. Here, in 1972, Tharp is driving Harry Schmidt's Blue Max Ford Mustang funny car while testing at OCIR. The very humble Tharp could also be found driving in top fuel; some of his top fuel rides were the Carroll Bros., Creitz and Donovan, "the Addict," and Candies and Hughes. Tharp had also driven other funny cars like Harry Schmidt's "Blue Max" Vega, Mike Burkhart's "Satellite," and Larry Huff's "Soapy Sales" Dodge Demon. One thing about Tharp was he never was without a ride.

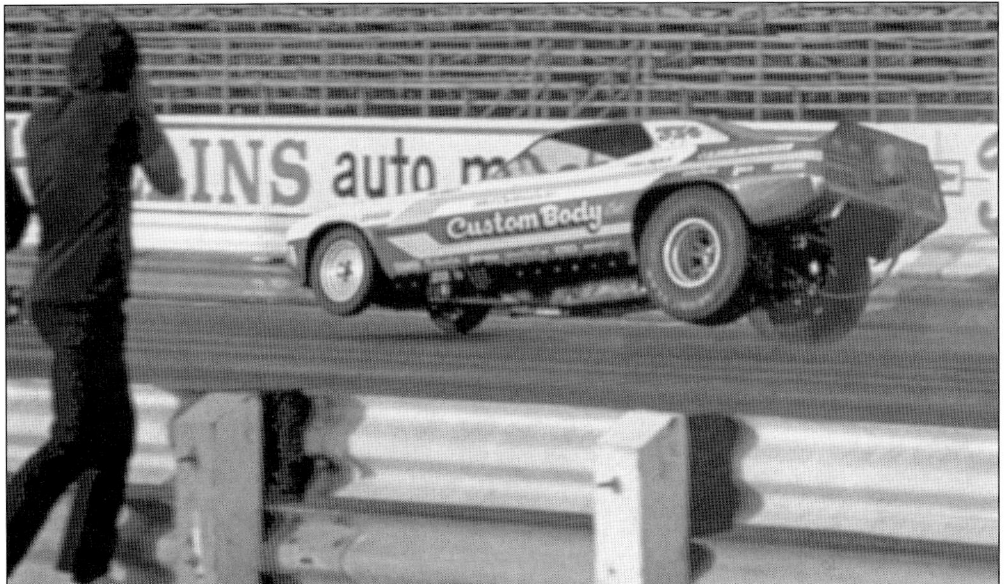

After winning the 1973 Super Stock Magazine Nationals at York, Pennsylvania, Tom Prock packed up the "Custom Body" funny car and headed to the OCIR Manufacturers Meet. The Utica, New York–based funny car did not seem to get along with the traction at OCIR as the car did the two-wheeled conga on the racetrack. No worries, though, as Prock kept the car off the guardrail and right side up. Fast forward to present day, and there is another Prock driving a funny car—Tom's grandson Austin, driving for John Force racing, became NHRA's funny car world champion in 2024.

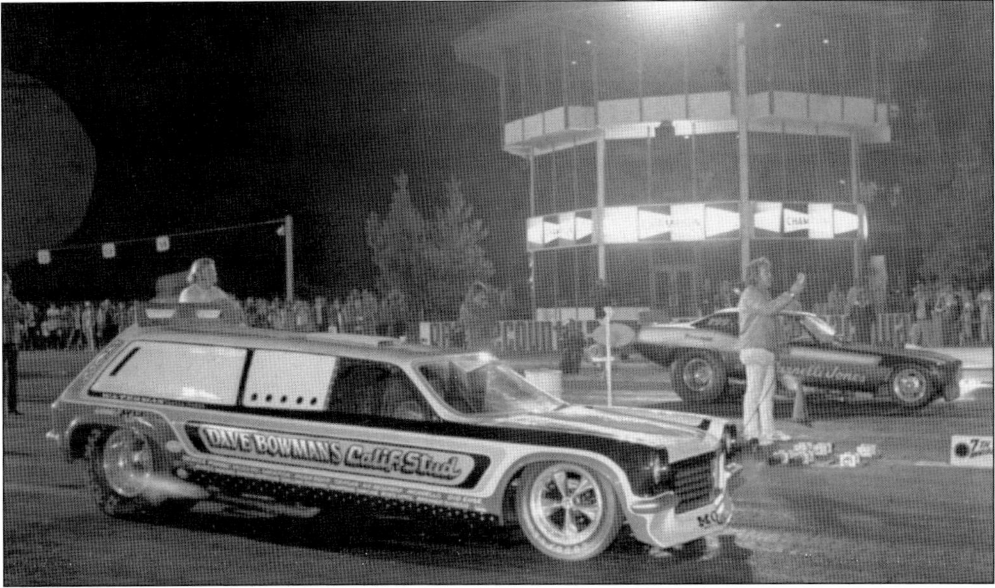

The funny car final round of the 1973 OCIR PDA race was Dave Bowman and his rear-engine "California Stud" Vega-panel funny car versus Danny Ongais in the Vels/Parnelli Jones Cuda funny car. Ongais would take the win, but it was a small victory for Bowman; his rear-engine funny car was only the second time a rear-engine funny car ever made it to the final round at a major event. Of course, the first rear-engine car to do that was the Dunn and Reath rear-engine Cuda. They won the 1972 NHRA Supernationals in Ontario, California.

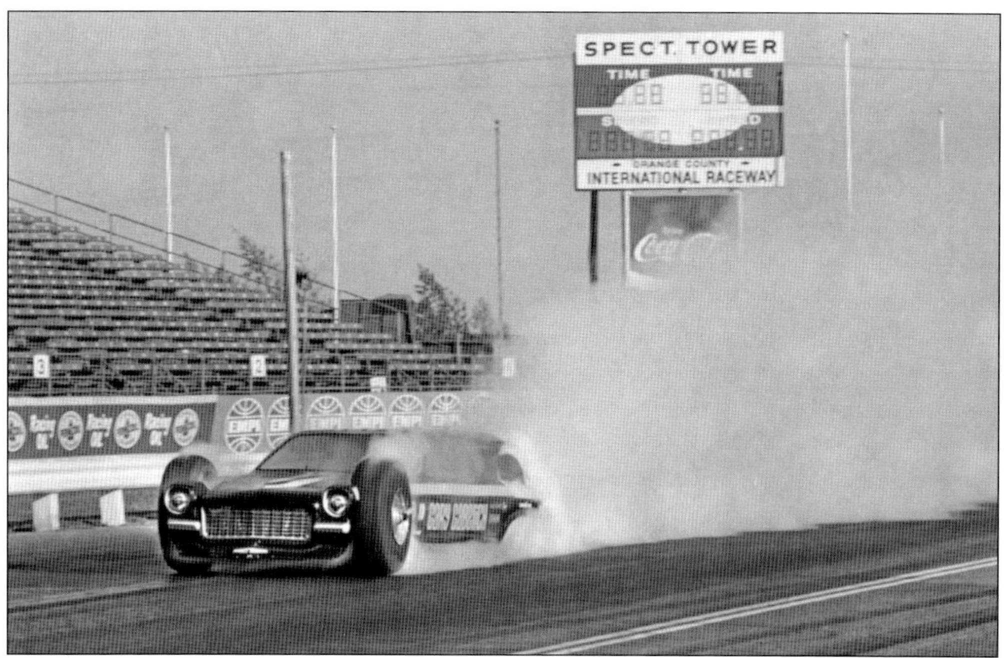

Photographer Mickey McIver captured the before and after of Gary Gabelich's four-wheel drive, rear-engine, Vega-panel funny car. Gabelich was testing his creation when he lost control and rode up onto the OCIR guardrail. The ensuing crash destroyed the car and severely injured Gabelich. Gary Scow, who was helping Gabelich run his car, administered first aid, and his quick thinking saved Gabelich's life. Gabelich recovered from his injuries, but the car was not rebuilt.

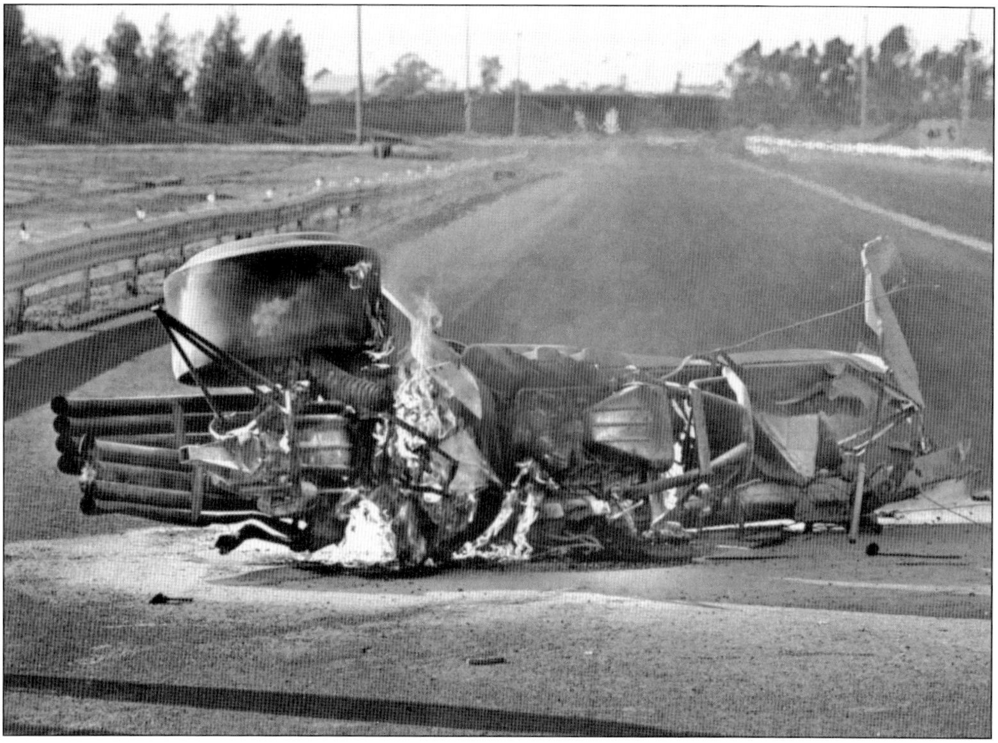

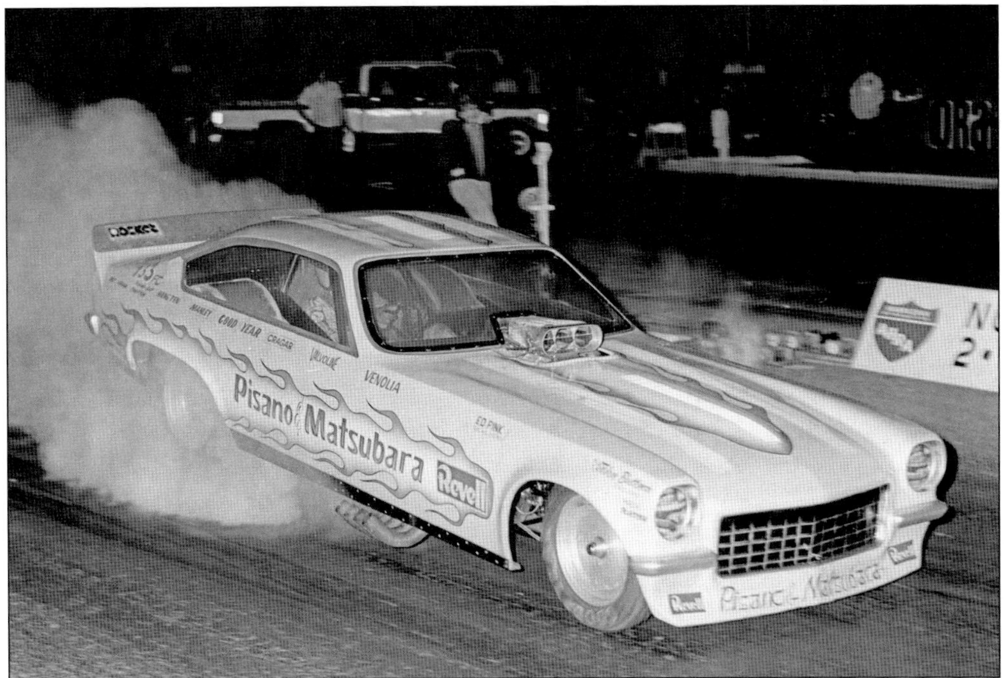

After being runner-up three times at the OCIR All Pro Series in 1973, Pisano and Matsubara finally found the winner's circle at the 1973 OCIR Manufacturers Meet. Two of those All Pro Series losses were to Tom McEwen. So, guess who they paid back in the final at the Manufacturers Meet? Why, none other than Tom McEwen. Driver Sush Matsubara also had low ET and top speed for the race at 6.49 and 225 miles per hour.

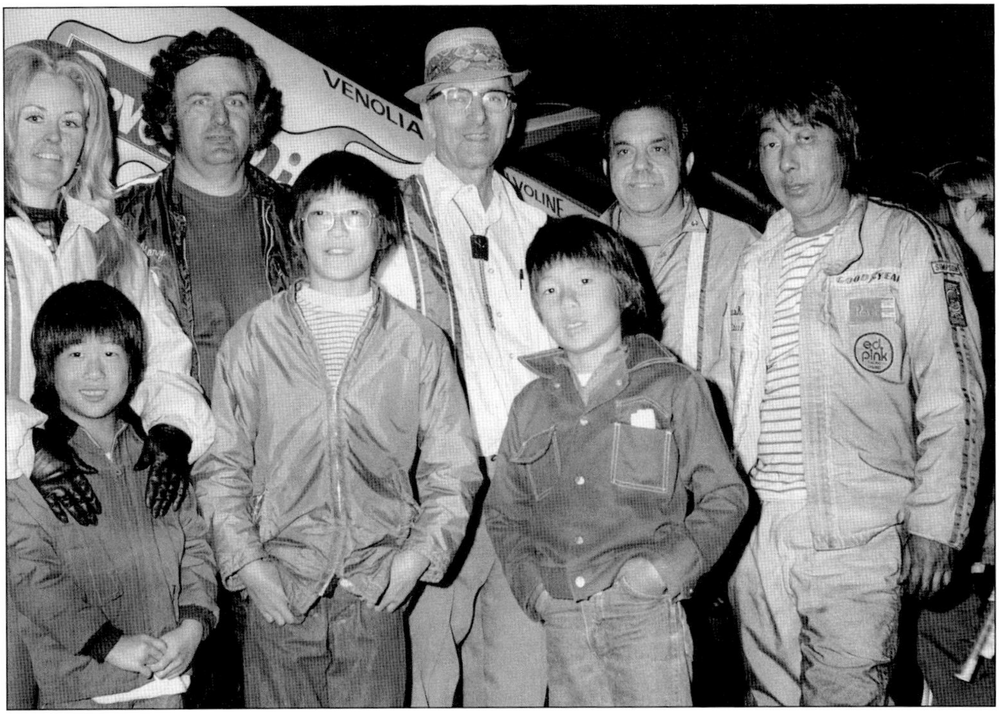

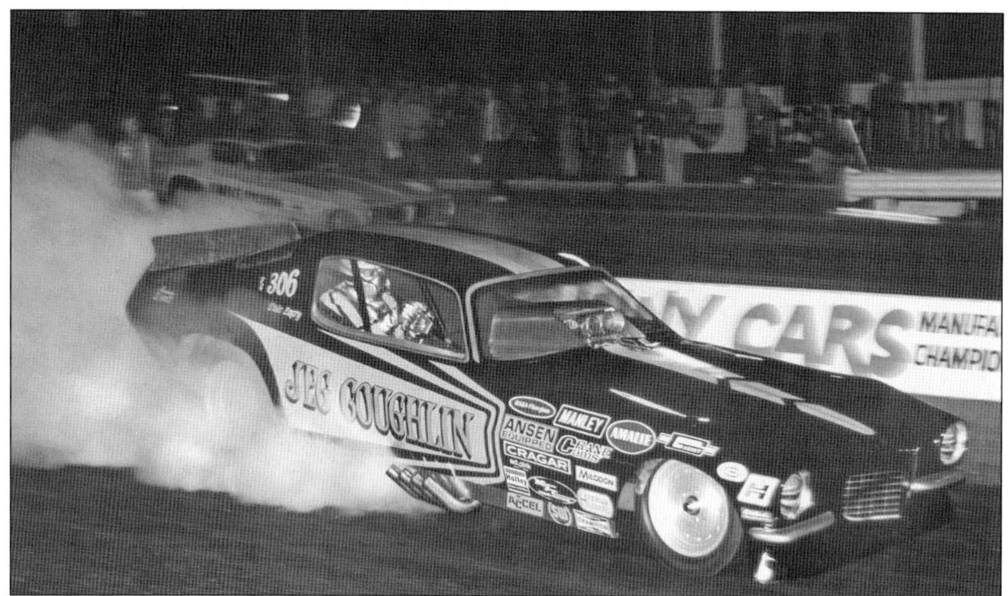

Coming to the West Coast in late 1973 was Dale "the Snail" Emery and Dee Gant with the Columbus, Ohio-based Jeg's speed shop Chevrolet Camaro–bodied funny car. Emery was a well-known driver among drag race fans; they remembered him when he drove Rich Guasco's awesome "Pure Hell" fuel altered. Emery and Gant's trip to SoCal proved to be a lucrative one as they won the East/West Funny Car Championships at Irwindale and the NHRA Winternationals at Pomona, California, at the beginning of 1974. Emery and Gant won funny car eliminator with the Jeg's Camaro.

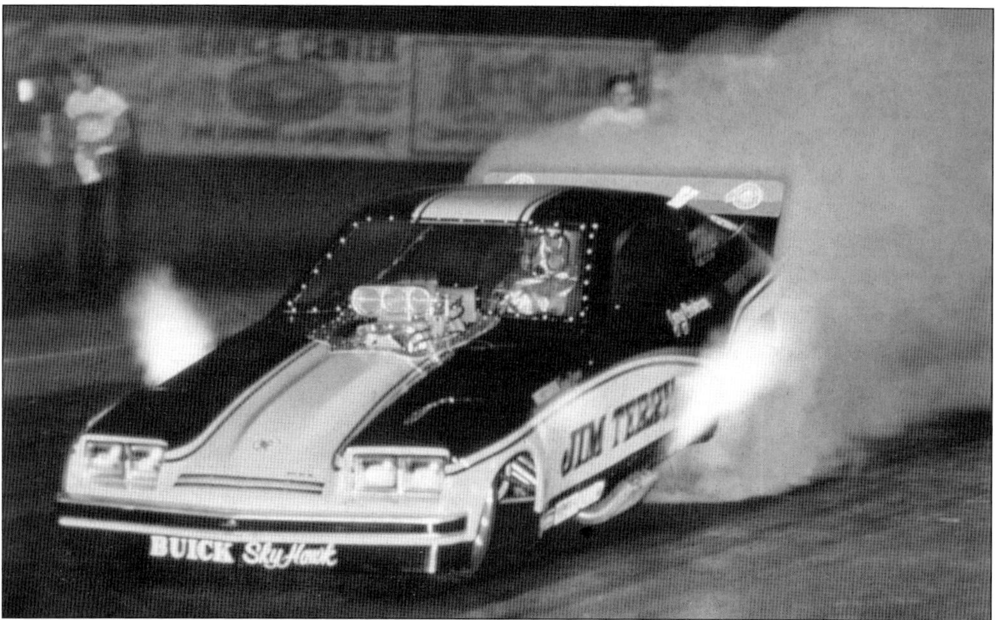

Longtime funny car owner Jim Terry went with something different in 1976. He traded in his Ford Mustang funny car for an all-new Buick Skyhawk–bodied funny car. Behind the wheel of the Skyhawk was veteran top fuel driver "Mr. C," also known as Gary Cochran. Because of job commitments, Terry and Cochran raced mainly in Southern California. Terry's choice of a Buick Skyhawk body gave Buick fans something to cheer about at funny car races in SoCal.

Southern California's Jeff Courtie was the ultimate craftsman in the funny car class. Courtie, with his homebuilt funny car, scored his biggest career win at the 1976 OCIR Nitro Championships on June 20, 1976. He drove his homebuilt Ford Mustang funny car to the win by beating Brad Anderson in the final round. The talented Courtie built the chassis, the aluminum interior, and the engine for his funny car. He also painted and lettered the body.

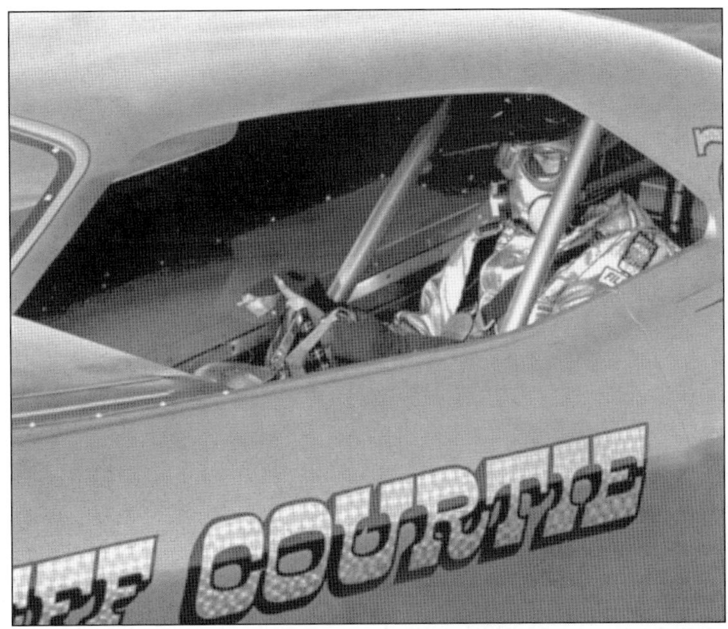

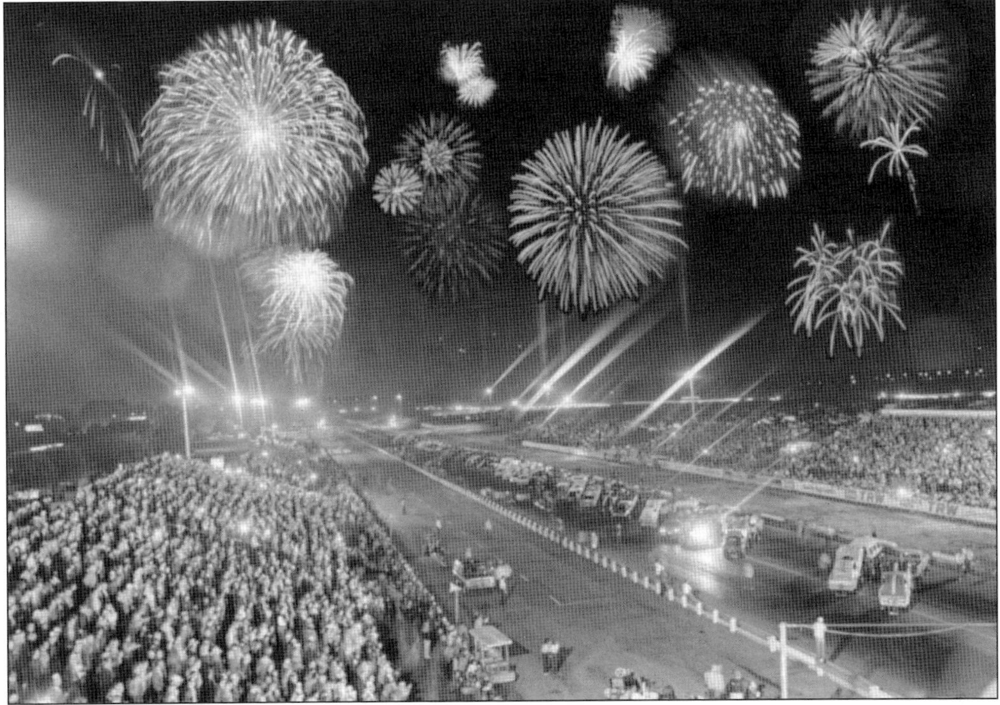

The OCIR manufacturers funny car event was the brainchild of manager Mike Jones. Jones promoted it into the largest gathering of funny cars in the world on one single day of racing. The race could feature anywhere from 70 to 100 funny cars with crowds topping 25,000. Part of the funny car show came prior to the actual race when the cars were lined up on the racetrack with their bodies up. Then Jones gave the signal, and a massive fireworks display filled the skies above the racetrack. To say it was mind blowing is an understatement. Photographer Richard Shute captured the pre-races festivities perfectly with his award-winning photograph.

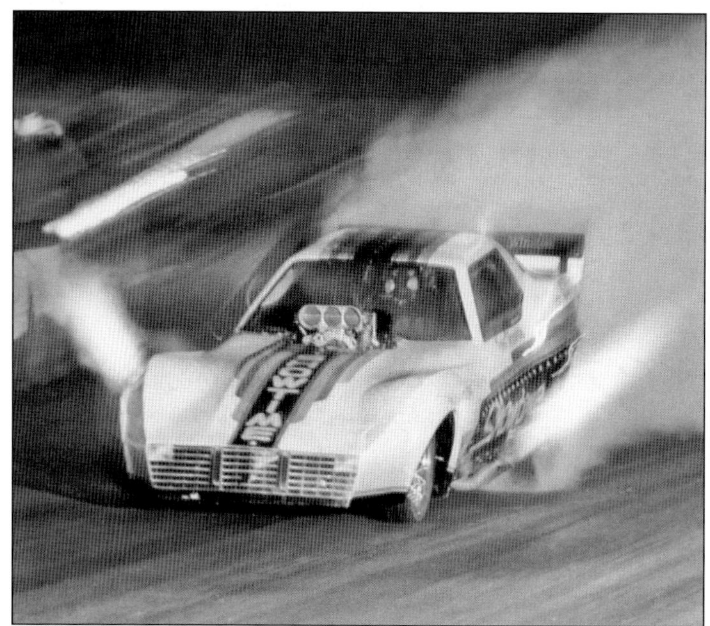

Funny cars at OCIR at night—there was nothing like it in drag racing. The nitro flames, noise, and the smell of tire smoke and nitro fumes filling the air is why manager Mike Jones loved to run his funny car shows at night—for the sheer beauty of night racing. Funny cars at night were eye candy to drag race fans at OCIR for 16 years. Pictured is Minnesota's Tom Hoover and his "Showtime" Chevrolet Corvette-bodied funny car becoming a creature of the night at OCIR.

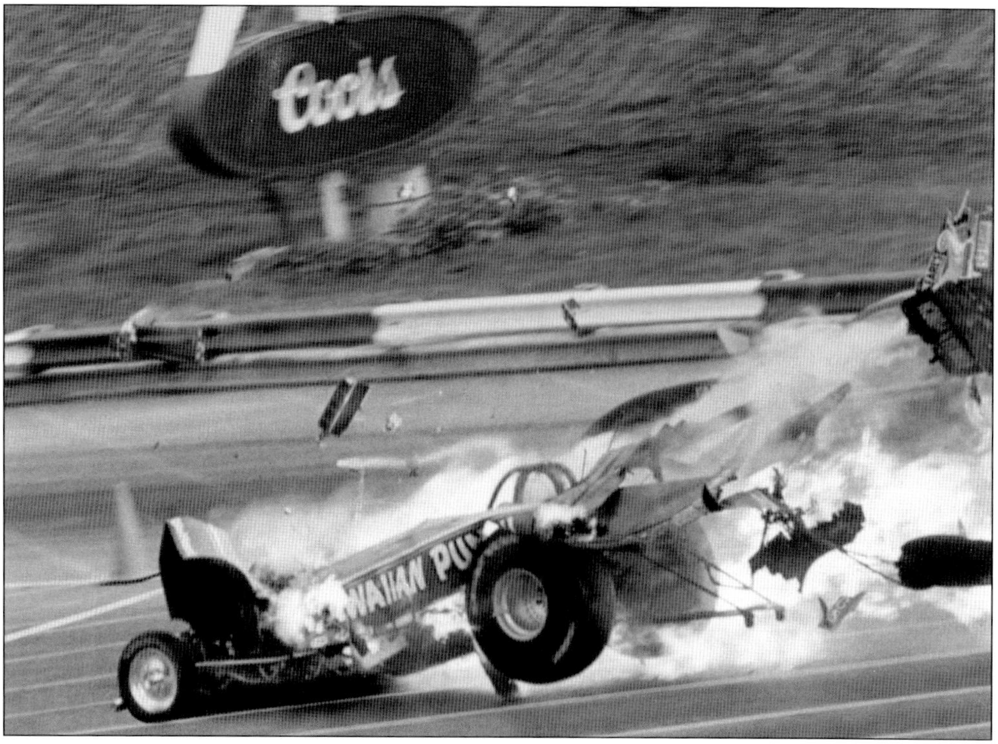

Photographer Don Gillespie caught this wild photograph of Roland Leong's "Hawaiian Punch" funny car exploding at the 1983 NHRA World Finals at OCIR. Driver Mike Dunn was shaken up but walked away from a body-less and engine-less funny car. Not only did the body blow apart, but the engine also came out of the chassis. Leong's car was pretty much a total loss, and he had the dubious honor of having the last big time funny car explosion at OCIR before it closed forever on October 29, 1983.

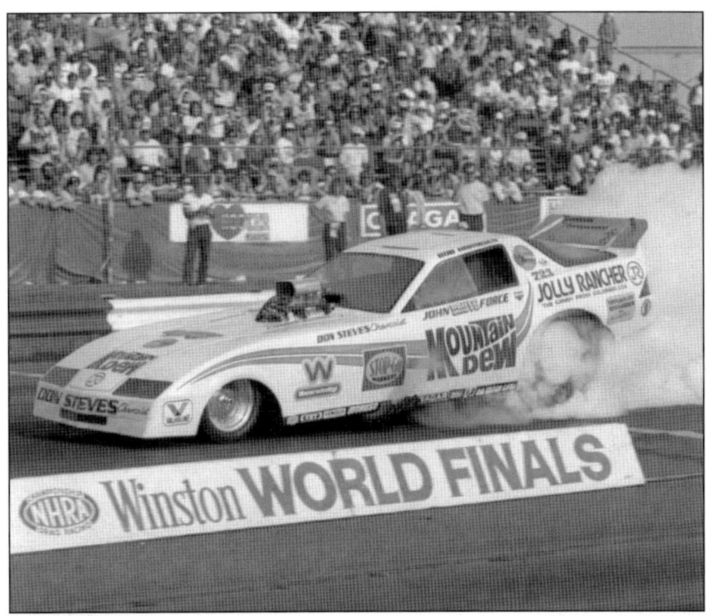

John "Brute" Force went full-time funny car racing in 1976; two years later he won the 1978 OCIR PDA race. In 1979, he was runner-up to Don Prudhomme at the NHRA World Finals in Ontario, California. Force capped off 1982 with a big win at the OCIR NHRA World Finals, and in 1983, at the same event, he was runner-up to John Lombardo. A few weeks after this race was OCIR's last drag race. Force would be runner-up to Kenny Bernstein in the last OCIR funny car eliminator.

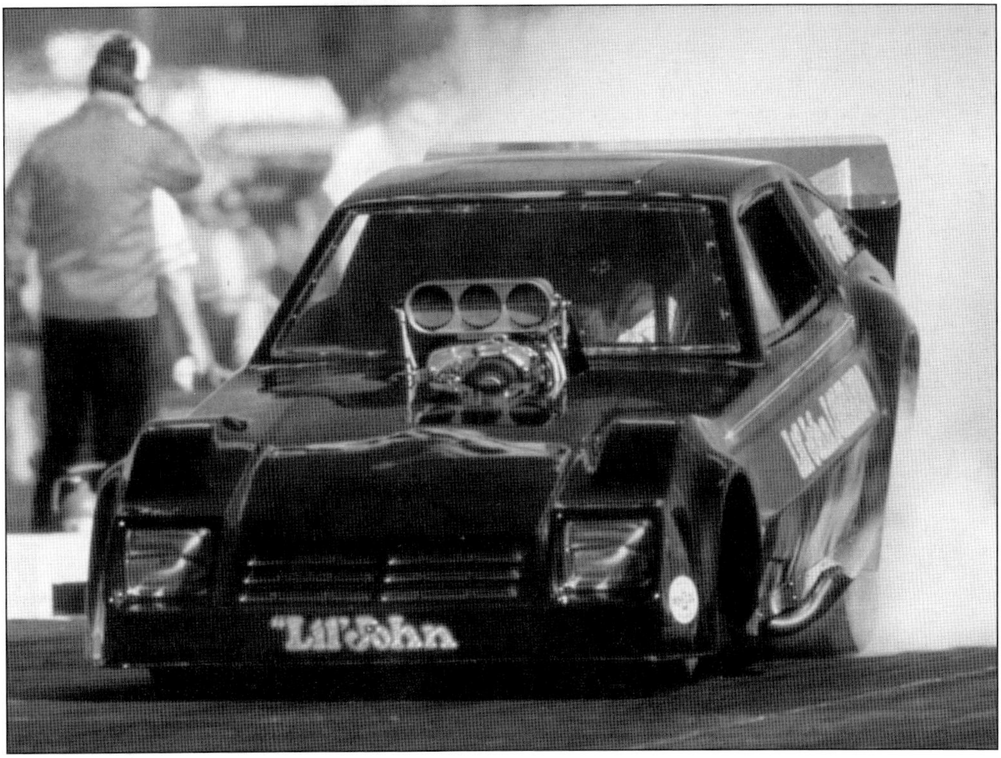

"Lil" John Lombardo vacated the seat of his Vega funny car to Pat Foster in 1974. Foster went out and won the 1974 OCIR Manufacturers Meet. Also in the 1970s, with Lombardo driving, he would win the 1977 OCIR Funny Car 500 and the 1977 OCIR Nitro Championships. Again in 1978, he won the Nitro championships, so that was back-to-back wins for Lombardo. The 1983 NHRA OCIR World Finals saw Lombardo defeat John Force for funny car honors. Pictured is his 1983 funny car.

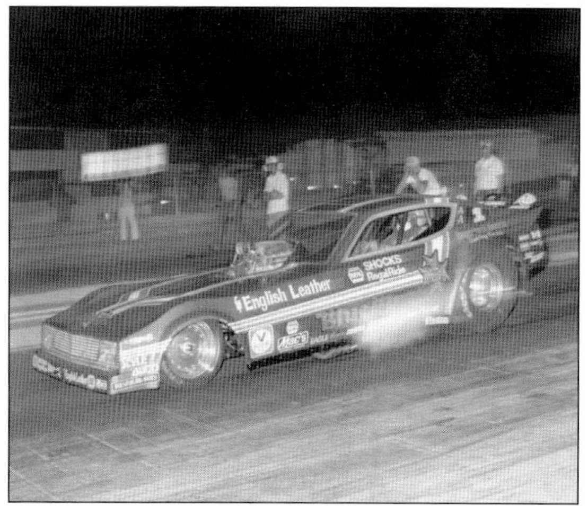

Texas does love their funny car racing, and Raymond Beadle did it better than most in the funny car class. The marketing businessman turned funny car racer won back-to-back OCIR Manufacturers Meets in 1979 and 1980 with his "Blue Max" Ford-bodied funny car. Beadle beat Jim Dunn in 1979 and Don Prudhomme in 1980. In 1970, Harry Schimdt's "Blue Max" won the OCIR Manufacturers Meet with Jake Johnston driving. In the mid-1970s, Beadle started driving for Schmidt and then purchased his entire racing operation. So, it became Raymond Beadle's Blue Max funny car.

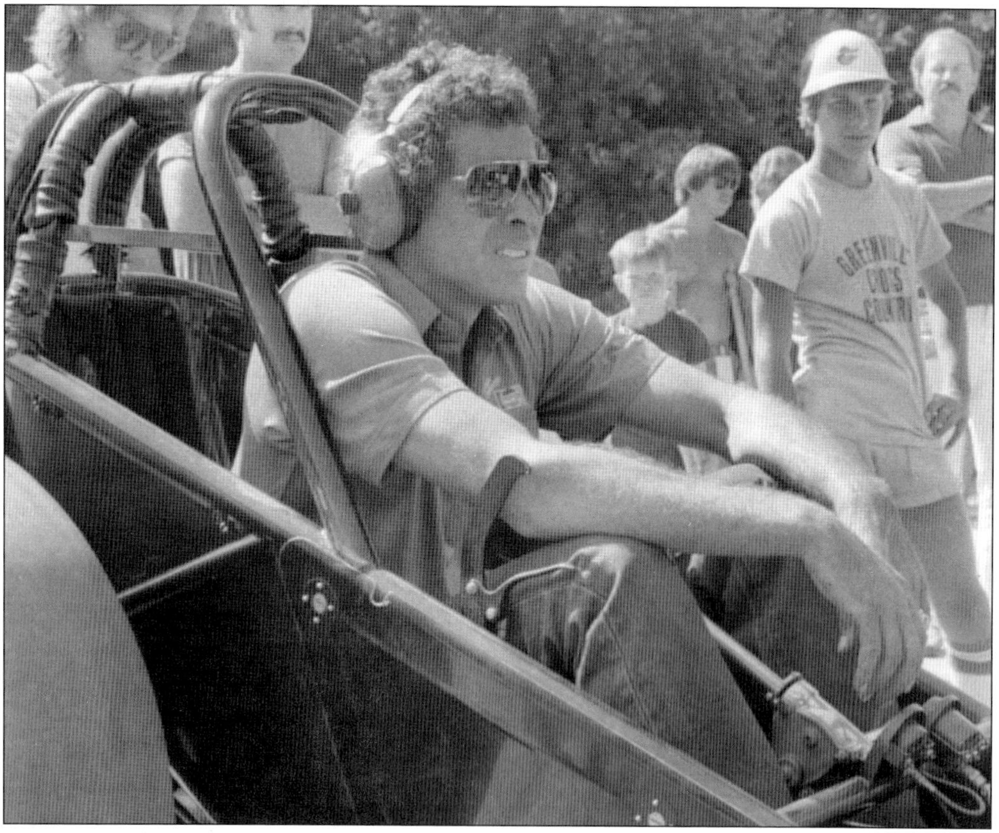

Don Prudhomme beat up OCIR's funny car records for 12 years, from 1971 to 1983. He started his OCIR record rampage in 1971 with 220.58 miles per hour and 226.13 miles per hour blasts and a record setting 6.62 ET. Then in 1975 at OCIR, he was at it again with a record-setting 6.18 ET at 234.96 miles per hour. On October 29, 1976, Prudhomme reset the ET record with a 6.15. Two years later, in 1978, he lowered the record to 6.00 ET. In 1979, he captured OCIR's speed record at 241.94 miles per hour, and to close out the OCIR record books forever in 1981, he laid down a 5.76. In 1983, with a 5.74 ET, Prudhomme became the quickest funny car ever to go down OCIR's 1320 (the quarter mile).

Three

And Yet There Was More to OCIR

Drag Strip and Road Course Racing

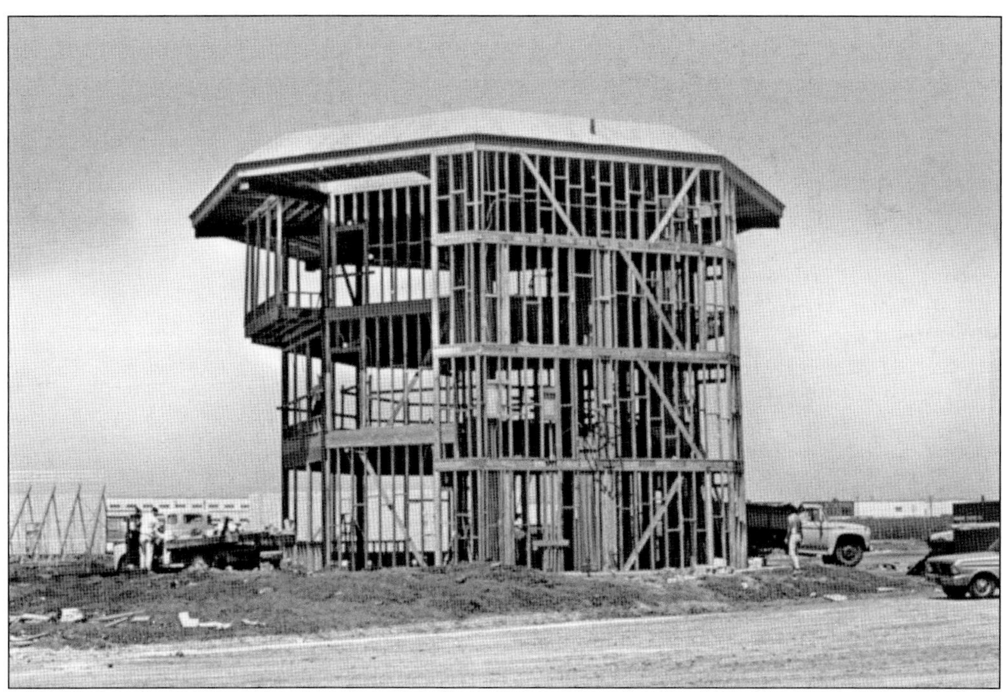

The one-of-a-kind, four-story, glass-enclosed tower and administration building was taking shape in the fall of 1966. OCIR featured custom landscaping and permanent restrooms and concession stands. It was the first racetrack to have reserved seating and permanent drinking water fountains. Another first for OCIR was its huge electric scoreboard—a feature only found at OCIR. (Photograph by Alan Earman; Don Gillespie collection.)

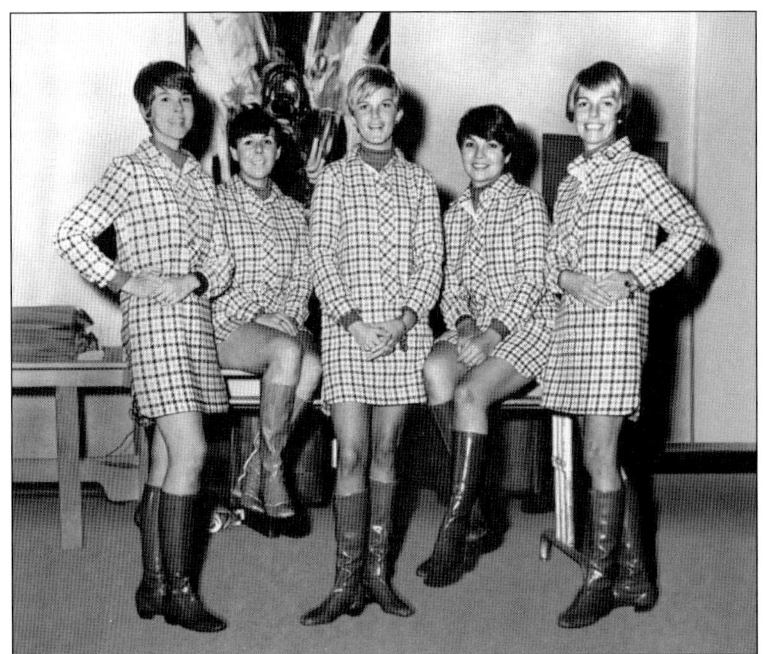

These lovely ladies are the OCIR tower hostesses. They made sure everything ran smoothly for the media, sponsors, and guests in the OCIR tower. Again, this was the only track that had this service. (Don Gillespie collection.)

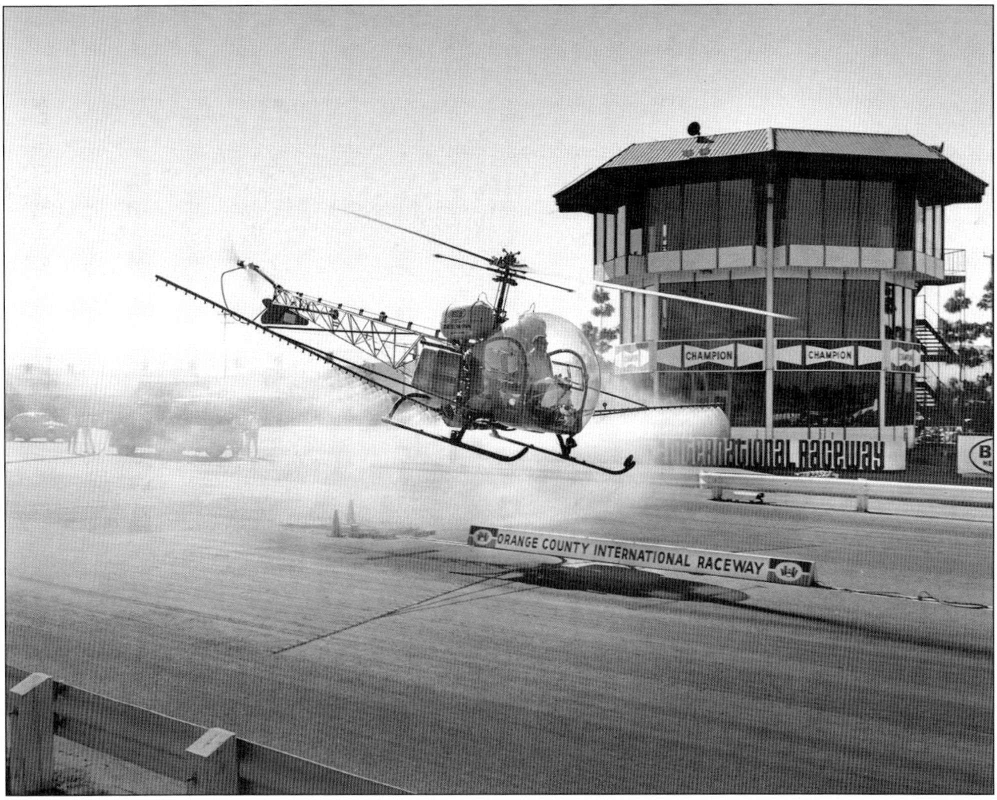

Track manager Mike Jones spared no expense to make OCIR the best place to race in Southern California. Here, in 1970, a helicopter sprays traction compounds the length of the OCIR quarter mile. Jones wanted the maximum "bite" for all racers who came to OCIR. (Don Gillespie collection.)

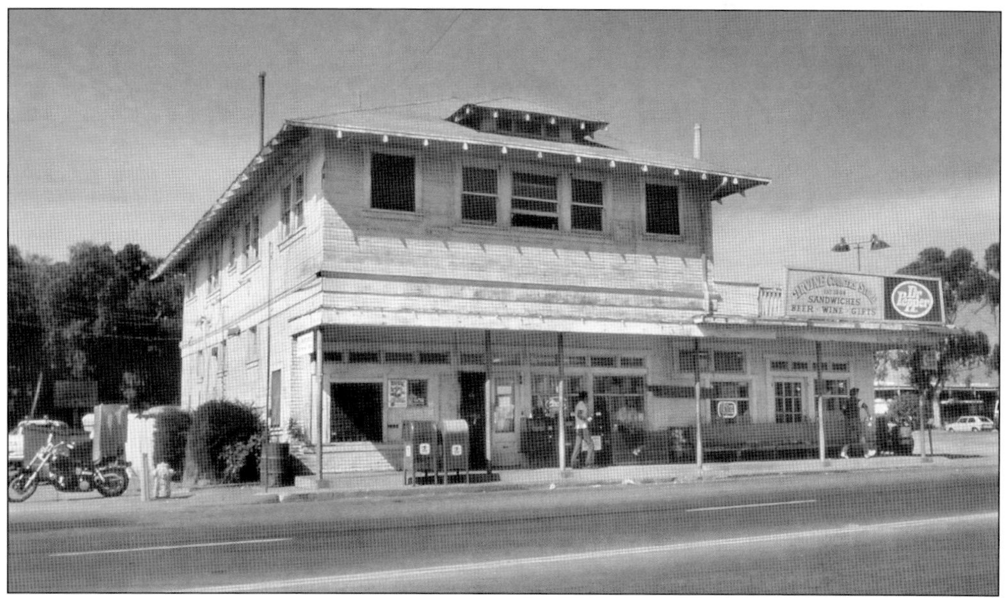

Driving into OCIR on its main road, fans and racers had to pass by the Irvine Country Store. This was a true landmark in the Irvine area and had been a general store and post office since 1909. Racers and fans would stop and gather food stuff, ice, and other goodies for the long day at the racetrack. When the track was torn down, the entire store was moved across the road where it still operates today. (Photograph by Alan Earman; Don Gillespie collection.)

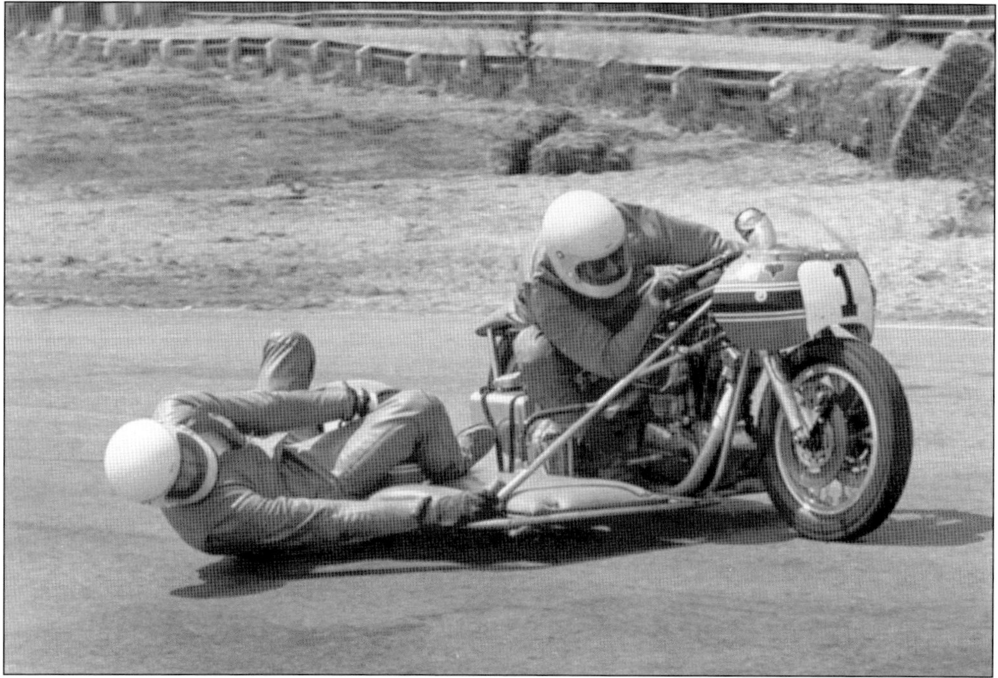

Since OCIR was a multipurpose racetrack, other forms of motor sports could be found racing from its opening in 1967. Formula kart road races, Grand Prix–style motorcycle road racing, SCCA road racing, and even a defensive driving school was featured at OCIR. Pictured is a side hack motorcycle road racer using the OCIR road course.

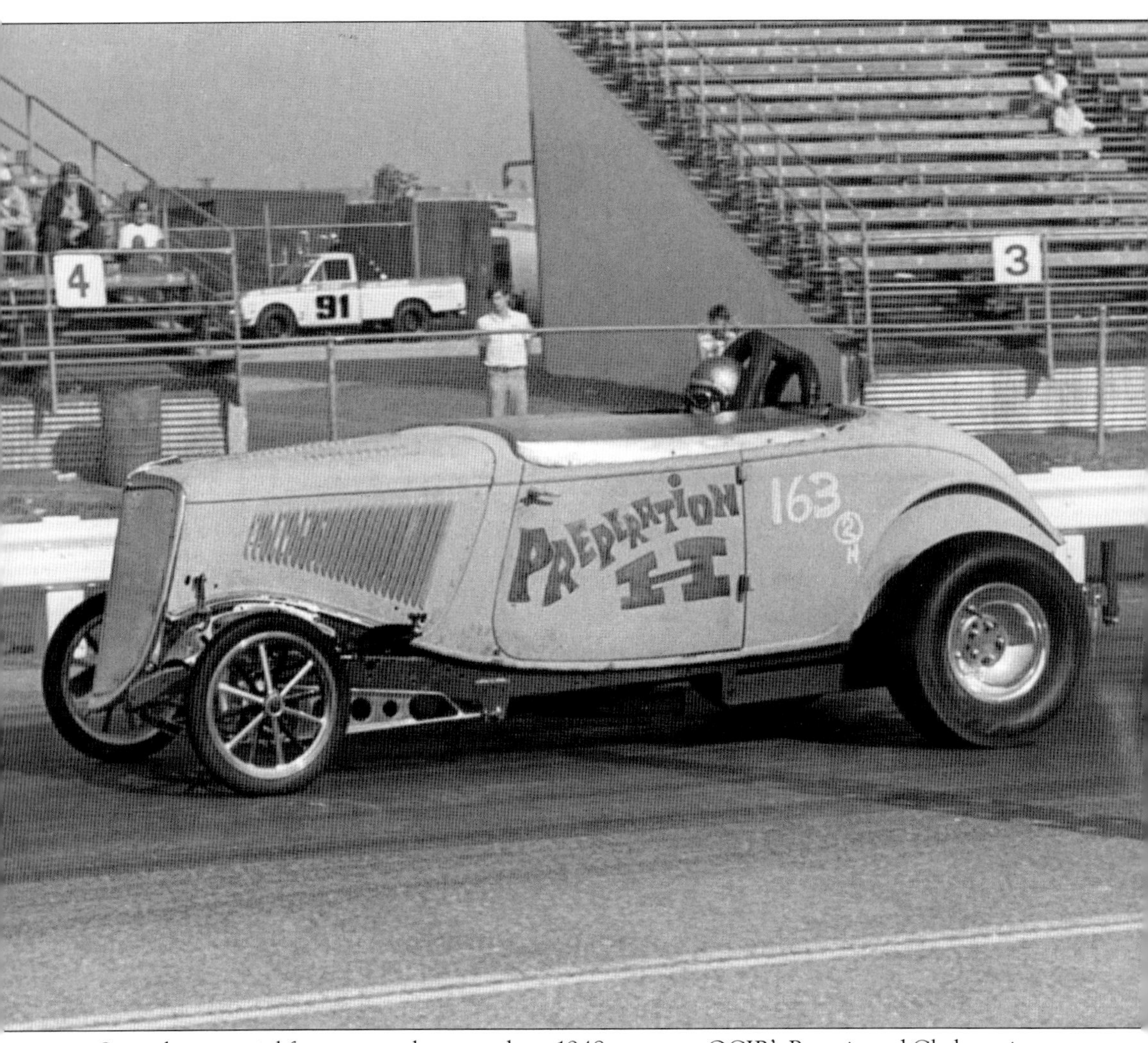

Something special for anyone who owned pre-1948 cars were OCIR's Bonnie and Clyde antique car races. It was a chance to blast down the OCIR quarter mile with pre-1948 street cars and street rods. Antique cars in all shapes and conditions came from all over California to race or to show their car in the show and shine area. In order to race, though, all cars did have to pass a safety inspection.

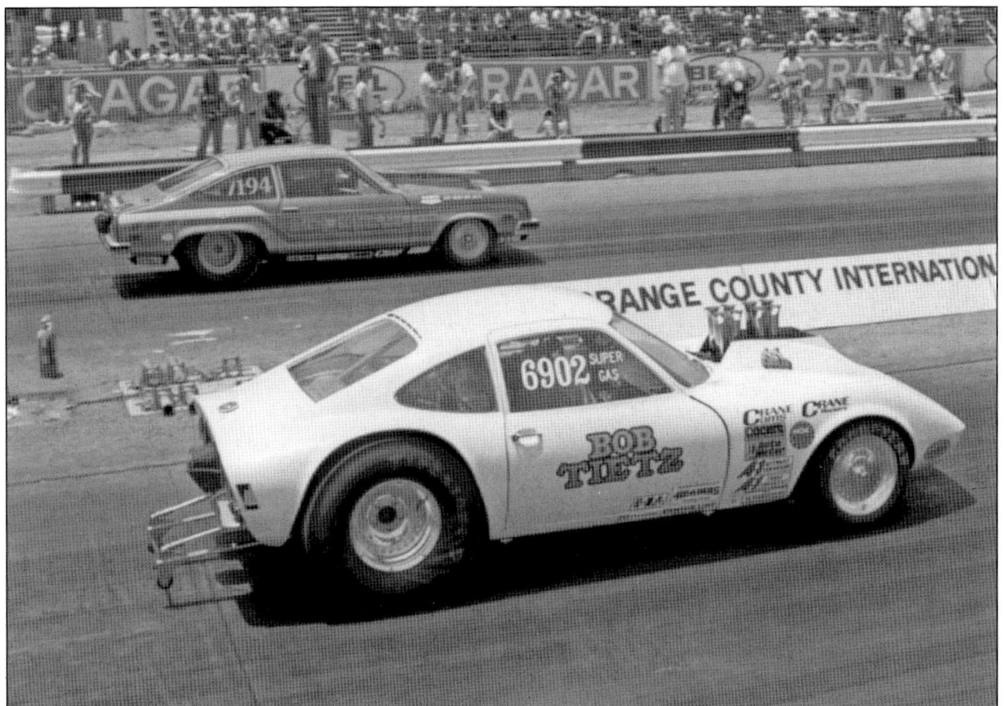

Super gas and pro gas racers helped keep OCIR open its final three years. These races featured the best of the best in both super gas and pro gas from all over California. Pictured are two of the best in super gas and a Northern California versus Southern California battle in pro gas. Above, in super gas, longtime racer Bob Tietz is taking on the Back-ordered Vega. Below, on the far side, is Northern California racer Ted Seipel taking on Southern California's Nicholson and Lemond. Many OCIR drag fans considered these classes the backbone of racing at OCIR.

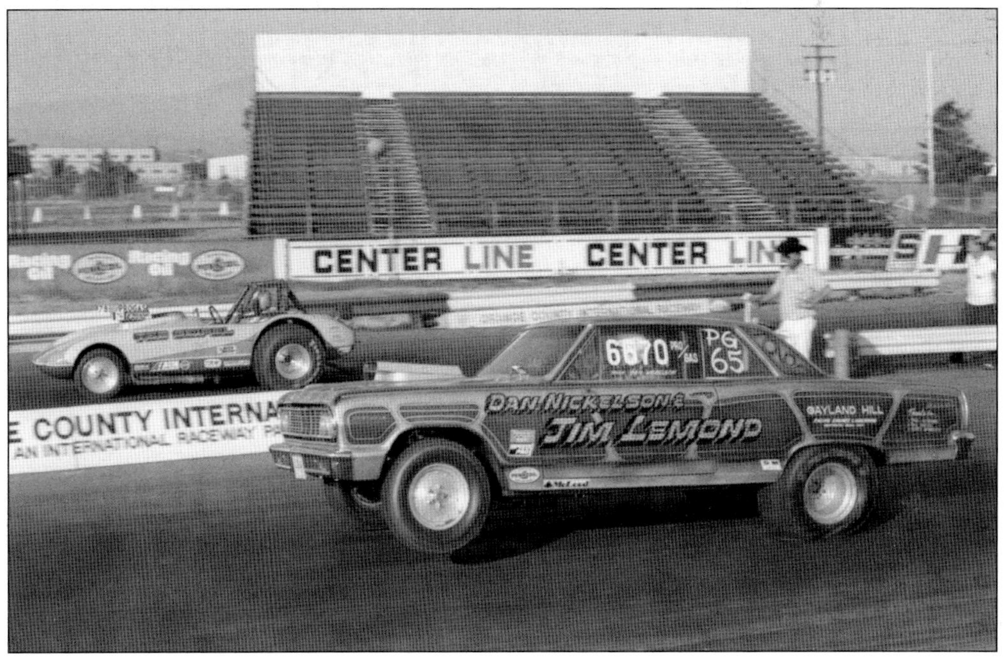

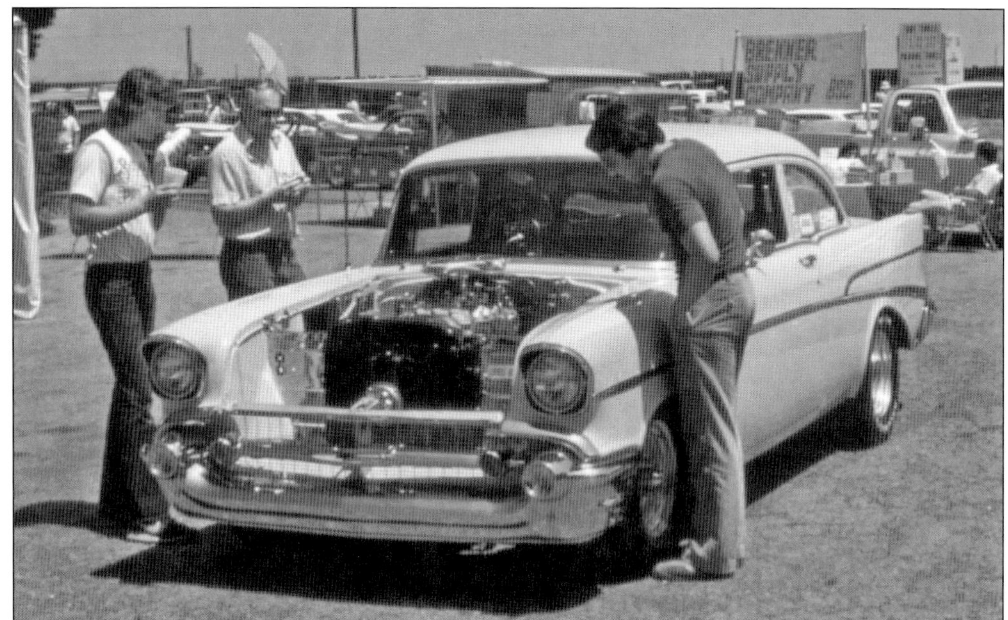

Super Chevy magazine held its first-ever Super Chevy Sunday at OCIR in 1981. The event featured an all-Chevrolet car show and an all-Chevrolet drag race. On display was the world's most famous magazine project car, *Popular Hot Rodding* magazine's Project X 1957 Chevrolet. In 1980, it became a "star" car when it was featured in the movie *Hollywood Knights*. The Super Chevy event was such a huge success that the magazine had Super Chevy events all over the United States for the next 14 years.

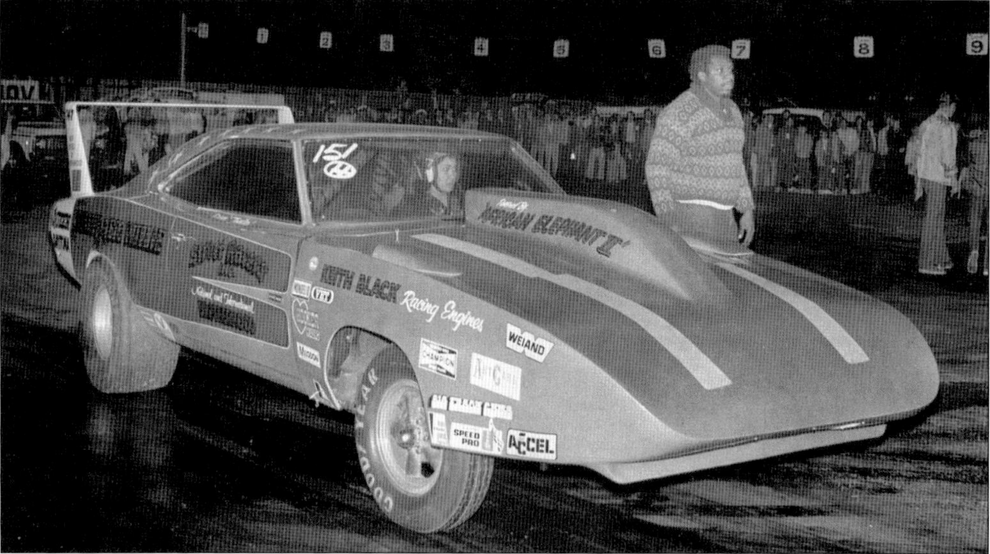

All day and all night drag races took place at OCIR on June 5, 1971. "Big Willie" Robinson and his International Brotherhood of Street Racers were the official/unofficial hosts of the races. Everything started on Saturday at 2:30 p.m. and ended at 3:00 a.m. Sunday morning. Pictured is Tomiko Robinson in her "Queen" Daytona getting ready to make a run; her husband, Big Willie, is standing just behind the front of the Daytona. Willie had a Cuda that he raced, but it was not finished at the time of the race. Willie and Tomiko have since passed away, but the cars are still around and living in Kentucky.

Volkswagen (VW) Beetle fans rejoiced when OCIR had its Bug-In once a year. The event was mobbed with VW Beetle race cars and show cars. The event featured all types of VW models, Bugs, VW vans, and rare VWs of all shapes and makes. The stars of the VW racing world battled out on the OCIR 1320 to see who the top bug was. Pictured is the "EMPI Lightning" VW Beetle race car making a wheels up pass at the event.

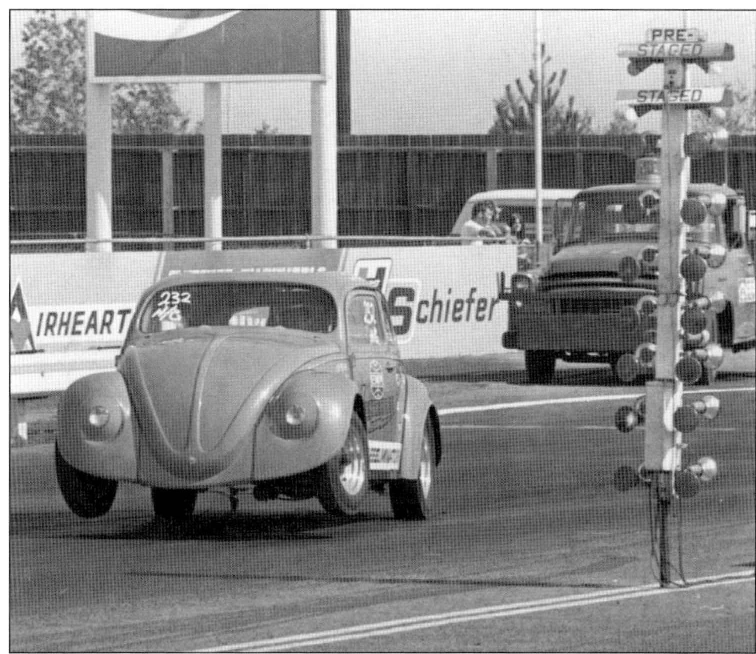

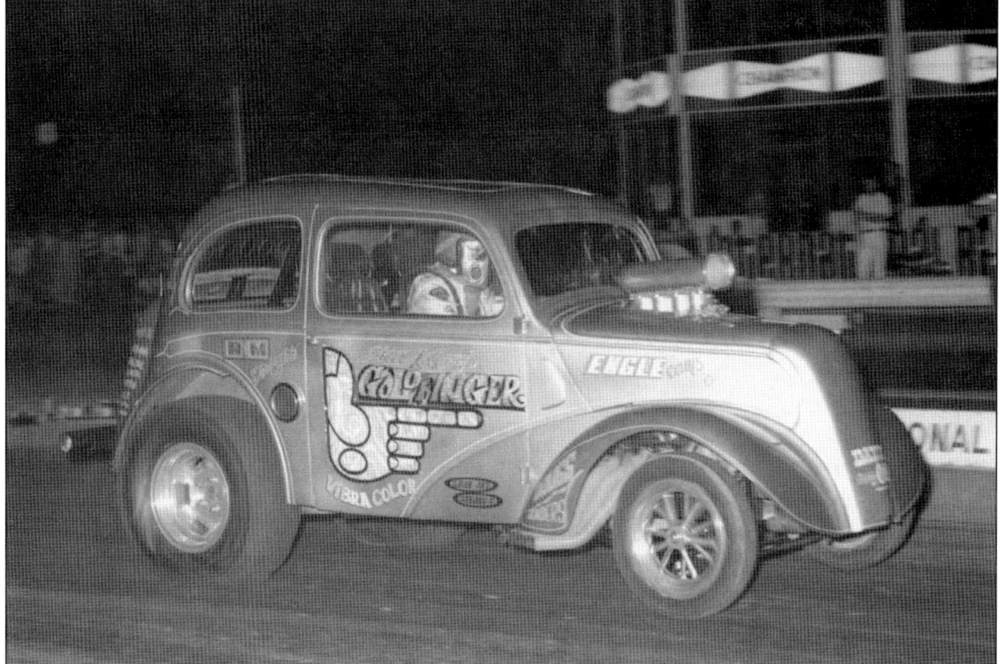

When OCIR opened in 1967, the gas coupe class was in decline. Stars of the class like Stone, Woods, and Cook were leaving the class and building funny cars. In 1968, Big John Mazmanian would follow Stone, Woods, and Cook and build a funny car. The influx of roadster and topless Corvette styles in the gas coupe class pretty much destroyed the true gas coupe feel that the class had to OCIR fans. Steve Korney and his "Goldfinger Anglia" gas coupe was one of a few that kept with the traditional gas coupe body style. The gas coupe class got so convoluted that in 1970 NHRA killed it.

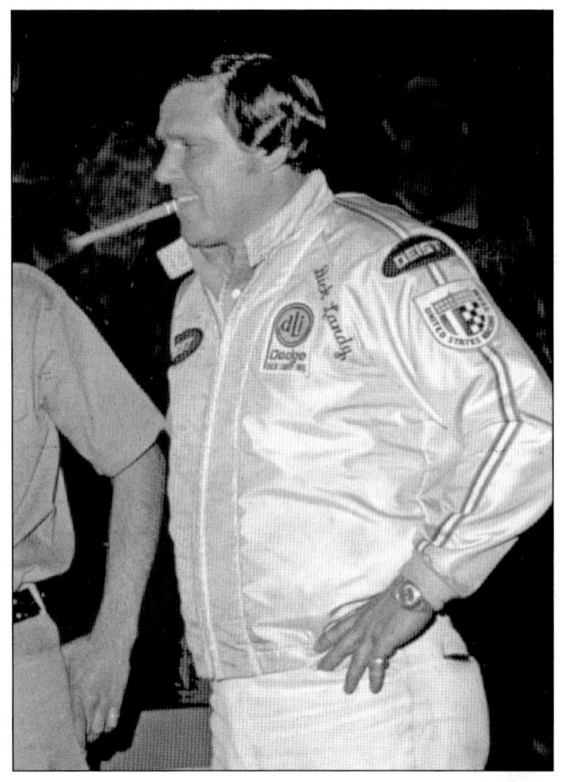

Cigar chomping "Dandy" Dick Landy left the world of super stock racing for a brand-new factory-backed Mopar pro stock ride in 1970. Landy and his factory-backed hot rod won pro stock at the NHRA Division 7 World Championship Series on July 19, 1970. The "Dandy" one was then runner-up to Bill Bagshaw at OCIR's Pro Stock Championships on October 10, 1970. There were another two runners-up for Landy, this time at the OCIR All Pro Series Championships in 1972 and 1973. At those two events, he lost in the final round to his archrival Butch Leal.

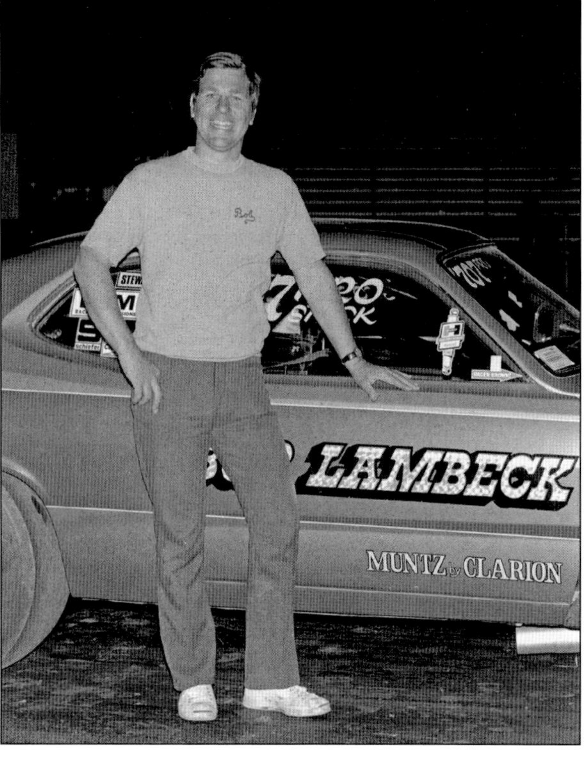

Bob Lambeck was one of those little guy super stock racers who went to pro stock in the early 1970s. At the OCIR NHRA Division 7 race on September 18, 1971, he was runner-up to Butch Leal. Besides racing in pro stock, Lambeck also kept racing in stock and super stock when his schedule allowed it. Lambeck toured the United States match racing and running in certain NHRA and pro stock events. He raced well into the 1990s.

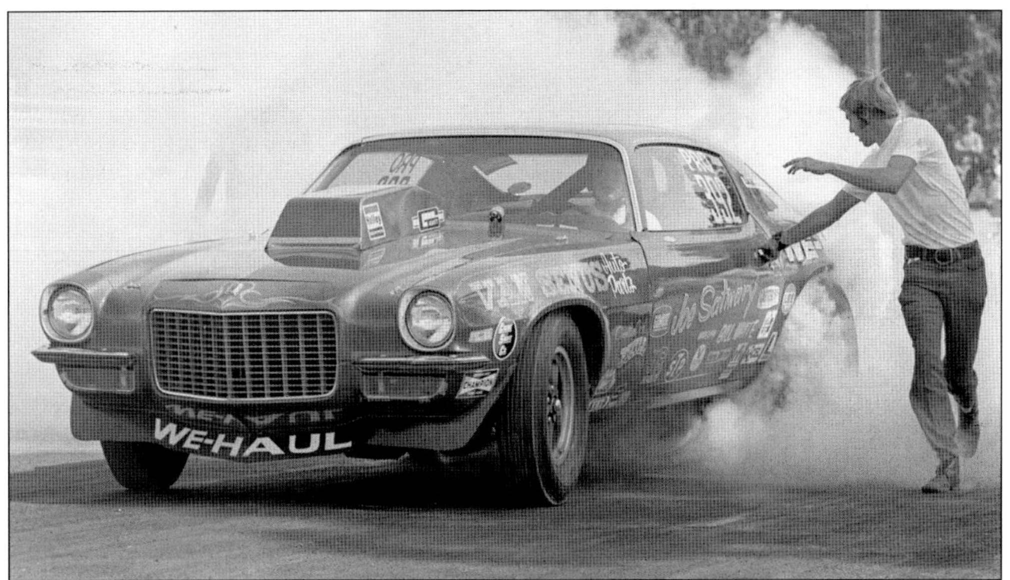

It is a very long tow from Hammond, Indiana, to OCIR, but Joe Satmary wanted to race his "We-Haul" Chevrolet pro stock at OCIR's Pro Stock Championships on October 9, 1971. Being the total underdog, he calmly waded through a tough field of pro stock racers to face Butch Leal in the final. And Satmary sent Leal back to Tulare, California, without the top eliminator prize. Satmary had done the impossible; he came and beat all those California pro stock racers at their home track.

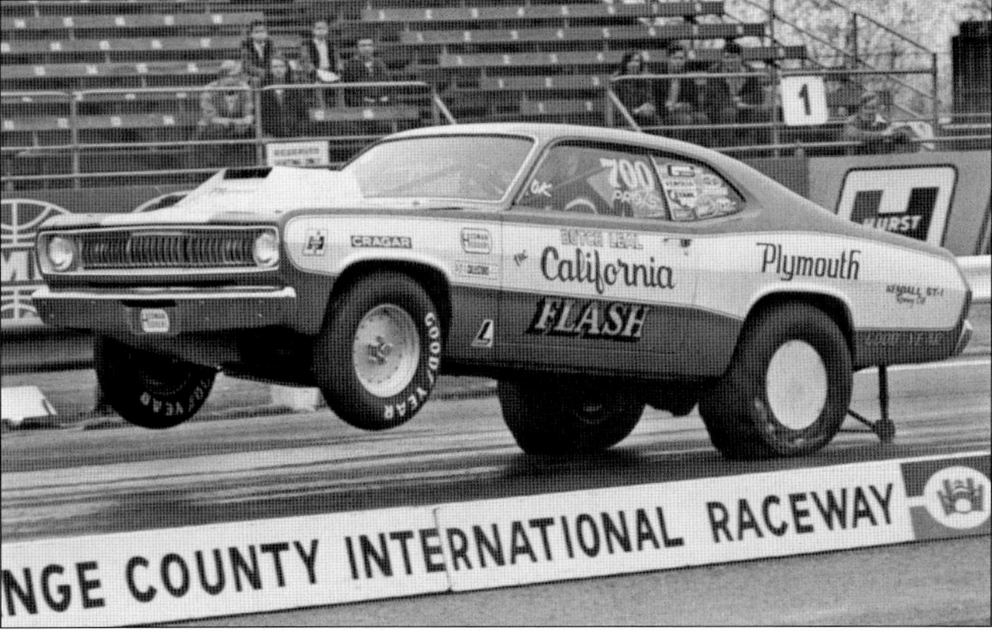

The "California Flash" Butch Leal could do no wrong at OCIR (almost). Leal flexed his Mopar muscle with victories or runner-up positions at the 1971 Pro Stock Championships (runner-up); 1972 Pro Stock Championships (won); 1971 and 1972 NHRA Division 7 World Championship Series races (won); and the 1972 OCIR All Pro Series, where he won three of the four races and won the pro stock title. In 1973, at the All Pro Series, he again won three of the four races and the pro stock title. Leal really liked racing at OCIR.

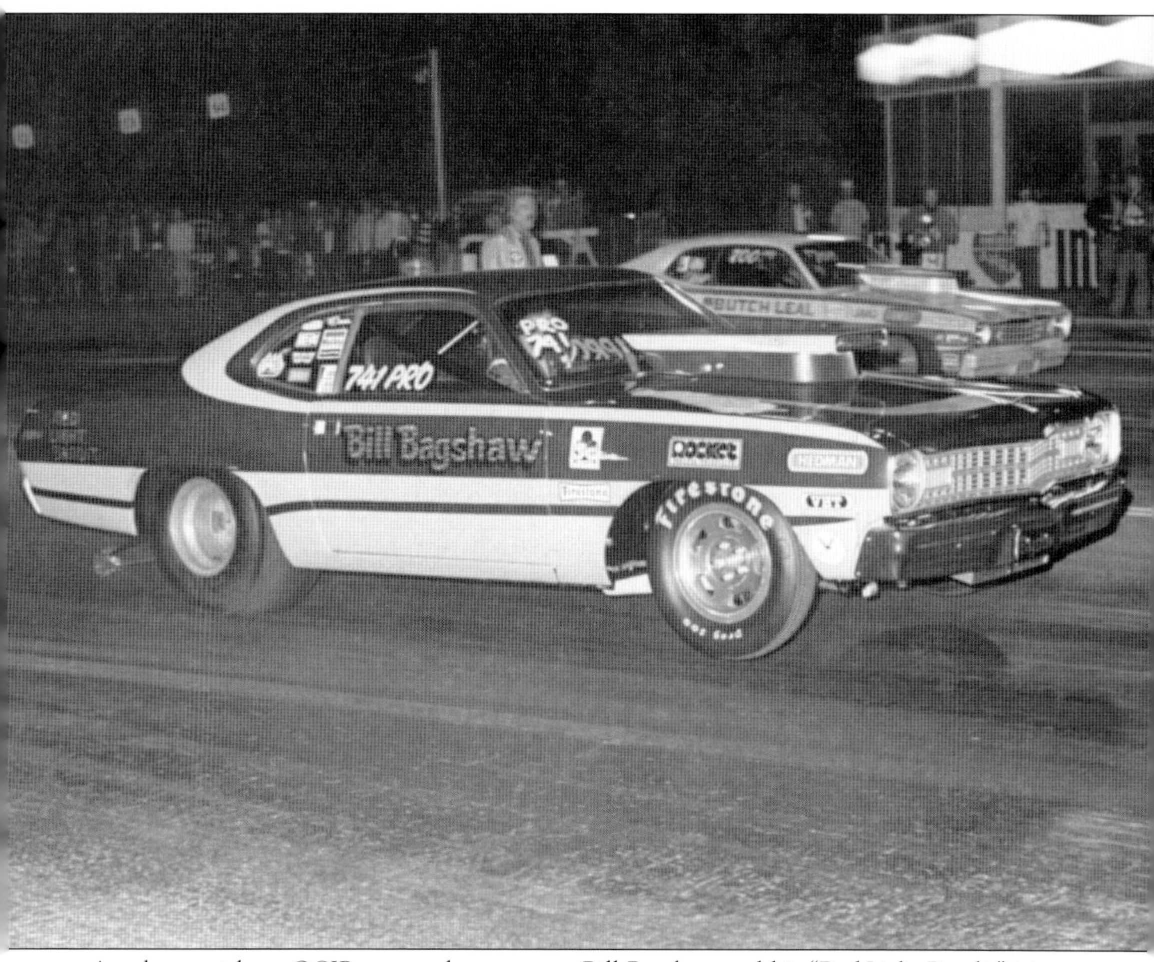

A welcome sight at OCIR pro stock events was Bill Bagshaw and his "Red-Light Bandit" Mopar pro stock. Bagshaw is a former super stock racer who turned to pro stock in 1970 when the class was introduced by the NHRA. Bagshaw toured the United States racing at major NHRA and AHRA events in the 1970s. He also match raced in the summer months and then returned home to SoCal in the winter to race at OCIR and Irwindale. He put himself in the OCIR record books with a 1972 runner-up to Butch Leal at the OCIR NHRA Division 7 World Championship Series race. Then, in 1973, Bagshaw was again runner-up to Leal at the OCIR AHRA Grand American race. But things changed for Bagshaw in a good way in 1974 when he beat Larry Huff at the OCIR AHRA Grand American race. With OCIR now back as an NHRA-sanctioned track, Bagshaw won the 1976 OCIR NHRA Division 7 race and then scored another big win a few weeks later, beating Mark Yuill in the pro stock final at the OCIR Funny Car 500. Bagshaw came away with the OCIR pro stock record with a 8.75 ET at 156.52 miles per hour.

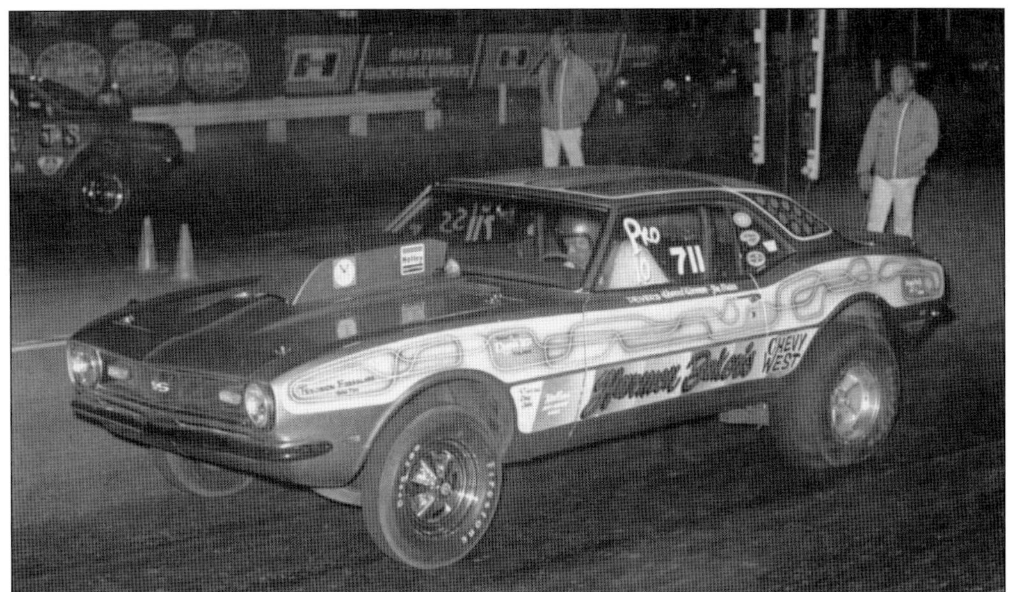

Before big money and factory-backed teams pushed their way into pro stock racing, there were racers like Jim Baker and his Chevrolet Camaro. Baker was considered the independent little guy pro stock racer—no big money just a racer at heart on a budget. Baker and a few others were the original pro stock racers in SoCal, most of which came from the super stock ranks. Their super stock race cars were converted to fit into the new pro stock class in 1970. But the arrival of factory teams and big money with their technology pushed racers like Baker out of the class.

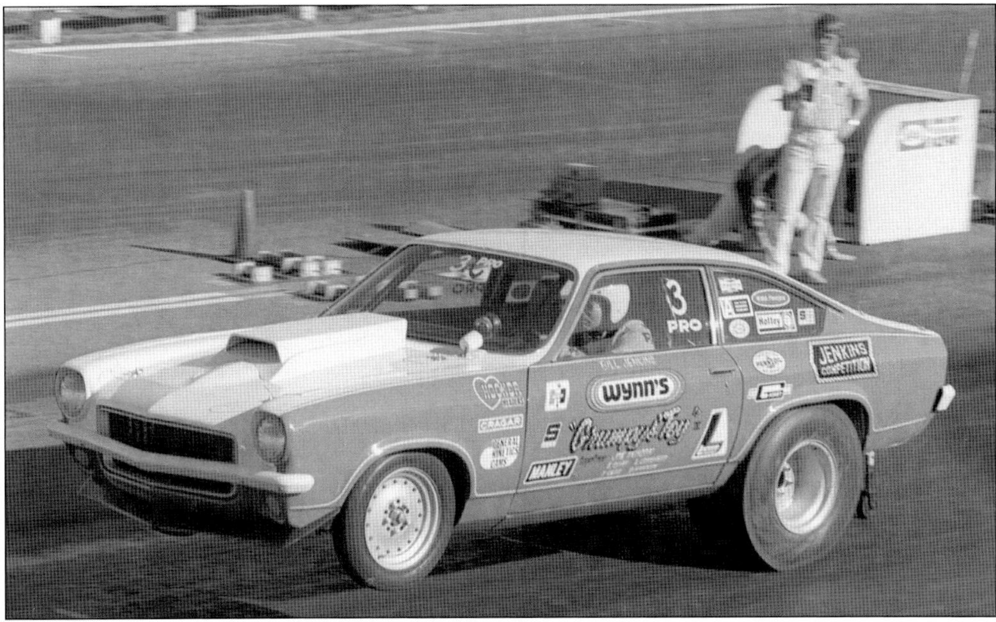

Coming all the way to OCIR from Malvern, Pennsylvania, was Bill "Grumpy" Jenkins and his 1973 pro stock Chevrolet Vega. Grumpy and crew rented the track for some test and tune time just prior to the AHRA Winternationals in Scottsdale, Arizona, and the NHRA Winternationals in Pomona, California. Jenkins and his new Vega did not race at OCIR; he would return some nine years later with a Chevrolet Camaro pro stock and race at OCIR's NHRA World Finals in 1982.

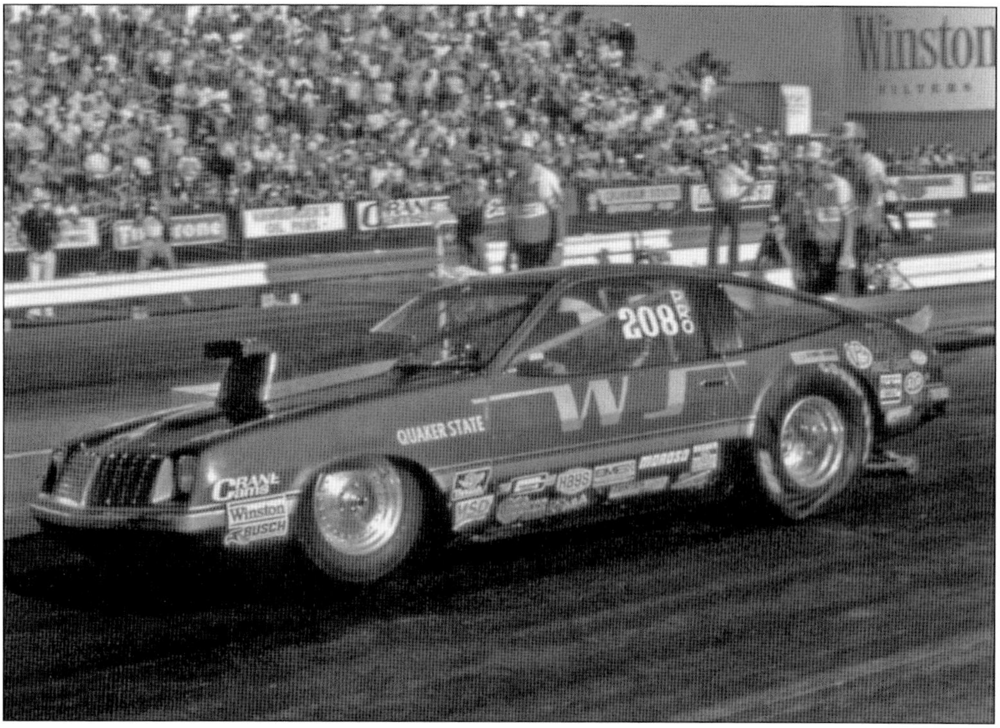

Georgia-based Warren Johnson enjoyed his time at OCIR in 1982 and 1983. First in 1982, he won the OCIR NHRA World Finals with his Oldsmobile Starfire pro stock. Then in 1983 at the same race, he beat Lee Shepherd in the final with his Hurst Oldsmobile pro stock. This made Warren a back-to-back winner of pro stock at NHRA World Finals.

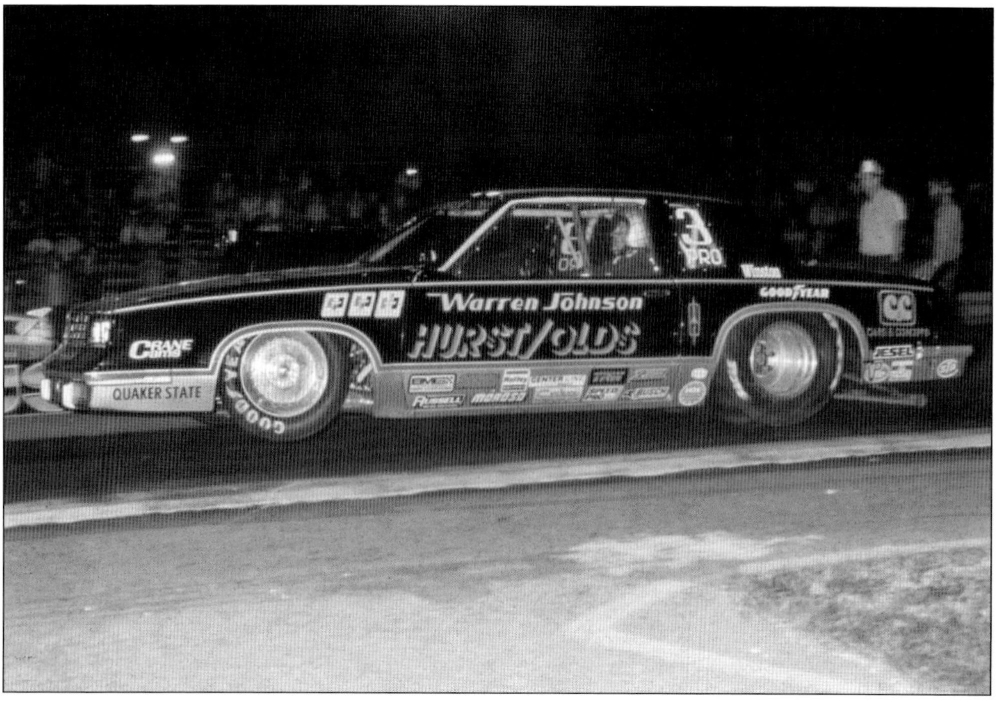

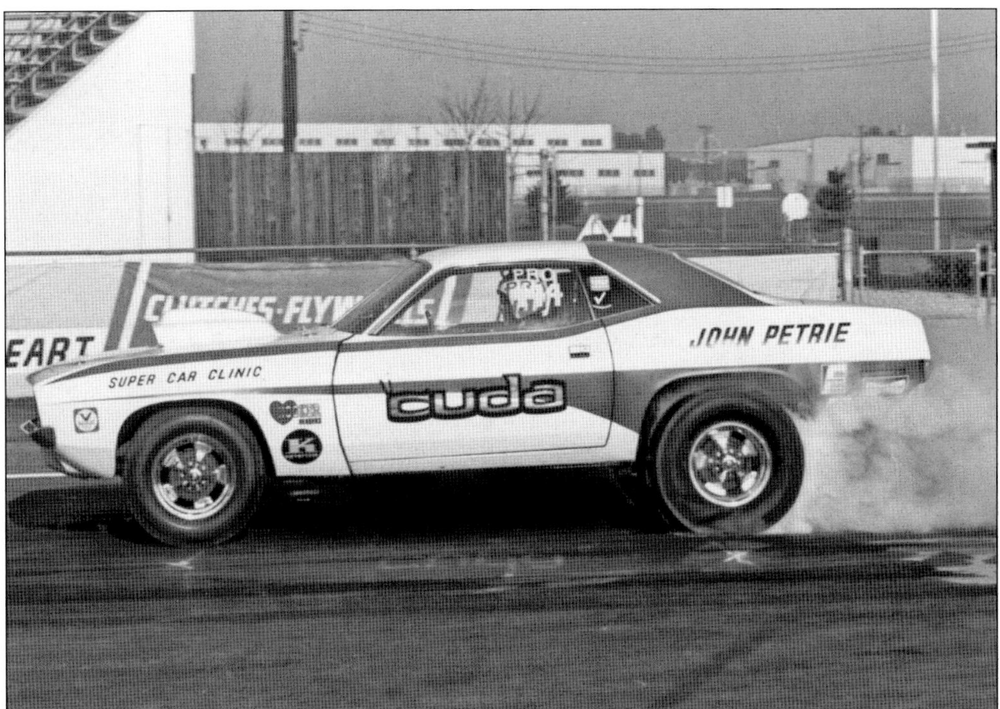

Former Canadian funny car racer John Petrie picked up a major sponsor when he decided to go pro stock racing in 1972. Mopar of Canada was Petrie's backer with a beautiful two-car race team and towing rig. Before heading out to tour the United States and Canada, he did a test and tune at OCIR. Petrie then raced in OCIR's All Pro Series season four. He only ran one event but scored a runner-up to Butch Leal on January 23, 1972.

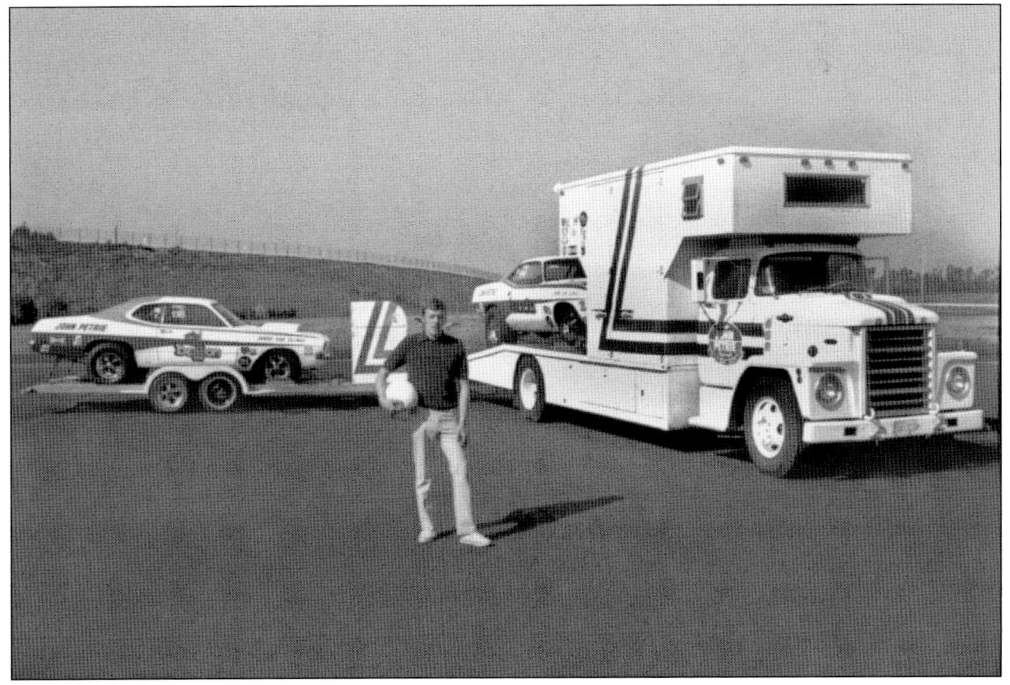

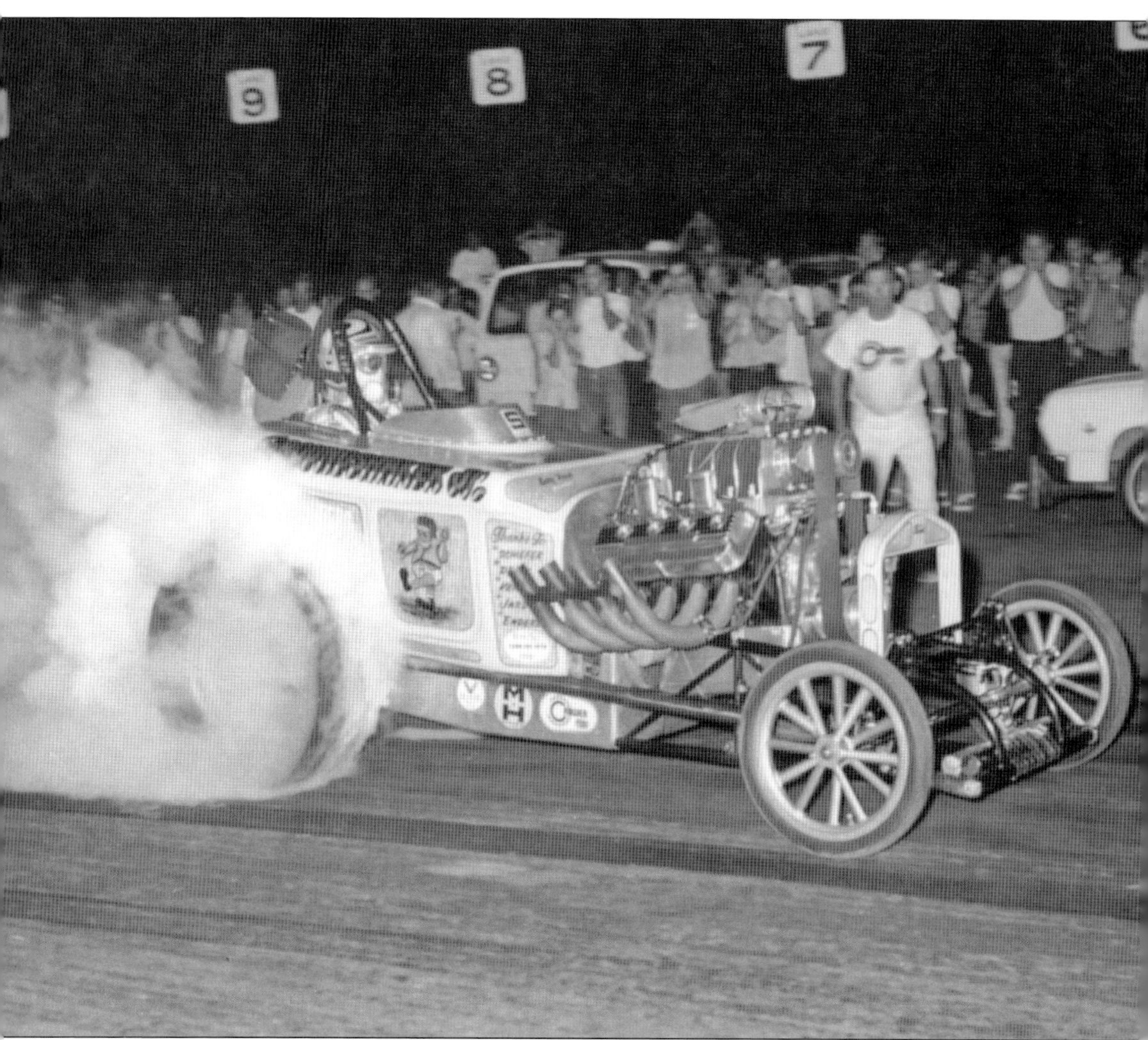

Winning the first-ever fuel altered race at OCIR at the 1968 Nitro Championships was Gary Read driving the Way, Hovan, and Okazaki fuel altered. Read beat Northern California's Burkholder Bros. for top honors. Pictured is the same car, but in 1969, it became the "Ground Shaker Jr.," a team car to the Ground Shaker top fuel dragster. Glen Way and Gary Read shared driving duties in Ground Shaker Jr. Tom Ferraro took Ground Shaker Jr. for a spin down OCIR's 1320 in 1968 and recorded a 7.77 at 203.60 miles per hour but did not back it up for an OCIR record.

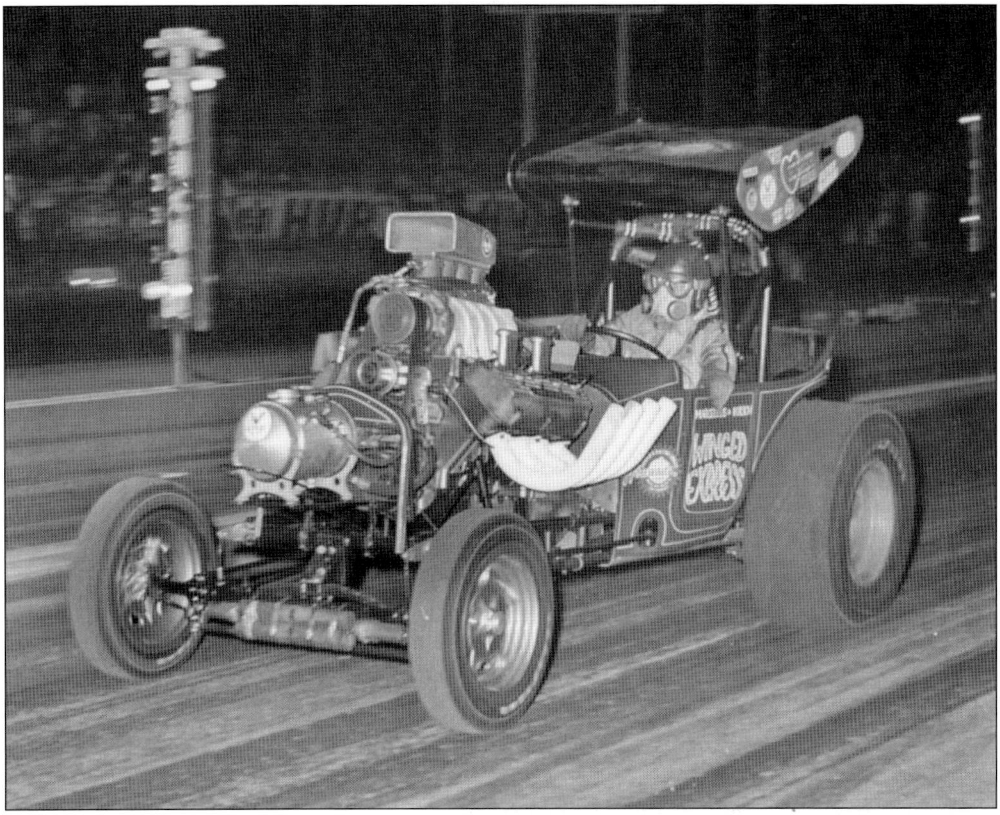

The legendary Willie Borsch and the "Winged Express" set the first fuel altered record at OCIR on September 2, 1967. Borsch recorded and backed up his 7.98 ET at 199.50 miles per hour for the record. At the 1969 OCIR Nitro Championships, Borsch beat Frank Harris, driving for Randy Bradford, for fuel altered honors. Borsch and the Winged Express also had low ET at 7.74 and on October 18, 1969, they set the track ET record for fuel altereds at 7.43.

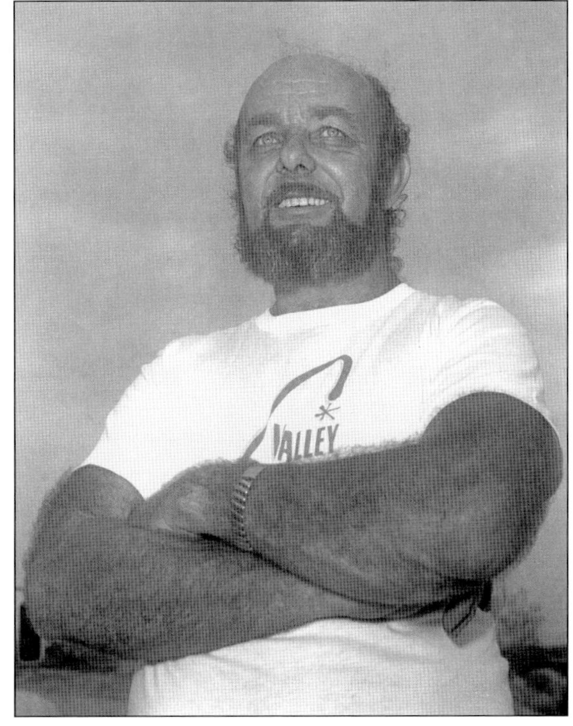

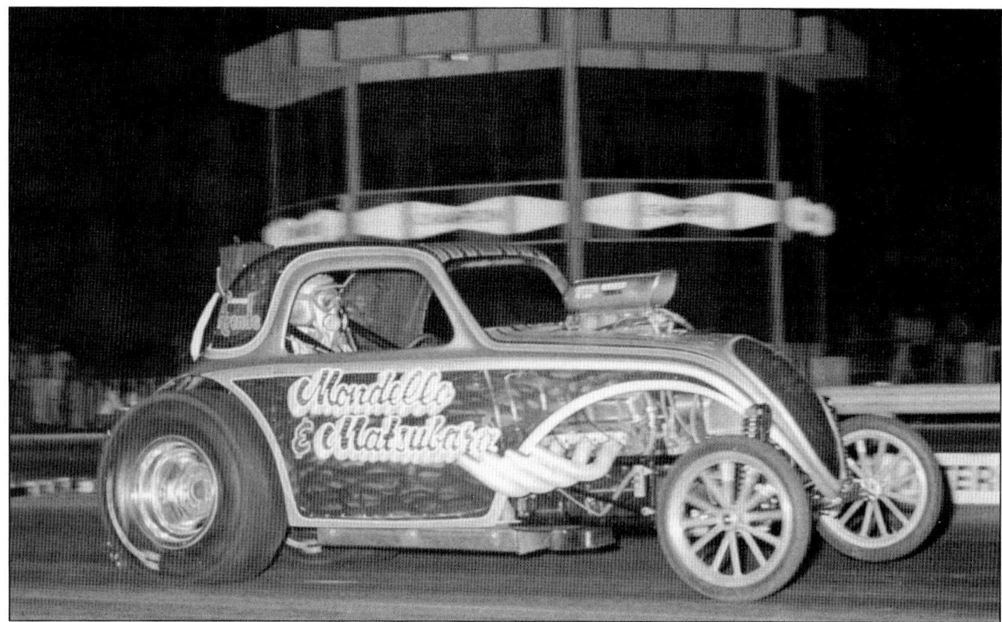

The big OCIR fuel altered bash held on September 27, 1969, saw Sush Matsubara driving the Mondello and Matsubara Chevrolet-powered, Fiat-bodied fuel altered beat the Winged Express and Willie Borsch for top eliminator. Matsubara cranked out a 7.57 ET at 193.96 miles per hour to outdistance Borsch's 7.64 at 204.98 miles per hour in the final. Mondello and Matsubara set the OCIR track record ET for fuel altereds the same day as their big win, a 7.51.

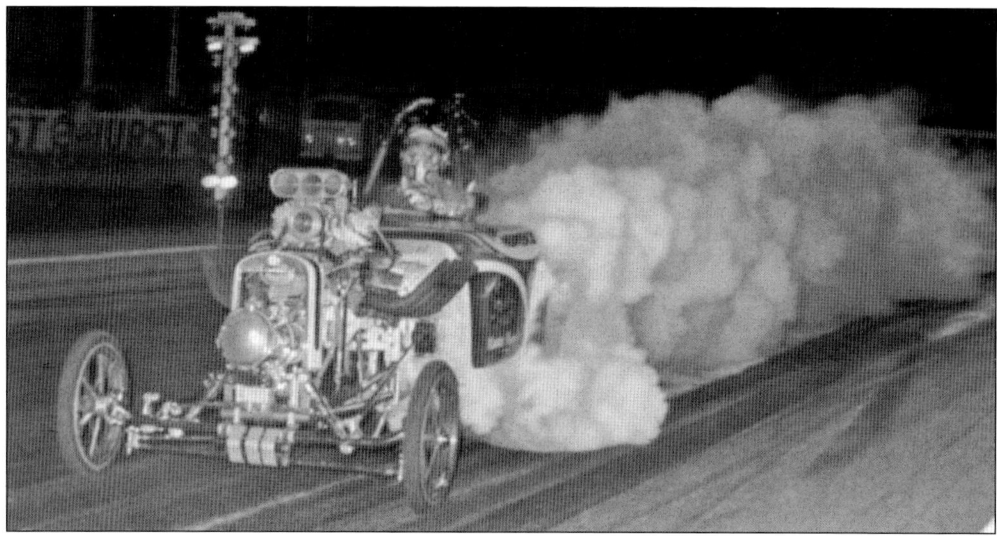

Just down the freeway from OCIR is the city of Anaheim. It is known for being the home of Disneyland, the Los Angeles Angels Major League Baseball team, and Leon Fitzgerald with his "Pure Heaven" fuel altered. Fitzgerald used his smarts when he saw Northern California's Rich Guasco name his fuel altered "Pure Hell." It was a perfect pairing for match racing—heaven versus hell. Fitzgerald and Guasco presented it to race promoters, and they loved the angle of good against bad. For about three years, they would match race until Guasco parked his fuel altered after a towing accident damaged the car on the way home from the 1969 NHRA US Nationals in Indianapolis. Fitzgerald was a regular at OCIR fuel altered events.

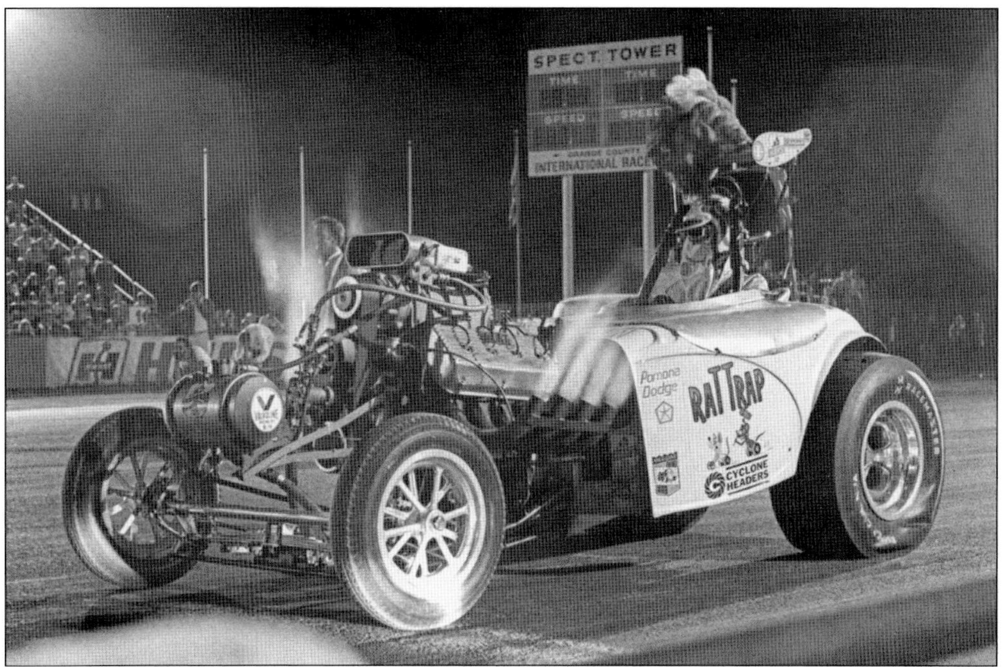

It was not a real fuel altered show at OCIR unless Don Green's "Rat Trap" was there in the late 1960s. It was a fan favorite and had a vast array of drivers, including Ron Boswell, Harry Hibler, and George "the Stone Age Man" Hutchinson (pictured). Green built his own 392 Chrysler Hemi and pretty much did everything himself. In 1970, he did build a new Rat Trap with "Dangerous" Danny Collins driving, but the fuel altered class was dwindling, so in 1972, Green went funny car racing with the Adolph Brothers and a new Chevrolet Camaro funny car.

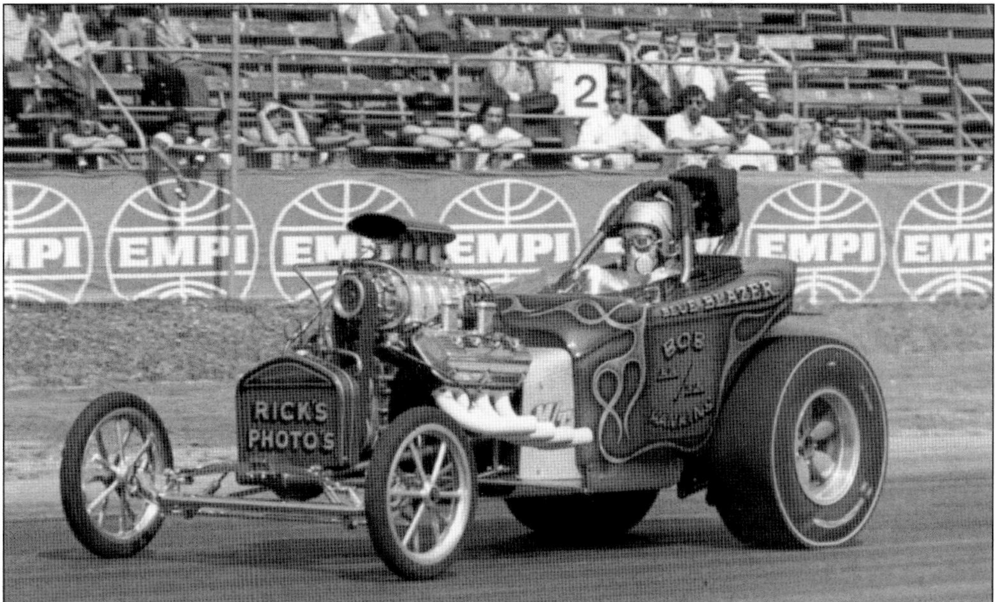

Bob Hankins and his "Blue Blazer" fuel altered scored his biggest win at the 1970 OCIR Nitro Championships. Hankins defeated Chuck Burch driving Glen Hyder's fuel altered in the final. Hankins would soon forgo the fuel altered class and join the ranks of funny car racing in SoCal.

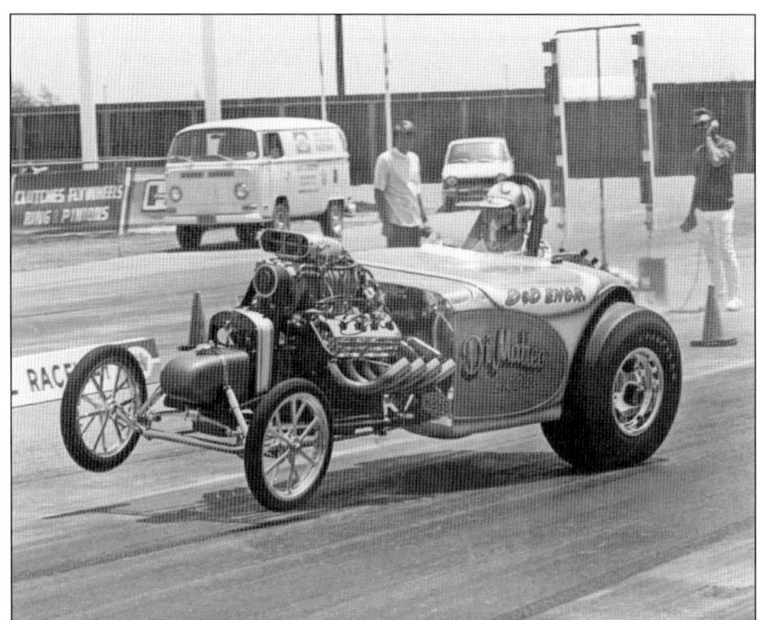

Doing little cha-cha moves off the starting line at OCIR is Bart DiMatteo driving the DiMatteo Brothers fuel altered. DiMatteo got the show and go fuel altered settled down and back on all four wheels. In the background is track manager Mike Jones, who is probably thinking, "What the heck is he doing to my racetrack!"

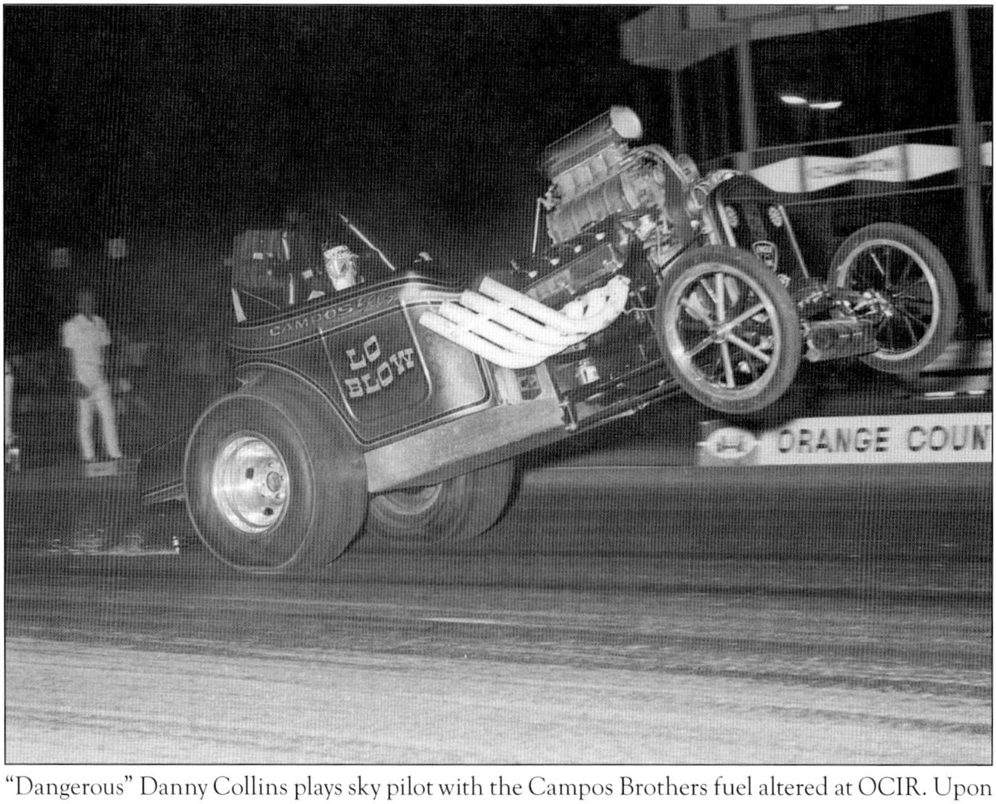

"Dangerous" Danny Collins plays sky pilot with the Campos Brothers fuel altered at OCIR. Upon landing, the car bent a few pieces in the front end but that is all in a day for a fuel altered racer. The Campos Brothers were longtime fuel altered racers; their car was given the name "Lo Blow" back in 1965. In 1965, the car had a side-mounted Potvin blower set up, and it was the only car in the class like that. In 1966, the car changed to a conventional blower set up but kept the name Lo Blow.

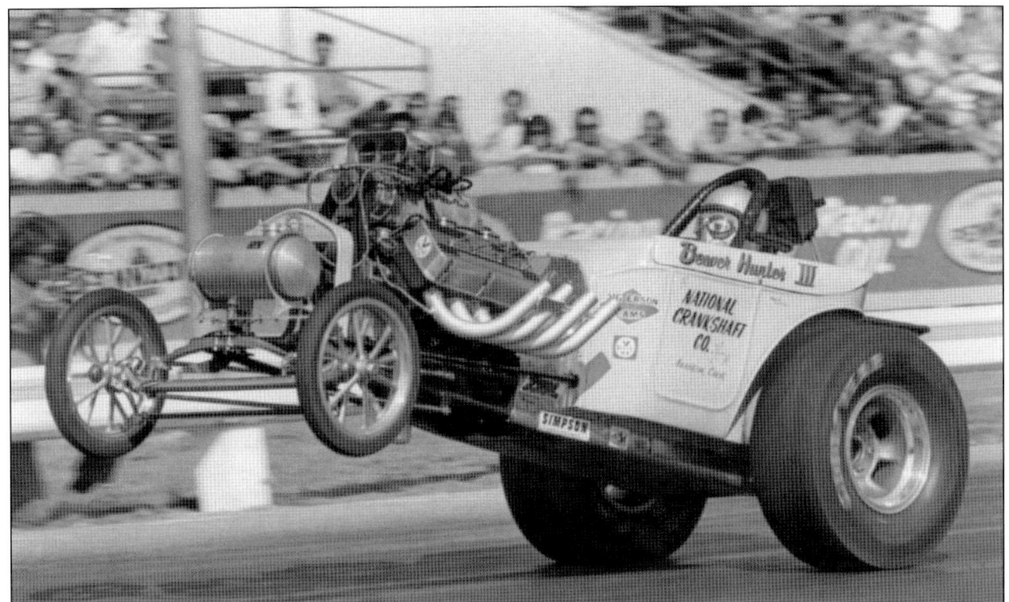

There are a couple of things that the "Beaver Hunter" fuel altered was known for in the early 1970s. The first was being a semi-regular at OCIR fuel altered shows, and the second was being the first nitro-powered ride for an unknown green kid named John Force. The car that is pictured, the "Beaver Hunter III" was badly damaged in 1971 when it crashed at the finish line while racing in Fremont, California. Fast forward 43 years, and it was restored and on display at the 2014 NHRA Hot Rod reunion in Bakersfield, California.

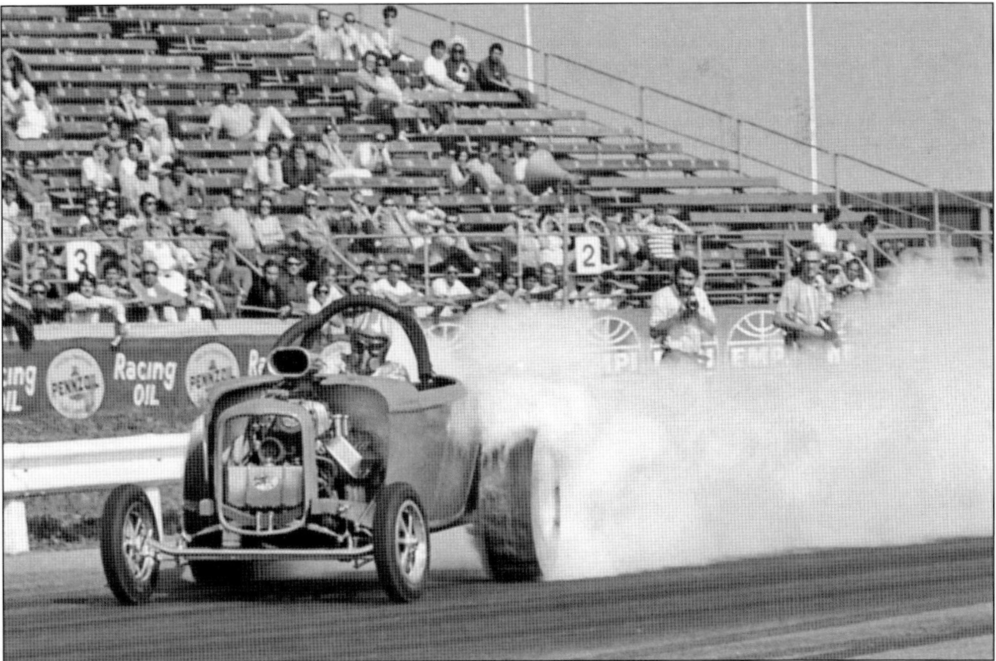

Bill and Butch Thurmond were owners of the only steel bodied fuel altered in Southern California. With brother Butch at the controls, the all-steel race car ran low ET and top speed at the OCIR Nitro Championships on July 6, 1968. Butch cranked off an 8.13 at 195.22 miles per hour.

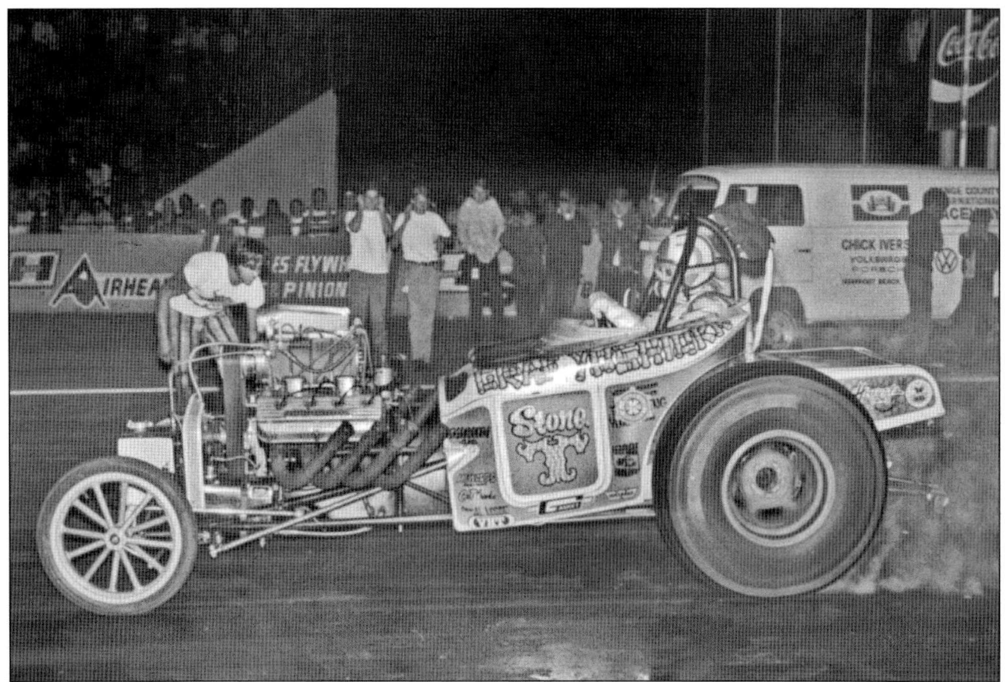

The partnership of Frank Graf and Mikio Yoshioka raced the awesome "Stone T" fuel altered in the early 1970s. At the 1971 OCIR Nitro Championships, the duo put away all competitors to win fuel altered eliminator. Yoshioka drove, and Graf tuned and built the car's 392 blown Chrysler Hemi. Right after their big win on July 3, 1971, they left to tour the United States with their Stone T.

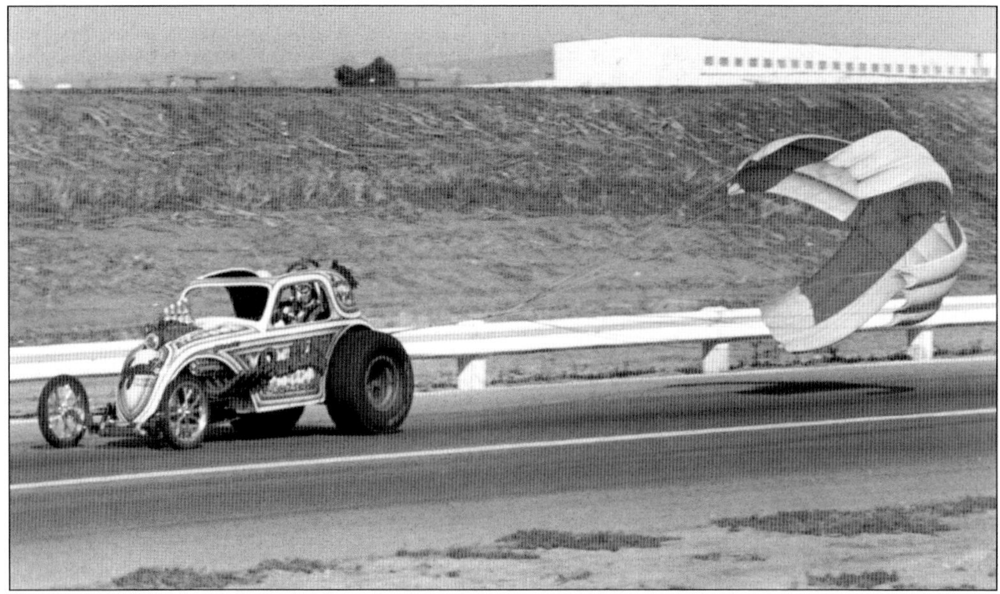

Northern California's Burkholder Bros. made the trek down to OCIR to race the best in the fuel altered class. Brother Pete tuned the 392 blown Chrysler Hemi, and brother "Hairy" did the driving of their new Fiat-bodied fuel altered. In 1967, they were runners-up to Gary Read at the Nitro Championships with their old car. Now with the new car, they would set the OCIR fuel altered ET record at 7.06 in 1971.

San Bernadino's Mike Sullivan was the world's quickest and fastest landscaper with his Fiat-bodied fuel altered. In 1970, Sullivan set the OCIR fuel altered track ET record three times at 7.30, 7.21, and 7.18. Sullivan was one of the few who stayed with the fuel altered class when it seemed like all other fuel altered owners were switching to funny cars. Sullivan would quit racing in 1973 instead of switching to a funny car.

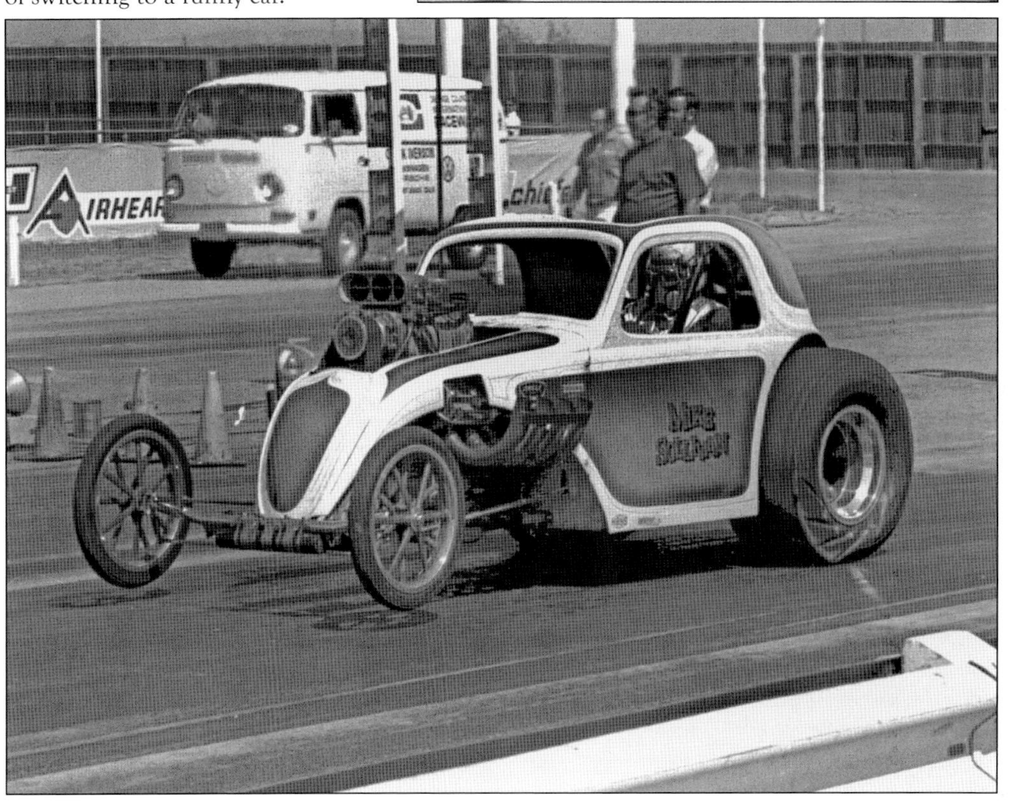

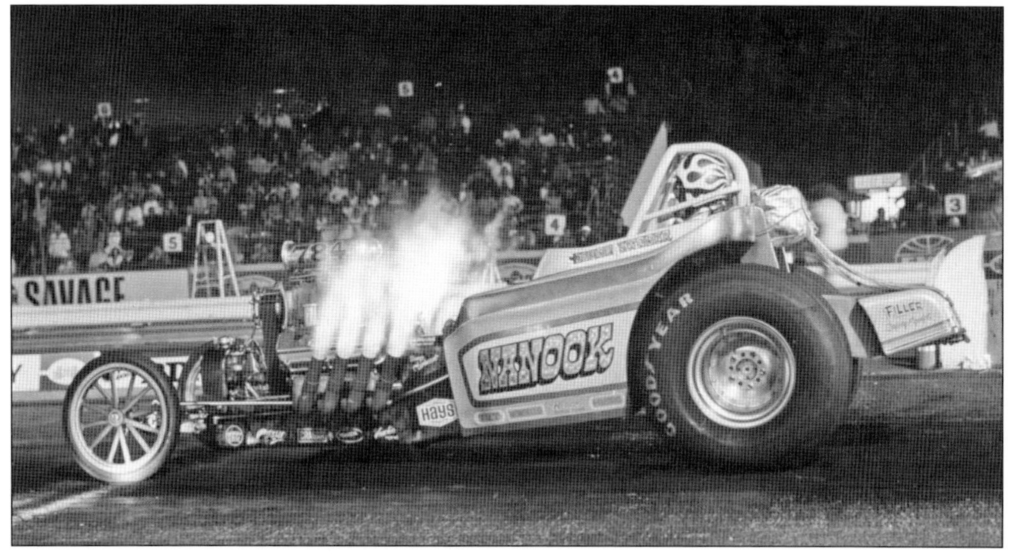

One of the most popular fuel altereds to ever race at OCIR was Dave and Lynn Hough's "Nanook." Dave held the record for ET and speed at OCIR in 1970 with 7.34 at 210.77 miles per hour. But the ET record would only stand for 21 days before fellow San Bernadino resident Mike Sullivan ran a quicker 7.30 ET. But Hough's miles-per-hour record would stand for six years until he broke both records with a 6.67 at 215.82 miles per hour at OCIR in 1976. Pictured is the 1973 version of "Nanook" at OCIR.

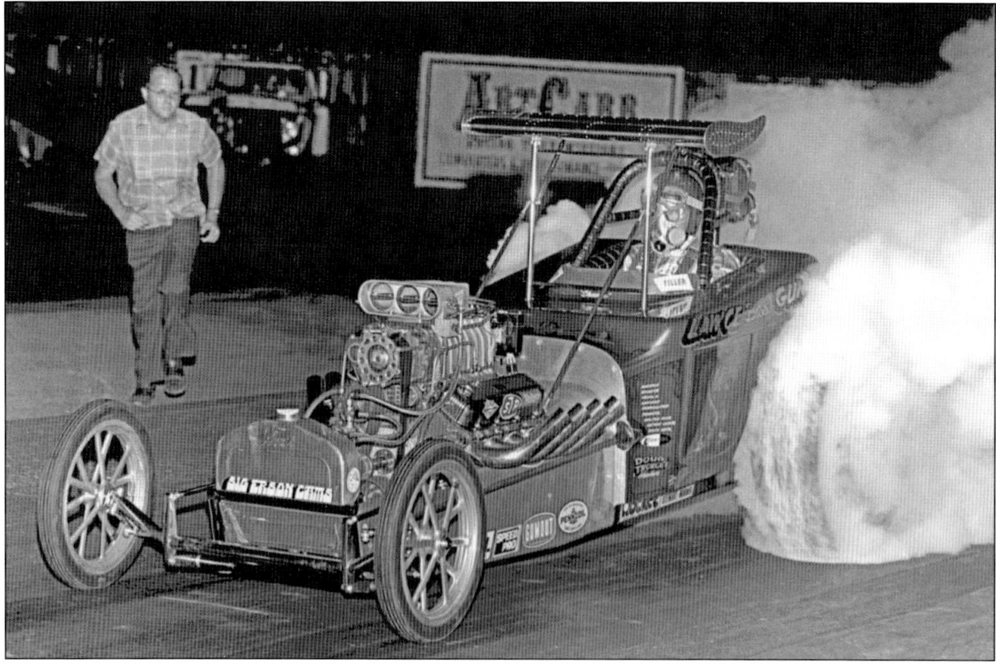

The Lawce Brothers and Sherm Gunn waded through a tough field of fuel altereds to win the 1972 OCIR Nitro Championships. Driver Sherm Gunn defeated Lee LeBaron in the final round. Gunn not only drove race cars, but he also built them at his business, M&S Welding, in Asua, California. One of the most well-known cars that came from the shop was the pro stock Ford Maverick of "Dyno" Don Nicholson.

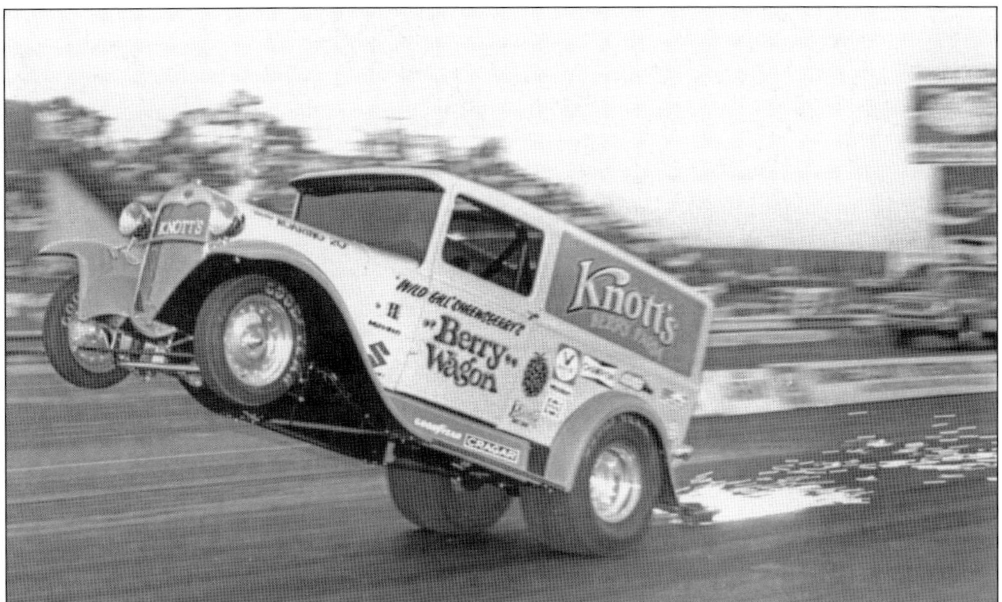

"Wild Bill" Shrewsberry went out and got himself a very big-name sponsor for his newest wheel stander, Knotts Berry Farm amusement park. Knott's Berry Farm was just down the freeway from OCIR so when it came time to unveil his new creation, it debuted at OCIR. The Knott's Berry folks were not just a name painted on the car, they had a replica built and proudly displayed in the middle of their park.

OCIR hosted the filming of action footage for the Shirley Muldowney motion picture *Heart like a Wheel*. "TV Tommy" Ivo and Kelly Brown did stunt driving for the movie. The movie received positive reviews and was well received by drag fans across the United States. The movie poster that is pictured is what Muldowney calls her Darth Vader look.

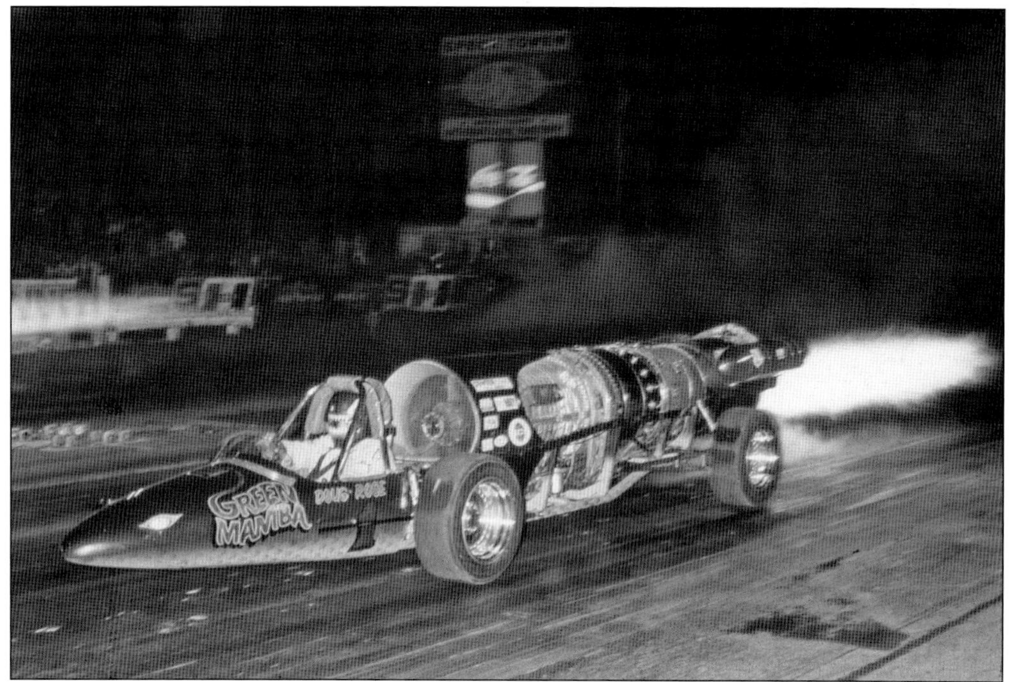

Longtime jet car racer Doug Rose was one of a few jet car owners/drivers ever to run at OCIR. Rose rallied NHRA into certifying jet cars so that they could run at NHRA-sanctioned racetracks. Rose got on the phone and called as many jet car owners as he could contact. They all would converge on OCIR at a certain date and be inspected by John Keeling, who was a certified jet engine expert and jet engine mechanic for a major airline. About a dozen cars showed up at OCIR and passed inspection; now they could run at NHRA racetracks thanks to Doug Rose.

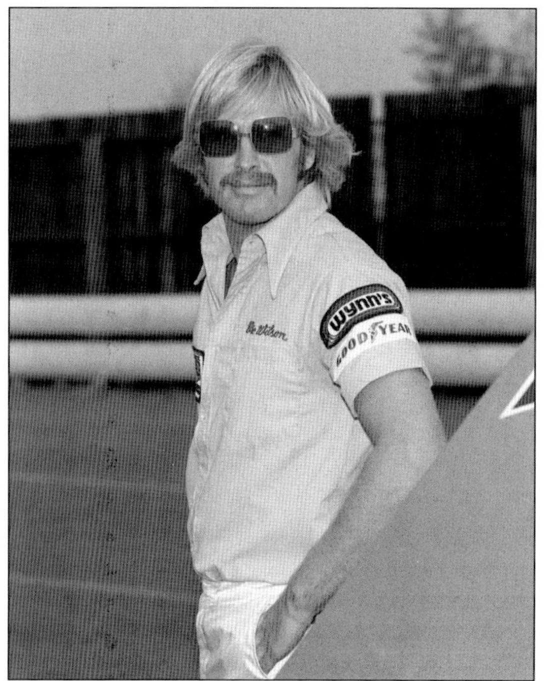

Who's the quickest and fastest person to ever go down the OCIR quarter mile? That would be Australia's Vic Wilson. He raced down OCIR's quarter mile in Bill Fredricks's "Courage of Australia" rocket car on November 11, 1971, at 5.10 ET and 311 miles per hour. After his record run at OCIR, Wilson packed up and went back to Australia, leaving Fredricks without a driver. The Courage of Australia was not driverless for long, though, as ex-rocket car driver John Paxson would fill the vacant spot left by Wilson.

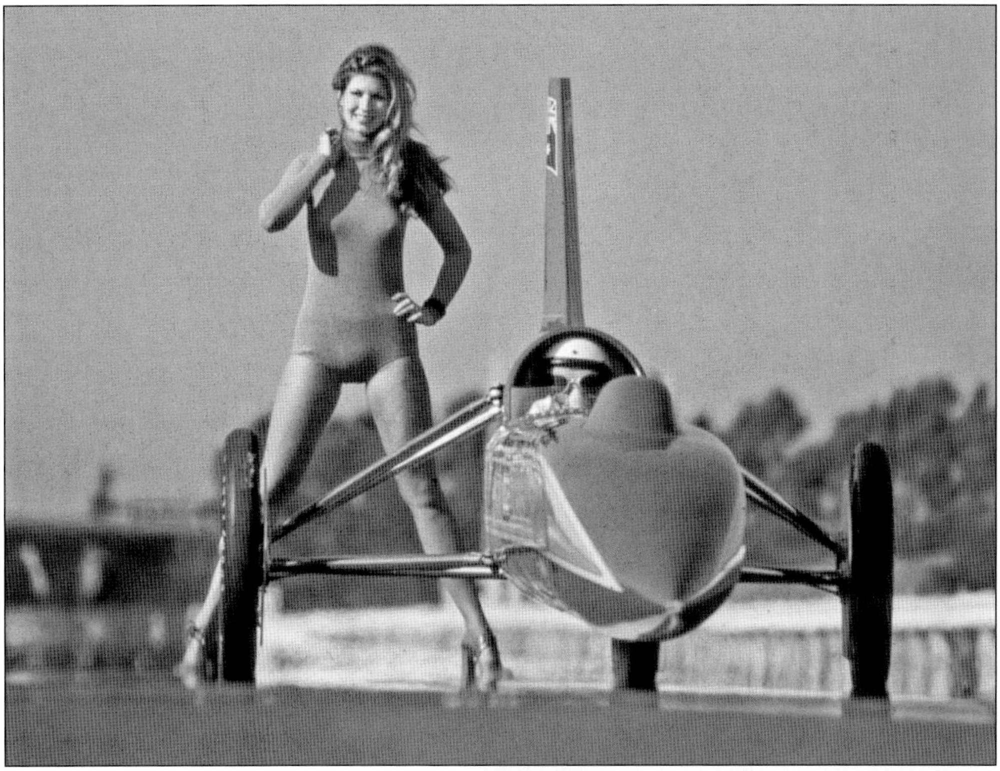

A bit of glamour came to OCIR in 1971 and 1972. Model Stephanie Rose posed with Bill Fredricks's Courage of Australia rocket car for *Drag Racing* magazine in 1971. Then, in 1972, she consented to be painted the same colors as the "Super Chief" funny car. Photographer Tom West applied the paint but forgot to leave a small patch of skin at the base of her spine bare. This caused her to get very ill because her skin could not breathe through the paint. West realized what he had done and quickly removed the paint from her lower back. She felt better almost instantly and continued with the photo shoot. At this time, Stephanie was the wife of jet car racer Doug Rose.

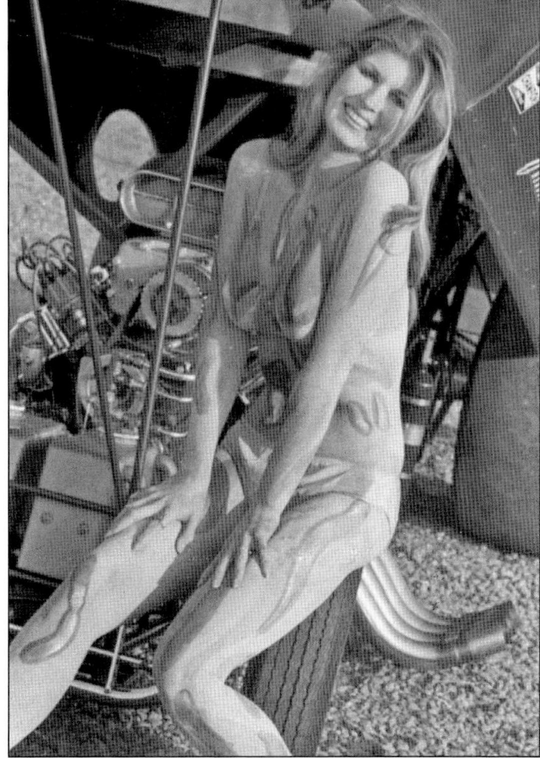

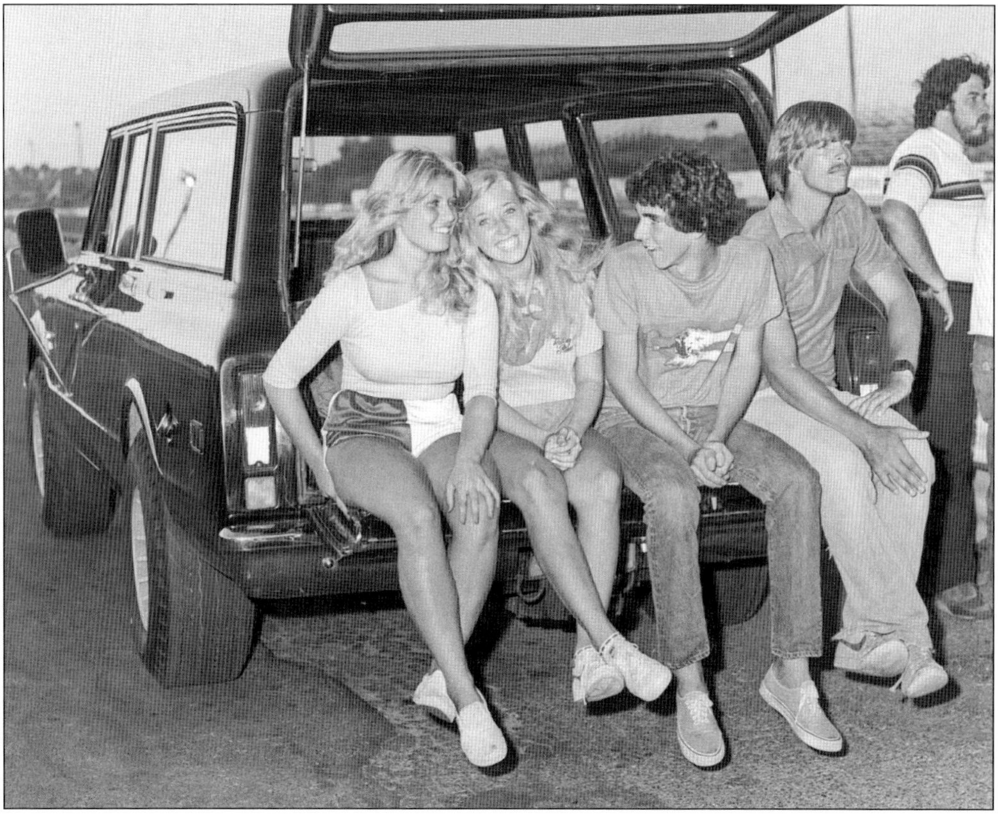

Southern California drag racing had sunny skies, cool cars, and of course, California girls. OCIR track manager Bill Doner took advantage of these elements with his Fox Hunt events. Doner figured let the women in for free and of course the guys will follow. Yes, it drew big crowds to the racetrack but not real race fans. The crowds were unruly, and things got out of control at one of the Fox Hunt races. The main concession stand burned to the ground and one spectator died and that ended the Fox Hunt events at OCIR.

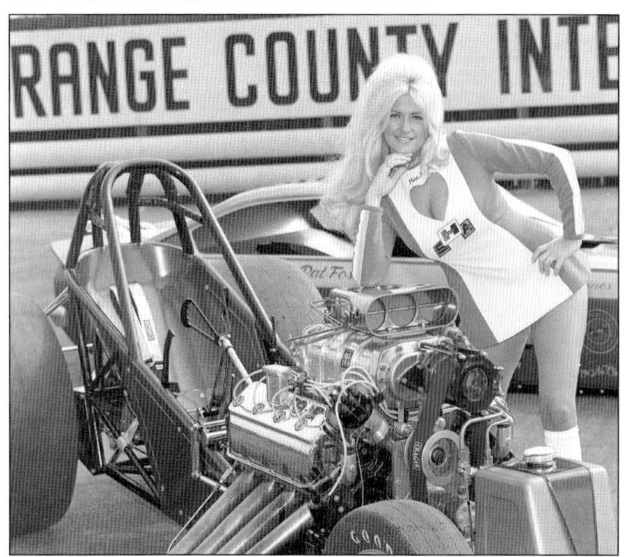

Hurst's golden girl Linda Vaughn lived just down the freeway from OCIR. So, when her friend, North Carolina's double-knit king Barry Setzer, asked her to shoot a few photographs with his new 1972 Chevrolet Vega-bodied funny car, she accepted his invitation. This was a rare photograph session for her; she usually did not do photo shoots with racer's cars, but Setzer and driver Pat Foster were friends, and of course, she lived close to OCIR.

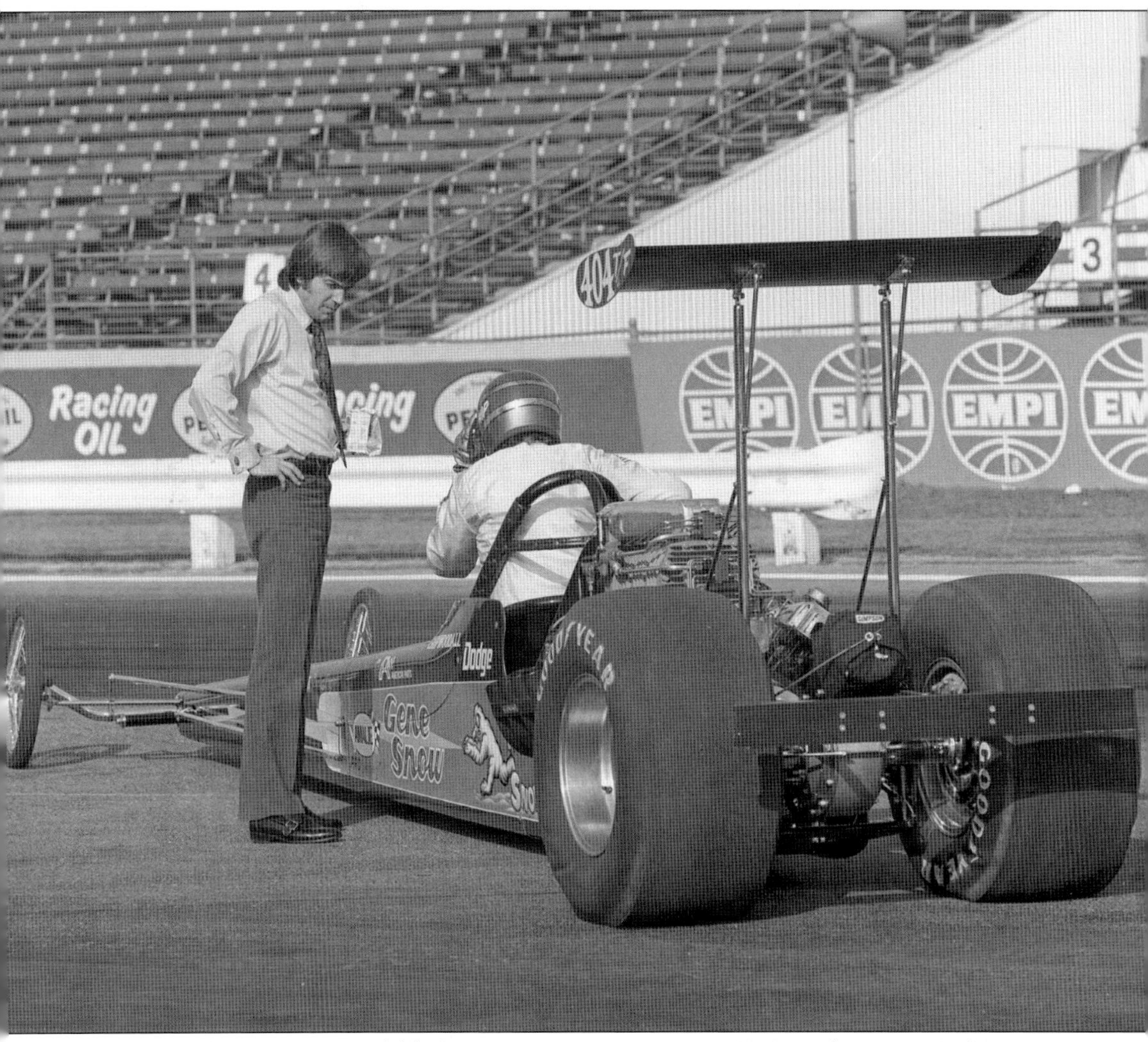

During the week, OCIR was available for racing car testing. Here, in 1972, track manager Mike Jones is checking out Gene Snow's all-new top fuel dragster and conversing with Chip Woodall, Snow's driver. Jones was a very much a hands-on track manager from 1967 to 1973. He designed the tracks logos and color schemes. He created the OCIR Manufacturers Meet, the Nitro Championships, the Funny Car 500, the East/West Funny Car Championships, and the All Pro Series. His ideas were seen in the electric scoreboard, permanent water fountains, paved pits, and restaurant-style food in the concession stands. One of his most popular ideas was the fireworks show that took place over the track just before the start of the manufacturers' funny car race. Mike Jones was true a showman at heart.

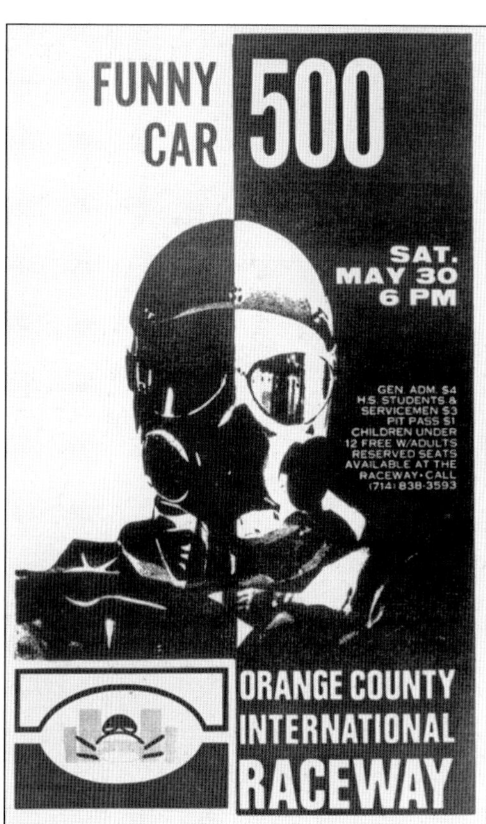

OCIR hosted two of the largest funny car events in the world: the Manufacturers Meet and the Funny Car 500. Funny car racers from 20+ states attended these events, filling the OCIR pit area with 70 to 100 funny cars for one incredible day of racing. Race fans planned their vacations around these two events, and they came from as far away as Europe to be part of these funny car spectacles. If a racer was lucky enough to win one of these events, it could mean more bookings to race in the following year; promoters loved to hype that their track would have the winner of either of the OCIR races.

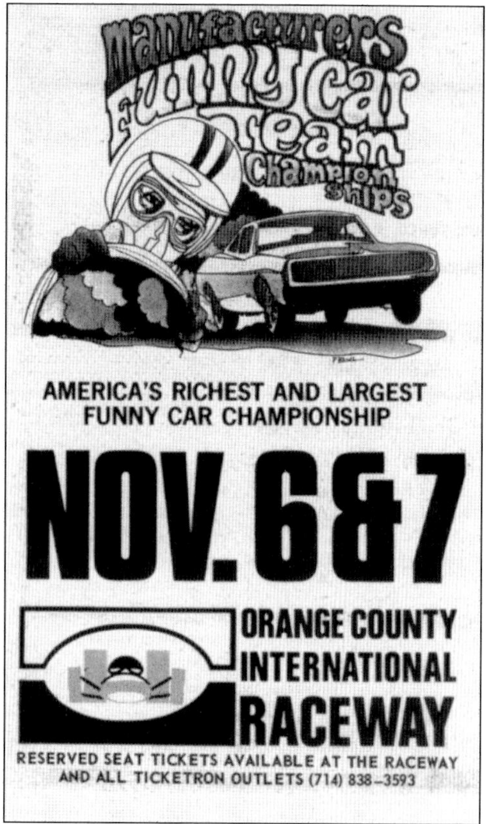

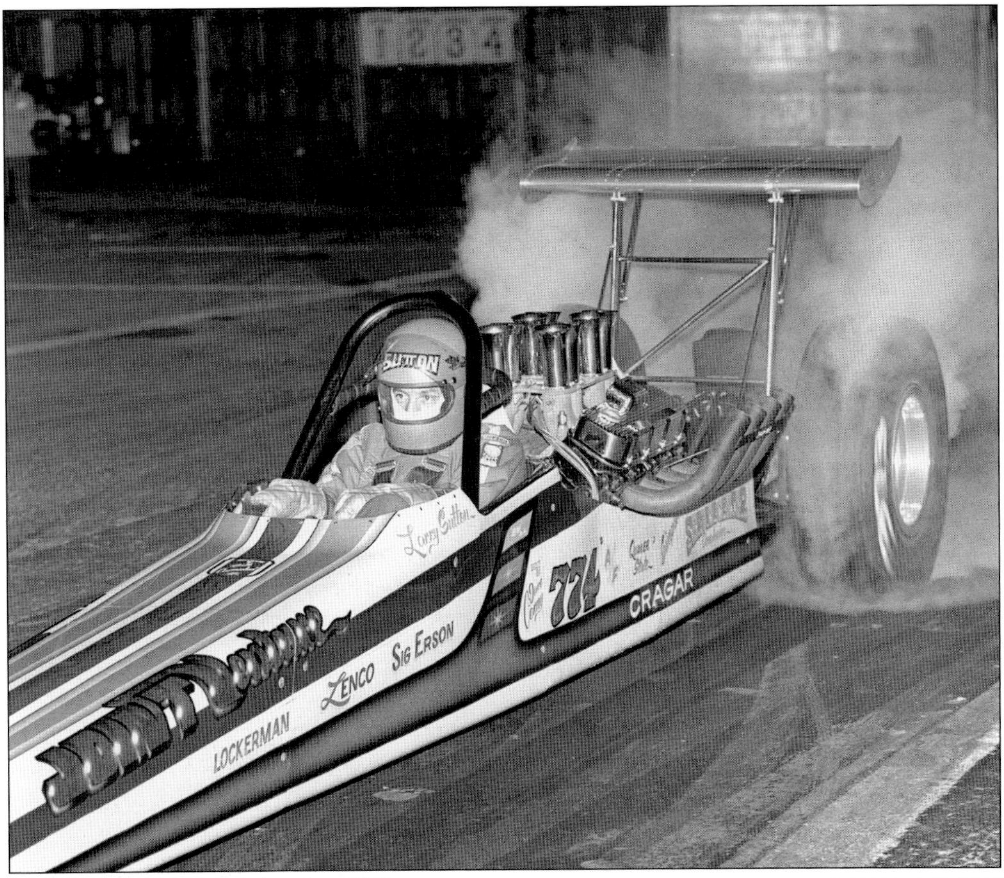

After Lions Drag Strip closed in 1972, starter Larry Sutton moved over to Irwindale. Then when Irwindale closed in 1978, Sutton moved to OCIR to start races. Sutton not only was a veteran starter but also drove race cars like the "Joint Venture" fuel dragster pictured. Sutton's other, faster ride was the "Circuit Breaker" top fuel dragster. In 1978, he drove the Circuit Breaker to top fuel honors at the last OCIR PDA race.

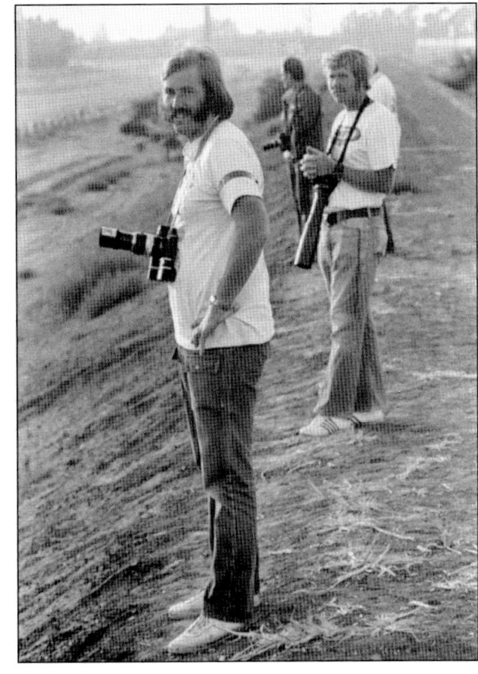

It was the vantage point at OCIR that photographers loved to shoot from—the hill at the finish line. Here, two of the best drag race shooters, Paul Sadler (foreground) and John Shanks (background), wait for the next pair of cars. These photographers covered the action at events at OCIR for magazines and trade newspapers.

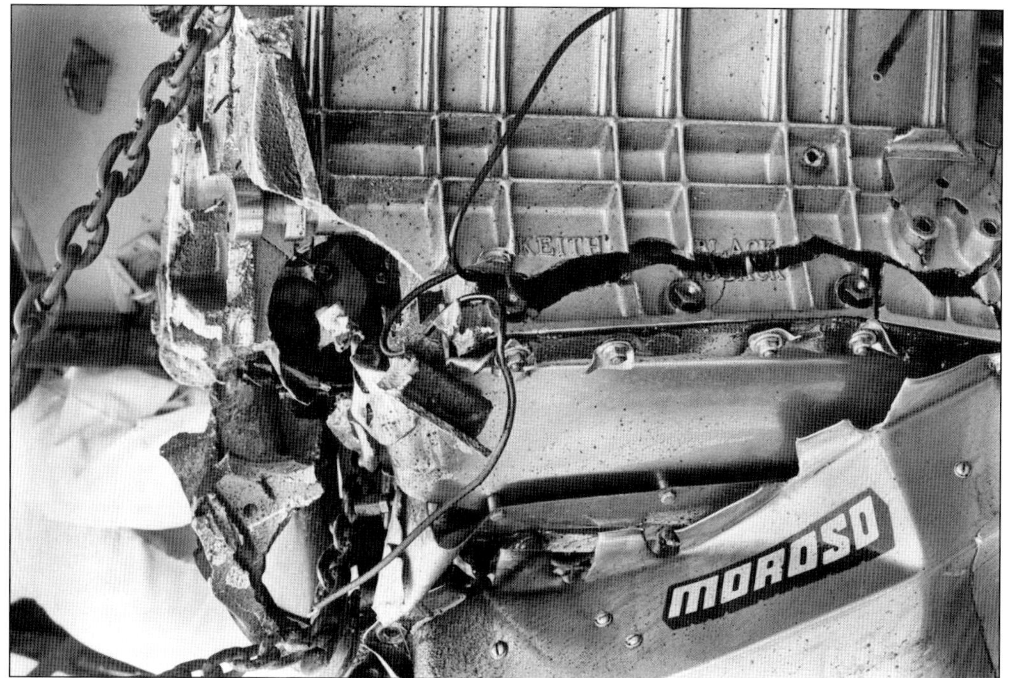

OCIR could be very hard on parts. In 1983, Roland Leong's Hawaiian Punch funny car found out how hard the track could be on engine blocks. The only thing this engine block was good for after running at OCIR was being a boat anchor. (Photograph by Don Gillespie.)

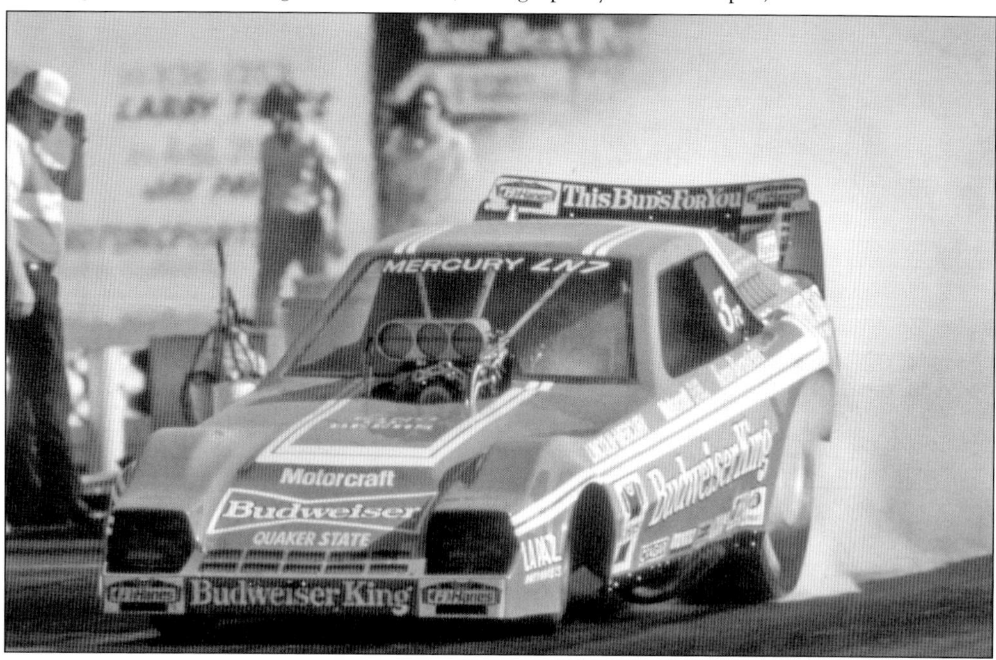

Kenny Bernstein took his brand-new 1983 funny car to OCIR for a *Popular Hot Rodding* magazine shoot early in the year. He packed up and went on tour and returned in the fall. He was just in time to win the last race at OCIR on October 29, 1983. He beat John Force in the final to become the last funny car winner before OCIR closed forever.

Canada's Gary Beck, driving for Larry Minor, beat a no-show Doug Kerhulas at OCIR's last drag race on October 29, 1983. Beck had the last car ever to race down OCIR when he made a single run for the title.

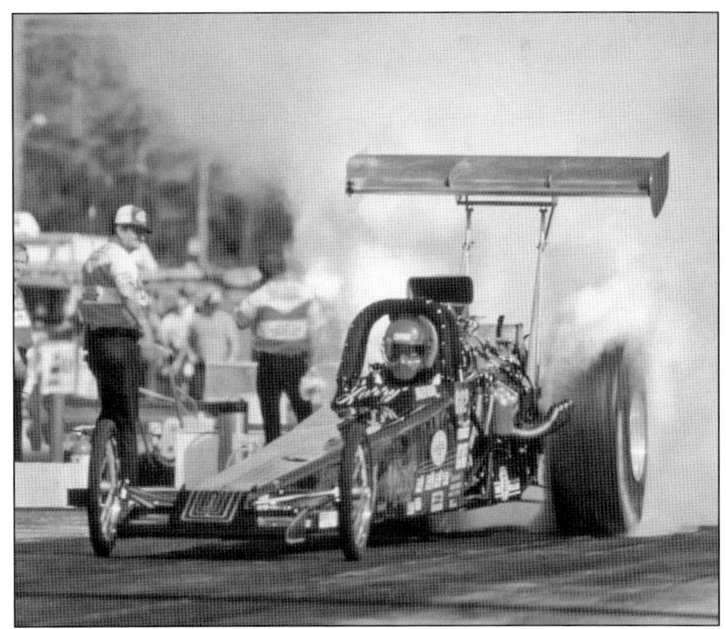

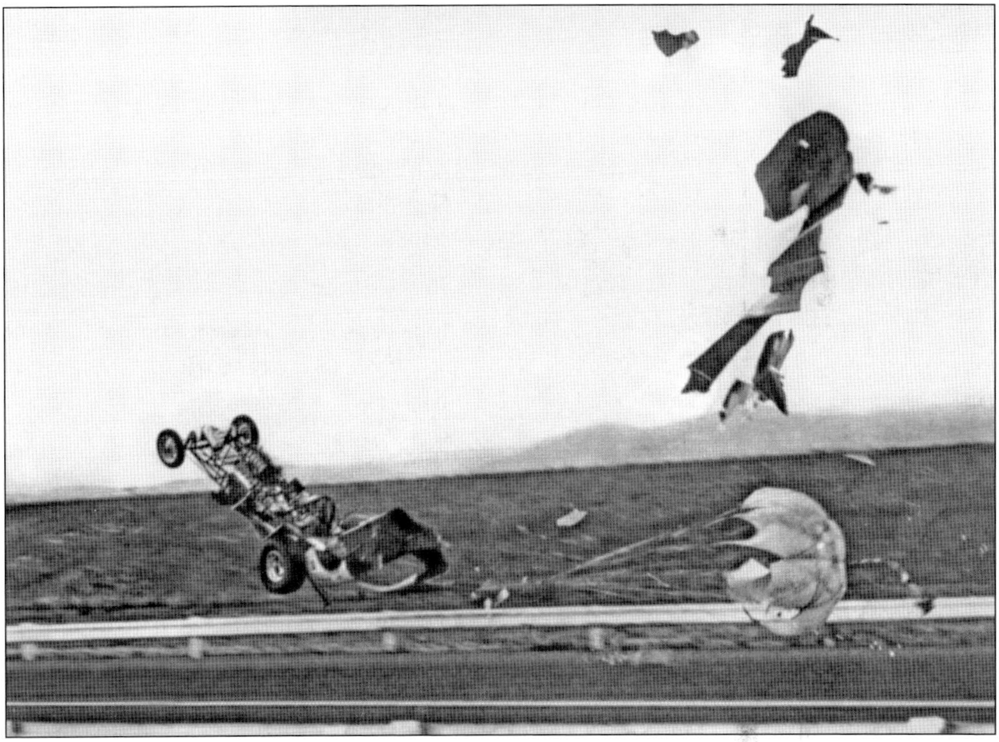

Many records were set at OCIR over the 16 years it was open, but one record that no funny car owner/driver wanted was "hang time" in a funny car. Setting that unofficial record at OCIR in 1970 at the Big Four Funny Car Championships was Bob Pickett and his AMC Javelin-bodied funny car. The photographer, the late Bob Kashler, caught Pickett in flight with his bodyless funny car at the OCIR finish line. Upon landing, the car stayed upright but injured Pickett's back. Pickett would heal and return with a Cuda-bodied funny car that stayed grounded. (Don Gillespie collection.)